ISLAND CRIMINOLOGY

New Horizons in Criminology series

Series Editor: **Andrew Millie**, Edge Hill University, UK

New Horizons in Criminology provides concise, authoritative texts which reflect cutting-edge thought and theoretical development with an international scope. Written by leading authors in their fields, the series has become essential reading for all academics and students interested in where criminology is heading.

Coming soon in paperback:

Visual Criminology
Bill McClanahan

Out now in the series:

Redemptive Criminology
Aaron Pycroft and **Clemens Bartollas**

A Criminology Of Narrative Fiction
Rafe McGregor

Transnational Criminology
Simon Mackenzie

Wildlife Criminology
Angus Nurse and **Tanya Wyatt**

Imaginative Criminology
Lizzie Seal and **Maggie O'Neill**

A Criminology of War?
Ross McGarry and **Sandra Walklate**

Find out more at
bristoluniversitypress.co.uk/new-horizons-in-criminology

NEW HORIZONS IN CRIMINOLOGY

ISLAND CRIMINOLOGY

John Scott and Zoe Staines

First published in Great Britain in 2024 by

Bristol University Press
University of Bristol
1–9 Old Park Hill
Bristol
BS2 8BB
UK
t: +44 (0)117 374 6645
e: bup-info@bristol.ac.uk

Details of international sales and distribution partners are available at bristoluniversitypress.co.uk

© Bristol University Press 2024

British Library Cataloguing in Publication Data
A catalogue record for this book is available from the British Library

ISBN 978-1-5292-2031-5 hardcover
ISBN 978-1-5292-2032-2 paperback
ISBN 978-1-5292-2033-9 ePub
ISBN 978-1-5292-2034-6 ePdf

The right of John Scott and Zoe Staines to be identified as authors of this work has been asserted by them in accordance with the Copyright, Designs and Patents Act 1988.

All rights reserved: no part of this publication may be reproduced, stored in a retrieval system, or transmitted in any form or by any means, electronic, mechanical, photocopying, recording, or otherwise without the prior permission of Bristol University Press.

Every reasonable effort has been made to obtain permission to reproduce copyrighted material. If, however, anyone knows of an oversight, please contact the publisher.

The statements and opinions contained within this publication are solely those of the authors and not of the University of Bristol or Bristol University Press. The University of Bristol and Bristol University Press disclaim responsibility for any injury to persons or property resulting from any material published in this publication.

Bristol University Press works to counter discrimination on grounds of gender,
race, disability, age and sexuality.

Cover design: Bristol University Press
Front cover image: Gettyimages.co.uk/James Gentles gentles360

Contents

Series Editor Preface by Professor Andrew Millie   vi
About the Authors   viii

1	Introduction	1
2	Idylls (and Horrors)	19
3	Isolation	42
4	Invasion	60
5	Integration	80
6	Insularity	98
7	Industry	111
8	Conclusion	129

Notes   139
References   141
Index   163

Series Editor Preface

Professor Andrew Millie, School of Law, Criminology and Policing, Edge Hill University, UK

I first became aware of John Scott and Zoe Staines' work on the place of islands in criminology after reading an article they produced for *Theoretical Criminology*, published in 2021. This article provided a case study of Pitcairn in the Southern Pacific, one of the world's more remote island communities and a place that in the early 2000s became synonymous with child sexual abuse. Scott and Staines had identified a truly new horizon for criminology, and I wanted to read more as they developed an island criminology. I was delighted when they agreed to produce this important new book that pushes the spatial, temporal, and imaginative boundaries of criminology.

The New Horizons in Criminology book series provides concise authoritative texts that reflect cutting-edge thought and theoretical developments in criminology and are international in scope. They are written so that the non-specialist academic, student, or practitioner can understand them by explaining ideas clearly before going deeper into the subject. For this book Scott and Staines chose not to produce an administrative account of what works in criminal justice in various island settings. Rather, they have fashioned an engaging text that uncovers a 'politics of place and belonging'. The book takes the reader on a journey to parts of the planet often overlooked by criminology, including the Caribbean, Iceland, Greenland, the Torres Strait Islands and back to the Pacific and Pitcairn where we learn about insularity, the possible negatives of social capital, and the 'normative nature of crime'. The definition of islands is also pushed, by considering desert, or land-locked 'islands' of the Australian interior.

At a time when there are calls to decolonize criminology, some of the islands featured in this book couldn't be further from the metropoles of the Global North. Scott and Staines are interested in definitions of crime and deviance in island settings, in what gets policed – and what does not – and processes of governance, discipline, and Othering. Colonialism and history play their part, but so too do notions of islandness, including the creation of islands as utopian idylls or dystopian horrors, in both fact and fiction. The authors explore techniques of 'islanding', with islands used to separate others for health or incarceration, or for the detention of asylum seekers. In this way the authors view islands as places of exclusion. Islands are regarded as literal prisons, but also as feeling like prisons. Scott and Staines consider islands as places of production and consumption – and islands have demonstrable relevance for corporate and green criminologies, for instance in terms of commercial exploitation and being on the front line of climate change, including threats to their existence from rising sea levels.

Alongside relevance for corporate and green criminology, the book is timely for those with interests in rural, cultural, transnational, indigenous, Southern, post-colonial, or decolonized criminologies. It is a rare book that is also useful for the rest of criminology, and beyond – including those with interests at the intersection between criminology and human geography. By studying lives at 'the periphery of peripheries', *Island Criminology* also tells us some disturbing truths about 'us', wherever we may live, and concludes by highlighting the importance of social integration and belonging rather than exclusion and Othering. The book is highly readable, challenging, and recommended.

About the Authors

John Scott is a Professor and Head of the School of Justice at Queensland University of Technology, Australia. His current research interests are in the areas of sexual and gendered crime and crime in remote places. He has published widely, including 24 books and major research reports and over 100 papers and book chapters, many with leading international journals and publishers. He has also had sustained success in attracting nationally competitive grants and industry funding. He is currently a member of the Australasian Research Council College of Experts, edits the Routledge Series *Crime and Justice Studies in Asia and the Global South*, co-edits *The Journal for Crime, Justice and Social Democracy*, and is Vice President of the Asian Criminological Society.

Zoe Staines is an Australian Research Council DECRA Senior Research Fellow in the School of Social Science, University of Queensland (UQ). Her research interests include welfare conditionality, neoliberal subjectivities, and decoloniality. She is particularly interested in exploring how social and penal policies combine to regulate, discipline, and punish those socially constructed as 'deviant', especially in settler colonial contexts, including remote spaces and places. Zoe has published in top-tier national and international criminology, sociology, and social policy journals, is co-author of *Compulsory Income Management in Australia and New Zealand* (Policy Press, 2022), leads the UQ Inequalities and Social Action Research Cluster, and is also Associate Editor of the *Australian Journal of Social Issues*.

1

Introduction

I

On 2 October 1629, seven men were hanged in the Houtman Abrolhos, a chain of 122 tiny islands and associated coral reefs, situated in the Indian Ocean, 60 km west of what is today the town of Geraldton in Western Australia. The executed were among the first inhabitants of the barren and windswept island chain. They were also the first people to be executed under European law in what would be known as New Holland, and then Australia, for mutiny and the horrific execution-style murders of approximately 125 babies, children, women, and men on the islands where they had been marooned for almost four months following the wreck of the Dutch East Company ship *Batavia*. Historians have likened Beacon Island (labelled by the Dutch '*Batavia*'s Graveyard'), the main site of the atrocities, to a modern-day concentration camp where the mutineers had experimented with various methods of killing (Sturma, 2002). Following these executions, which had been preceded by torture and the amputation of limbs, two other European mutineers, convicted of lesser crimes, were marooned on the Australian mainland. These men were never seen again, being the first of many Europeans to seemingly vanish in the vast depths of the island continent. They were also the first known European inhabitants of Australia.

The story of the *Batavia* had been something of a sensation in its day, only to be subsequently forgotten. With the unearthing of human remains from shallow graves by archaeological digs on the islands during the 1960s, interest was revived. Historians examined the Dutch archives to find a rich body of materials dating from the period, including diaries, ecclesiastical pamphlets, and polemics, which can be variously likened to pre-modern criminologies or 17th-century true crime tales. Like other famous wrecks of the period, *Batavia* proved a versatile source for writings, from the sober to sensational. As with other dystopian narratives, much of the writing then, as with more recent analyses, asks how such social disintegration and crimes could be possible, with answers often reflecting on the character and psychology of the mutineers' leader. To date, the mutiny has been the subject of academic conjecture, several popular histories, documentaries, plays, poems, and even a three-act opera (Titlestad, 2013). Remains of the ship and victims of the massacre are housed at the Shipwreck Galleries in Fremantle, forming its main attraction.[1]

The continued interest seems justified, given that *Batavia* was something of a '*Titanic*' of its day. Not unlike the *Titanic*, the *Batavia* was the flagship of one of the most powerful maritime companies in the world at the time and sank on her maiden voyage, carrying a diverse cross section of European society, travelling to the Dutch East Indies. The story also offered seemingly stylized heroes and villains, including a character whose evil seemed then, as now, unfathomable and whose nature and motives have been subject to enduring conjecture. Not the least, the story was one of horror that provides a counter narrative to the settler colonial myth of the peaceful arrival of the British convict fleets on the Eastern Coast of Australia from 1788. In brief, the story is outlined below, with much of what follows drawn from historian Mike Dash's excellent (2002) account of the tragedy.

II

The *Batavia* struck a coral reef at night and proceeded to break up, with 40 of the 341 passengers drowning in the writhing waters and dangerous corals that surrounded the ship and separated it from nearby islands. Those passengers and crew that managed to reach Beacon Island soon found themselves facing starvation and dehydration in a hostile environment. Some men remained for several days on board the disintegrating wreck until it broke up, pillaging the ship's stocks and belongings of the wealthier crew until the final destruction of the ship after several days. Those who had reached Beacon Island soon discovered it bereft of water and for five days suffered the extreme effects of dehydration and exposure, a further number of wreck survivors perishing, before the tides brought limited water and stores ashore from the wreck.

Meanwhile, the ship's commander, Francisco Pelsaert, along with 48 of its most senior sailors, including the captain, took a longboat to search for water on the Australian mainland. Having failed to find landfall after several days, they made the fateful decision to abandon the castaways and try to reach the Dutch East Indies, some 900 miles from the wreck. They departed hastily without notice, fearing that to return to Beacon Island would risk taking on more survivors, which would swamp the already overloaded longboat.

Pelsaert's second in command, Jeronimus Cornelisz, a former apothecary and alleged heretic who had been formulating a mutiny prior to the wreck, took charge of the remaining survivors and, at first, appeared to be acting in their best interests by sending some of the most capable men to nearby islands to search for water. Some of these men were variously executed or marooned on islands in the Houtman Abrolhos chain. All the while Cornelisz recruited a party of mutineers, secured all available weapons for these men, and set about murdering wreck survivors to reduce strains on the limited resources left on the island, with the aim of reducing the island's population to about 45 people. He had also hatched a plan that should Pelsaert return with a rescue ship, a small number of remaining mutineers would forcefully seize the vessel and embark in piracy, before eventually establishing a new kingdom based on the proceeds of their crimes.

Murders were at first carried out as executions under the authority of an island council resided over by Cornelisz, and under the pretext of some crime having been committed, such as theft of rations or conspiracy to mutiny. But this quickly gave way to autocratic sentences ordered in an increasingly casual and arbitrary fashion (Dash, 2002, p 172). Corneliez soon abandoned any pretence to piety and become autocrat of the island, espousing a new code of Libertine philosophies and heretical beliefs, including the idea of a Devil and Hell being nothing more than fables (Dash, 2002, p 166). He also denounced his former status as 'under-merchant' for the new status of 'Captain-general' of the islands.

The increasingly random and unprovoked nature of atrocities on Beacon Island has largely been blamed on Cornelisz' 'burning need for novelty and stimulation' (Dash, 2002, p 138). Similarly, among the other mutineers, daily routines held limited appeal for those who had come to enjoy the power of taking life, so that these men became well-practised killers whose murdering sprees were carefully planned and became trivial events to quash boredom (Dash, 2002, p 142). Indeed, 'in the end he [Cornelisz] and his men were slaughtering for mere entertainment' (Dash, 2002, pp 172, 180). Men who appeared reluctant mutineers were cajoled or forced to take part in killings to prove their loyalty to the new regime, soon becoming enthusiastic accomplices. Members of the inner circle proved themselves worthy through the individual butchering of between 12 and 20 people. Initial drownings soon gave way to gratuitous stabbings and throat cutting, and victims were murdered with axes, daggers, pikes, cutlasses, and morning stars before being buried in shallow graves, sometimes pre-prepared for groups (Dash, 2002, p 142). The murders of the *Batavia*'s survivors began with the weakest members of the group, which included those who were enfeebled and ill. Cornelisz was presented as adept at manipulating and recruiting others to engage in such acts and, although he had attempted to use his skills as an apothecary to unsuccessfully murder a baby (comatized and subsequently killed by an accomplice), he himself only *ordered* the savagery. It was said he took pleasure not in conducting the murders himself, but in corrupting others, especially young people, to do so (Dash, 2002, p 138; Titlestad, 2013). Of the 20 women who had survived the wreck, those who were pregnant or too old to interest the mutineers were killed and the seven remaining reduced to the status of sex slaves to be shared among the mutineers, while Cornelisz reserved the reputedly most desirable passenger for his personal abuse (Dash, 2002, p 169).

The only man left on the island who could challenge the authority of Cornelisz was a minister of the Dutch Reformed Church, who was lured from his tent so that his wife and five of his children could be massacred. One daughter was spared in order to become a 'wife' (sex slave) of one of the mutineers while the minister was reduced to a state akin to slavery and mocked by the mutineers. As such, one of few authorities left on the island that could constrain the men was neutralized (Dash, 2002, p 167).

A small group of approximately 20 soldiers, led by a loyalist named Webbe Hayes, who had been marooned in the early days of the wreck had managed to find water on one of the islands and survive from the myriad birdlife and fishing available. They had learnt of the murders from others fleeing Beacon Island. They built a crude limestone fortress, made makeshift weapons, and engaged in skirmishes with the mutineers who had become determined to eliminate them before a rescue party should arrive. As fate would have it, these men were engaged in a final desperate battle with the mutineers as a rescue ship approached the islands. A race to the rescue ship ensued with the loyalists managing to narrowly beat the mutineers and alert Pelsaert and the rescuers to their plans. After a short struggle, the mutineers were overpowered and captured. Of the fate of those mutineers not mentioned above, a further five were hanged on their trial in the Dutch East Indies and several were subject to extreme corporal punishments. Cornelisz proved himself resistant to confession and to the very end refused to admit to or take responsibility for his actions, several times retracting his confessions. Having had both hands severed with a crude chisel, he was likely barely conscious from loss of blood when he was taken to the gallows.

III

In 2019 the Houtman Abrolhos Islands were declared a national park by the Western Australian government. Sometimes described as the 'Galapagos Islands of the Indian Ocean', the Houtman Abrolhos are home to much biodiversity, including two local species of mammals, and are one of the world's most important seabird breeding sites. Nonetheless, they remain, as they were in Cornelisz' day, largely uninhabited and off-limits as a conservation habitat, the exception being seasonal fisherman. Day trips to the islands for fishing, bird watching, snorkelling, and diving are widely promoted (Muncipal Dept. of Tourism in the West, 2021).

The islands are also, perhaps unsurprisingly, a site for 'dark tourism', not only owing to the *Batavia*, but also to 19 lesser-known wrecks around the archipelago, including the wreck of the *Zeewijk* (1727), which was also notable for two boys having been convicted of sodomy and marooned on separate islands in the chain. Not surprisingly, few human remnants or constructions remain on the islands from these early incursions, the one notable exception being the first known European structure built in Australia – the limestone fort that the *Batavia* loyalists built to defend themselves from the mutineers.

IV

As previously noted, many attempts have been made to interpret the events of 1629. Whatever the cause of the events, interpretations often tell much about the interpreter and their respective cultural milieu. The earliest modern account of the events presented Cornelisz as charismatic, yet pathological and suffering from paranoia and other delusions: a charlatan capable of persuading men that wealth and new freedoms could be theirs should they follow him. Many interpretations tend to draw sharp distinctions between the evil of Cornelisz and the leader of the loyalists, Hayes, who was promoted and became a hero following the events. A statue of Hayes stands on the mainland in the town of Geraldton. The simplicity of such accounts lends dramatic effect to a tale of enduring appeal. Cornelisz represents an archetypal villain and Other, but one whose obvious flaws make him someone who can be at once understood in his humanity; and therein lies the horror. He embodies aspects of the worst elements of the modern world that would find wider expression in later historic atrocities. At any rate, accounts have tended to psychologize and individualize the events to the detriment of space and place.

Dash (2002) reinforces these conclusions and goes so far as to draw on the modern diagnostic tool DSM-IV to argue that Cornelisz was a verifiable psychopath. Yet, his account also offers sociological observations that the most loyal of the mutineers enjoyed a special status on the islands, which allowed them to feast on the limited ships stores rather than hunt and scavenge for food and rainwater. They had better clothes, larger tents, and freedom of movement on and between islands that was denied to loyalists. Notably, these men who had been of lower social status in their European homelands, had for the first time in their lives enjoyed freedom from the social constraints that had governed them. As we will iterate in the following pages, the realities of distance, isolation, and boundedness present possibilities for resistance to dominant regimes, along with supporting the power that such regimes hold. This is true to the extent that one social order was replaced by another; indeed, one that could be characterized as 'carnivalesque', but nonetheless 'order' was not absent from the lives of the mutineers. For example, in the confinements of his island kingdom, mutineers were actively encouraged by Cornelisz to blaspheme and swear. They were also absolved from the requirement to attend religious services, rejecting the rules of an order that until then had constrained them. Nonetheless, oaths of loyalty and trust were made by the mutineers to Cornelisz, to each other, and to what was essentially the new order of the island (Dash, 2002, pp 131–67). In this way, the mutineers can be compared to modern criminal groups such as mafia and gangs. Neither the mutineers nor the mafia exist in a social or moral void.

Further, what shocked the early modern mind (blasphemy and heresy) is not what shocks or draws contemporary attention to the events of 1629, this being the extreme brutality of the violent crimes and that they were carried out collectively and systematically. But such actions are recognizable when we consider the islands as a colonial landscape and the mutineers as colonizers. To understand the brutality, one must understand the powers associated with the colonial enterprise in addition to the social orders of 17th-century Europe.

Interestingly, Titlestad (2013) draws on the 'political theology' of Carl Schmidt to argue that in asserting a state of emergency in his island kingdom, Cornelisz had assumed the sovereign powers which drew on the monarchy that the Dutch Republic had replaced, observing that dictatorships, not unlike psyches, are rooted in time and place. The mutineers also mimicked the autonomous and often violent and coercive powers of the Dutch East India Company, which they served (Parthesius, 2010). Cornelisz thus exercised a realpolitik that in a commissary dictatorship drew a sharp distinction between friends and enemies (in this case consumers of scarce resources and potential threats to power).

Titlestad (2013) observes that one of the more interesting of the myriad of political, psychological, and theological interpretations of the event is in Arabella Edge's *The Company* (2000). This presents Cornelisz' perspective and likens him to the Marquis de Sade. The difference is that, while Sade 'could only dream of a citadel where he could enact all his fantasies', the Abrolhos archipelago allowed Cornelisz, for a time, 'to reign supreme'. Once again, it is space and place that makes possible otherwise unrealizable fantasies/crimes. Following from this, the islands arguably represented a human laboratory comparable to the manufactured environments of the modern Milgram Experiment (1963) or Stanford Prison Experiment (1971). Milgram, interested in the psychology of genocide, required diverse participants in his study to obey an authority figure and perform acts conflicting with their ethics and beliefs. Although its method has since been questioned, the Stanford Prison Experiment argued that the insularity and confinement of a prison, as opposed to personality traits, facilitated abusive behaviours.

All the hypotheses regarding the events of 1629 focus on the actors but largely fail to account for the stages in which the dramatic events were set, these being the closed confines of ship and the bounded territories of the

Houtman Abrolhos Islands. In this way, the role of geography – so integral to the creation of the drama surrounding the narrative – is absent from the analysis of the crimes. The ship and the islands blur into one to the extent that both might be regarded as akin in some respects to what Goffman (1961, p 15) referred to as 'total institutions': locales that are all encompassing, eroding barriers between different spheres of life (sleep, leisure, work), to provide 'something of a world' while barring 'social intercourse with the outside'. What makes the events of 1629 so disturbing is not so much that the islands came to be *devoid* of social order, but that an order that we are still familiar with today, including one informed by both humanism and Judaeo-Christianity, could be so spectacularly subverted and replaced by another order that similarly drew on those traditions.

Cornelisz' island kingdom is clearly a dystopia, representing an enduring narrative of islands as sites of horror or strange and Other places. There are plenty of examples, historical and fictional, that might be drawn upon to illustrate the way in which islands – bounded, often small, and isolated – generate crime and criminal cultures. To take one example, although he was unlikely to be at all familiar with the *Batavia* story, William Golding's *Lord of the Flies* (1954) chillingly makes murderous castaways of modern British grammar school boys. As we return to throughout this book, such accounts are balanced against an alternate imagery of islands as a utopian 'paradise' or 'idyll'. And, indeed, today what was once known as '*Batavia*'s Graveyard' is renowned as a site of vitality for its biodiversity and is reimagined, as it could never have been for a castaway, as an enclave of beauty and leisure.

For Baldacchino (2012) island geographies lend themselves to near absolute human domination. They can exist as personal property and be treated according to personal whims. For example, nearly a century after the wreck of *Batavia* and marooning of the mutineers, Defoe would have his castaway, Robinson Crusoe (1719), survey the island on which he was isolated with a kind of megalomania: 'with a secret kind of pleasure to think that this was all my own, that I was king and lord of all this country' (Defoe, 1719, p 99). In one sense, Crusoe is a rugged survivalist tale, but it is also one of imperialist greed resulting in conquest, slavery, robbery, and murder (Baldacchino, 2012, p 105). Small islands also present as extreme sites in the colonial project, providing laboratories and models for exploitation and domination. McCusker and Soares (2011, p xi) explain:

> The Western gaze, rooted in what Bill Ashcroft describes as the 'imperial passion for perspective,' frequently imagined the island as an inferior, marginal or easily dominated space, as an obvious site for subjugation and organization by the colonizer. Thus the island was a natural colony for the European, not just, as Rod Edmond and Vanessa Smith note, 'because of the desire to possess what is paradisal

or utopian, but because islands, unlike continents, look like property.' Their supposed vulnerability and isolation, and their (imagined) small geographic scale, meant that islands were both arche-typal and prototypical sites of the colonial experience. Historically, the island was considered as an ideal locale, or even a laboratory, in which to materialize the colonial will, free from undesirable alien influences emanating from the outside.

In the most extreme manifestations of the colonial project, islands offered a particularly complete model of domination and exploitation, exemplified in the plantations of the Caribbean and the Indian Ocean, whose histories of genocide and slavery testify to the supreme acquisitiveness of the Western gaze. At the height of imperialism during the 19th century, *The Coral Island*, one in a long line of Robinsannades, as with the trope, does little to hide visions of racist imperial conquest: 'We've got an island all to ourselves. We'll take possession in the name of the king; we'll go and enter the service of its black inhabitants. Of course we'll rise, naturally, to the top of affairs. White men always do in savage countries' (Ballantyne, 1858/1867, pp 27–8 cited in Baldacchino, 2012, p 105). As Baldacchino (2012, p 105) points out, though, islands are also sites of complexity and contradiction:

> With their beguiling simple geography, small islands invite us to consider them as comprehensible and manageable totalities. ... Islands help to unleash and encourage the indulging of atavistic desires for power and control, encouraging humans (usually men) to think that their island world is an enticing tabula rasa; for all seasons and for all tastes. Which is why, then, anything goes. This sounds like a recipe for a natural collapse into patriarchal authoritarianism. And yet, if one reads the specific political science literature, this extols small, often island, jurisdictions as paragons of democratic behaviour.

Indeed, little over a hundred years before the *Batavia* tragedy, Thomas Moore had presented the ideal political commonwealth as the Island of Utopia, its bounded and exclusive geography making it an ideal site for a political experiment (Baldacchino, 2012). And so it is that islands are places of the imagination and, as we show in this book, sites of both idyllization and horror. As we build on in the chapter that follows, the island-idyll is a symbolic place into which various meanings of islandness are condensed. Idyllization is produced by mainlanders, as well as by islanders themselves, and sources nostalgic yearnings for an imagined community remembered as purer, simpler, natural, and stable. It can provide an escape from city and/or mainland life and the problems considered to manifest it, leading to a sense of belonging. In the idyll, the island presents as a space of bucolic tranquillity and communion with nature – an authentic place of retreat from the mainland (Bell, 2006, p 152). Idyllization and horror inform the social construction of crime and, with it, fear of crime.

Drawing on Durkheim's work, Erikson (1962) presented deviant forms of behaviour as a valuable resource in the community, providing clarity to the extant social order. He had earlier commented on this process in terms of 'boundary maintenance', highlighting the social production of deviance rather than its causes (Erikson, 1962). The denser social networks which social disorganization theorists have described in some small-scale societies are only achieved through a clear articulation of social order and social disorder, with much social activity operating to highlight what resides within and outside the boundaries of 'communities'. While small communities tend to have a strong sense of identity, defined through geography, the problem exists: who is defined as belonging to the community in terms of residing in it and contributing to its prosperity? For example, racial and ethnic discrimination have been reported to be common in many small-scale societies (Coorey, 1990; Cunneen, 1992).

V

The social networks and symbolic landscapes of islands are not produced in a social or geo-political vacuum, free of historic and current power relations or the social figurations such relations produce. Moreover, they have material effects. Organization, as presented in terms of tightly integrated and/or well-resourced social groups, allows for clear articulations of disorganization and inferiority, often defined in terms of criminality. Such articulations can inform a group's integrity, with ideology defining the normative boundaries of a group. This is the case in small-scale societies, which although often being resource poor, regularly have what is termed 'social capital', which exists and is mobilized through tight-knit social networks. The politics of who belongs in such societies may define Otherness in terms of internal or external threats to 'the (imagined) community' (Anderson, 1991). So it is that in a remote or small-scale society, the Other may be a particular social group or 'drifter' or other 'stranger' passing through a town, or even the 'town drunk' who embodies a certain disorganization that threatens the whole.

Other places can also exist as threats to local cohesion. This may be, in the case of a rural town, the metropolis, or in the case of an island, the mainland. Scholars have recognized this definitional capacity in terms of islands with reference to what we have referred to as 'islandness', especially how a sense of belonging is informed by feelings of being in place. Not only is group membership important to belonging, but 'ownership' of place is equally important. Memmott et al (2006, p 41) observe that people are dependent upon place for social identity and places are also dependent on people for their identity. It should also be added that discourses of belonging write the contributions of some people into the landscape and others out. Antonisch (2010, p 650) observes that the politics of belonging has a side that claims belonging and a side that grants it. Communal bonding shapes the scale of the crime threat and informs a socially constructed criminogenic order in which some crimes are marked as extreme threats to the social order and others are dismissed or ignored. In this way, talk about crime is always about *more* than just 'crime'.

VI

Norbert Elias' figurational sociology can be helpful in understanding how 'problems' are socially constructed and strategically deployed in small-scale settings. In particular Elias' account of established–outsider relations, developed through a classic community study with Scotson in the late 1950s, is especially informative. What is valuable about the study is the way in which the authors examined a 'community' without marked ethnic or class differences: a place akin to many islands, with their relatively 'flat' social structure. Winston Parva (pseudonym) in the late 1950s, was a suburban settlement on the outer fringes of an industrial city located in the Midlands of England. Elias and Scotson (1994) document a social cleavage between the older and newer residents who had been relocated there after the war. The older or 'established' residents of Winston Parva presented as a cohesive and tightly integrated group, while the newer residents, or 'outsiders', were less cohesive and subject to stigmatization from the established group. Typically, the newer or 'outsider' group were presented as lacking in civilized standards, especially those pertaining to bodily integrity and control. For example, they were blamed for various forms of social disorder in the community and characterized as dirty, uncouth, and violent. A good deal of what 'villagers' habitually said about Estate families was vastly exaggerated or untrue (Elias & Scotson, 1994, p 101).

To explain the social dynamics of this place, Elias avoids traditional explanations of stigmatization and discrimination associated with forms of stratification such as educational, occupational, religious, ethnic, and class differences. Indeed, social exclusion and stigmatization can exist independent of any of these variables. Both social groupings in Winston Parva were working class and exhibited similar socio-cultural characteristics. The only significant difference evident between the groups was merely the social oldness and cohesion or organization of the established group, while the newcomers had lacked the time to build up social cohesion and, subsequently, lacked common identification and shared practices. In this way, Elias and Scotson (1994) examine a group's ability to organize itself as an important power differential. They argue that an established group tends to attribute to outsider groups the 'bad' characteristics of that group's 'worst' section — its perceived 'anomic' minority. Blemishes perceived in some members of the group were transferred to all members of the group. In contrast, the self-image of the 'nomic' group is based on perceived attributes of a minority of its members (Elias & Scotson, 1994, p xix). The more unequal the balance of power is between groups, the more distorted is the image of outsiders produced by the establishment group (Mennell, 1992, p 138). Established groups not only treat others as inferior, but also make them feel inferior, which can have a paralysing effect on groups with a lower power ratio (Elias & Scotson, 1994, p xxiv). Stigmatization impinges on self-image, being that of an outsider, resulting in a demoralization (Elias & Scotson, 1994, pp xxiii–xxiv). Notably, praise, blame, and gossip are important elements in such relations. Gossip, for example, provides a means by which people can demonstrate 'their fervent adherence to their own group norms by expressing their shock and horror at the behaviour of those who don't conform. The high organisation of social networks among established groups facilities the flow of gossip and also reinforces integration of the group' (Elias & Scotson, 1994, p 89).

An account of established–outsider relations may be helpful in understanding how social problems are defined and maintained over periods of time. It may also account for the complex dynamics of power relations in small-scale settings. It draws attention to the intimacy and density of socio-spatial relationships that characterize many small-scale societies, including islands. Elias' work is especially illuminating with regard to bounded and small-scale societies where notions of length of residence and age of families have been shown to affect social dynamics, being important indicators of status and authority (Wild, 1974). It is also useful in understanding colonial and neo-colonial practices, such as how Indigenous groups come to be defined as outsiders in their own lands and have been repeatedly characterized as an uncivilized and even parasitic presence in the landscape from which they have been displaced, being excluded from social, political, and economic life of communities (Whyte, 2018). One mark of this incivility is a perceived capacity for violence. It also explains how processes of colonization, which involve the displacement and disruption of social networks, are vital in maintaining hegemonies. Countering such imagery may be difficult and certainly requires high levels of organizational capacity, which an eradication or erosion of culture denies. In relation to this, crime is also thought to be the product of a lack of shared values and beliefs and inability to solve common problems. We can look at social problems in small-scale societies, such as islands, in terms of claim-making activities which are always a form of interaction between social groups. Most of the time groups that have more membership, money, greater discipline, and better organization will be more effective in having their claims realized (Spector & Kitsuse, 1973, 1977).

VII

According to *The Island Studies Reader*, approximately 600 million people (10 per cent of the world's population) live on islands (Baldacchino, 2007), though this is contingent on how 'island' is defined. Definitions tend to span characteristics of both space (that is, geographical features) and place (that is, cultural and social features). In English, the word island is derived from Anglo-Saxon tradition, rather than Classical cultures, and tends to refer to spatial qualities – essentially denoting a land mass surrounded by water. English includes several distinct words to describe water-bound land masses, perhaps signifying the early importance of the construct to trading and colonizing islanders. For the Vikings, land surrounded by water was not, however, an island unless it was only navigable by a boat with a rudder in place. This might contrast landlocked societies where islands have held relatively less significance, and where few words exist that denote the kind of insularity that is often considered a place-based characteristic of islands (Royle & Brinklow, 2018).

Biologists tend to define 'small', isolated bodies surrounded by water as islands, though often not clearly defining what is meant by 'small' (Jedrusik, 2011, p 202). Thus, although in terms of their spatial characteristics islands may be simply defined as relatively confined terrestrial systems, bounded by sea, this is potentially too broad. Papua New Guinea, Borneo, and Madagascar might, for instance, be considered islands by this definition, but they are also large land masses (>500,000 km^2). Under Jedrusik's (2011, p 202) classification, however, islands are considered to be smaller than 10,000 km^2, while a continent is in excess of 50,000 km^2. Thus, the large floating land masses of Papua New Guinea, Borneo, and Madagascar do not qualify as islands according to Jedrusik (2011). Using Jedrusik's (2011) definition, we can nevertheless identify several hundreds of thousands of islands worldwide, with only 18 of these having a surface area greater than 10,000 km^2. And yet, islands show much cultural, geographic, social, political, and economic diversity; it is often debated whether they have anything in common, *besides* being surrounded by water.

Contemporary island nations are often comprised of diverse cultural and linguistic groups, frequently formed by colonial geographies. They are what Anderson (1991) might call 'imagined communities', whereby national cultures are, as with elsewhere in the world, represented in objects such as flags, anthems, dress, institutions, and languages (Connell, 2003). There may also be significant diversity *within* islands, and/or across island archipelagos. Melanesia, for example, is home to 20 per cent of the world's languages, while the Melanesian Solomon Islands, which are made up of nearly 1,000 smaller islands spread across nine groups, are home to 70 different languages (Dinnen & McLeod, 2009). Thus, notwithstanding Jedrusik's (2011) spatial criterion, the way in which islands are understood varies widely according to cultural and temporal settings. The place-based characteristics of islands are also relative. Australia's comparative isolation often sees it presented as an island, regardless of its size and continental status. And for those living on the Australian island state of Tasmania (located off South-East Australia), Australia is the 'mainland'. Similarly, for the Ulster Nationalists, Great Britain is referred to by the politically potent term 'mainland'. While for the British, Europe is the 'continent'. In William Shakespeare's *Richard II*, for example, John of Gaunt cites the imaginative and physical geographies of the 'British' Isles: 'This fortress built by Nature for herself, against infection and the hand of war, this happy breed of men, this little world; this precious stone set in the silver seas, which serves it in the office of a wall, or as a moat defensive to a house' (Shakespeare, cited in Dodds & Royle, 2003).

Overall, it might be said that islands possess unique geological, geographical, and cultural histories owing to their limited population, isolation, and resource scarcity (Dodds & Royle, 2003, p 487). Indeed, island isolation leads to their being imagined as complete worlds secured by natural boundaries, with seclusion and remoteness often considered to be central features (Jedrusik, 2011, p 202). In fact, the word island resembles terms for isolation in many European languages, but isolation here has as much to do with geographic distance as it does with the place-based nature of the communities and cultures living within island geographies. It is also the case that both geographic and cultural isolation can ebb and flow, being challenged for example in periods of rapid globalization (Jedrusik, 2011, p 202). Indeed, islands and islandness are complex, changing, and paradoxical (Thomas, 2007).

'Islandness', a concept popularized in island studies, is a term that has proven difficult to define. Conkling (2007, p 192) cites qualities of islandness as independence, loyalty, a strong sense of honour, handiness (polydextorous and multi-faceted competence), earthy common sense, fragility, opinionated machismo, tolerance of eccentricity, fragile discretion, highly individualized expressions of spirituality and superstition, a complex oral tradition, and canny literacy and intelligence. These are very broad and mostly positive, seeing islands as places of social capital and underwriting a darker side to island experience.

The idea is that being bounded or surrounded by water contributes to a psychological and sociological sense of boundedness and belonging and of difference and sameness, inclusion and exclusion in what has been termed 'the island effect' or articulation by compression. Being bound geographically reinforces a shared sense of purpose and identity among islander dwellers, while also reinforcing a connection to place. Islandness can be reinforced, for instance, through stories, such as folklore and other cultural traditions (Mountz, 2015) and islands have been considered among places (seashore, valley) where people feel strong attachment, and which have persistent appeal to the imagination (Aldrich & Johnson, 2018). Islands are often exotic and imaginative places to the outside world, but for locals, islandness is frequently expressed in determination to remain on the island and live as an economically self-sustaining community, despite the sometimes-experienced effects of population and economic decline (Amoamo, 2012, p 422). Islanders share characteristics imposed by boundedness and isolation and such qualities transcend local cultures. Often islandness is felt instinctively by those local at islands but is articulated by outsiders to islands (Conkling, 2007, p 192).

Island metaphors can serve to highlight rugged individualism, but also its opposite (Hay, 2006). Islands can create feelings of safety and community, but they can also be places that are stifling and confined from which people seek to escape *from* 'community'. Islandness could, for instance, be used interchangeably with insularity. However, one advantage of the term is that it is value-neutral, not having negative or positive connotations that terms such as insularity do (Hay, 2006). For small islands in particular, all that exists can be seen and regulated, giving them a panoptic quality that can lend itself to secrecy and exploitation, depending on who is doing the 'looking' and with what intent. In this sense, 'Visibility is a trap' (Foucault, 1977, p 200), and islands are thereby often viewed in myriad utopian and dystopian translations as natural and social laboratories (Connell, 2003, p 555). This raises debate as to whether islands are best characterized by *vulnerability*, *resilience* (Hay, 2006), or as we return to throughout this book, perhaps both. Indeed, tropes of islandness, which we argue are experienced *not* as binaries, but on a continuum, include: tradition/modernity, dependency/autonomy, roots/routes, globalization/particularity, and vulnerability/resilience (Aldrich & Johnson, 2018).

These functional thresholds for determining an island are not merely historical artefacts or curiosities. For example, the United Nations Convention on the Law of the Sea 1982 (Part VIII, Article 121) does allow exclusive economic zones to be awarded where places are incapable of sustaining human habitation or economic life on their own (Royle & Brinklow, 2018). Meanwhile, island studies, or 'nissology' (McCall, 1994; Baldacchino, 2004), has also invested much energy into defining the term 'island', as well as different island 'types'. There are Indigenous and colonized islands, resource rich and resource poor, continental and oceanic islands, and urbanized and wild islands (Hay, 2006). There is also debate over whether the physical hard edges of islands should be considered their boundaries. In many instances, the beachscape might be conceived of as a liminal space of islandness; a border that is ever shifting and changing in response to the movement of surrounding waterways and seas (Breidenbach et al, 2020). Indeed, a key focus of nissology has been to ask: what is the essence of islands and how are they different from other geographical and social formations? Are islands only water-bound places or should we develop a more elastic understanding of the term, free of physical boundaries? Is earth itself to be conceptualized as an island, for example (Fletcher, 2011, pp 20–1)? Analogous definitional concerns have troubled rural criminology, despite demographers having developed very concise definitions of the 'rural' specific to national contexts. Thus, in seeking to draw together nissology and criminology, we engage with these (and other) definitional questions throughout this book. We also, however, start below with some rough parameters for how we engage with the concept of islands from herein.

In the chapters that follow, we view islands as typically being non-urban and peripheral or isolated settings. Their borders are often 'natural', as opposed to being socially generated through politics or struggle (Hay, 2006, pp 21–2). Conceptually, we think of islands as being centrally characterized by three integral and often interlocking elements: (1) isolation/separateness; (2) small scale (though we do not always adhere fervently to Jedrusik's [2011] relatively rigid spatial criterion of islands as being <10,000km^2); and (3) some notion of security/protection. They are seemingly complete worlds secured by natural boundaries (Connell, 2003, p 555), with their 'natural' security often being reinforced/multiplied and/or eroded as socio-political uses of islands change over time and across space.

Our preference here is to think of islands in terms of both space *and* place. This enables us to look beyond objective geographic markers to consider other contextual factors, including how identity is socially constructed within these settings and how this might also link to constructions of deviance and crime. Ethnographic research has been used to illustrate, for example, how 'belonging' can be powerfully associated with islands, being rooted in a sense of community, and common heritage. It is also apposite to note that inhabitants of the Turks and Caicos Islands and of the British Virgin Islands were traditionally called 'Belongers', while the Japanese word for island, *shima*, can also mean 'community' (Royle & Brinklow, 2018). Thus, islandness also denotes particular imaginings of social cohesion; perhaps the insularity of even a large 'island' with a large population survives and is demonstrated in the majority vote for Brexit in the 2016 referendum to leave the European Union (EU) (Royle & Brinklow, 2018). Even though, as we note above, technology, transport, and globalization constantly challenge understandings of island isolation and independence, a sense of connectedness is nevertheless a crucial aspect of the island experience and water may not always be seen as a *barrier* to its realization. For instance, Tongan scholar and writer Epeli Hauʻofa wrote about the Pacific Ocean traditionally serving as a road, binding Pacific peoples together (Royle & Brinklow, 2018). In this view, therefore, the Ocean is interpreted as the *uniting* feature of Pacific Island communities, as opposed to a geographic marker of *separation* and *isolation* (as water is typically conceptualized in island studies – as in moats, for instance).

VIII

In the following chapters, we grapple with these (and other) definitional and interpretive complexities to examine how the place and space of islands can inform criminological thinking. This is not an administrative endeavour to make various arms of criminal justice systems either on islands or elsewhere function better. Nor is the driving question whether islands simply have more or less crime than other locations (though this does, at times, find its way into our discussion). Instead, we are interested in how crime and deviance are defined in island settings, which crimes are policed and visible as well as which crimes are not, who defines crime, and who is/is not subject to regulation. We are also interested in the ways that island settings, as well as features of islandness, have been mobilized socio-politically to govern and discipline deviant Others, including under (settler) colonialism. Vitally, all of these questions are informed by what we refer to here as the *politics of place and belonging*.

While the physical and demographic diversity of islands must be appreciated, we argue – and seek to show in this book – that there is a need to understand crime in islands as places of exclusion (detention centres, prisons), production (agriculture, industry), and consumption (tourism, retirement sites). Accordingly, the book is organized into key themes that enable us to delve into and more deeply explore how the space- and place-based characteristics of islands can inform criminological theorizing across these areas. In the chapter immediately following (Chapter 2), we spend some time setting out a place for island criminologies within the broader context of Southern and decolonizing criminologies. This chapter serves as something of a 'literature review', though we do not claim to be systematic or comprehensive in our presentation of relevant literature, choosing, rather, samples representative of the type of criminological research that has been conducted to date around islands. Drawing on spatial and place-based criminologies, we discuss the promise that island criminologies hold, in terms of similarly pursuing a shift away from what has been an almost exclusive focus in criminology on the metropole, and towards a deeper understanding of criminology at the so-called 'peripheries'.

In the next chapter (Chapter 3), we more deeply explore isolation as a defining characteristic of islands, charting how this feature of islandness has informed the treatment of *polluted* and *criminal* bodies across time and space, with the techniques of 'islanding' deployed by health and penal institutions often becoming interwoven and sometimes appearing as indistinguishable from one another.

In Chapter 4, we turn our focus towards islands as sites of invasion, considering how islanding can also be deployed as a form of erasure within a larger (settler) colonial toolkit of surveillance, normalization, and domination. In doing so, we extend our theorizing of island spaces to include islands situated on *terra firma* and bounded by the natural barrier of the desert. This enables us to develop a more elastic understanding of *island* as an imaginary that can affect different types of spaces and places.

In Chapter 5 we examine the issue of integration in relation to policing in the Pacific, where most research on policing islands has been conducted. We argue that small-scale and remote societies are more likely to develop a 'localistic', as opposed to 'legalistic', approach to policing. What little theoretical work has been done on policing in small places has highlighted the issue of integration and how it might both enable and limit the task of policing. We examine this issue with respect to the problem of gendered violence in island societies.

Much of the research literature on social capital assumes a consensus perspective that aligns 'the common good' with mainstream or official functions. However, just as social capital and dense social networks have been theorized in criminology as being crime protective, they can also be crime productive when the norms adopted by networks are criminogenic. In Chapter 6 we further develop aspects of the analysis in the previous chapter to examine how integration may also breed a kind of insularity. While insularity may not be crime *productive* per se, it may indeed enable conditions where certain crimes can remain hidden and be left unaddressed. We examine a series of sexual crimes committed on the very remote Pitcairn Island in the Pacific to better understand the normative nature of crime and responses to crime.

We return to notions of island exploitation in Chapter 7, critically discussing how islands have also been frequent backdrops to extractive industry, often rooted in (neo-)colonialism, that has repeatedly resulted in irreparable damage to island spaces and places. Drawing on perspectives from green criminology, we ask questions about how islandness has enabled criminal destruction of land and peoples to go relatively unchecked and unseen. This, we argue, raises significant questions about social justice for island communities into the future, particularly as the threat of climate change looms large over island spaces and places, rendering many islands as sites that are now dealing with an imminent threat of disappearance as sea levels rise.

While we take some initial steps towards charting island criminologies here, we also intend this book as an invitation to others to take more seriously the role of islands and island imaginaries in understandings of deviance and crime. Indeed, islands encapsulate and draw together myriad features of socio-political life in ways that are unique and have historical as well as contemporary relevance – particularly as we continue to grapple with the increasing precarity and uncertainty that are enduring features of the current Age of Anthropocene. Thinking through islandness in this context raises significant questions about past and future social justice, safety, and security; at their most auspicious, islands may indeed present a much-needed microcosmic window into the future, and of the shape of things to come, by revealing past and sometimes hidden or forgotten places and spaces.

2

Idylls (and Horrors)

> Looking down on the islands and the expanse of water of the carceral archipelago, we wonder about the relationship between the parts and the whole, and the difficulty of distinguishing figure and ground. Are prisons islands – discrete yet connected or might it be more fruitful to think of water itself as the constraining phenomena? Land or water as preferred metaphor for confinement? Fixed locations or fluid spaces of betweenness? (Or the air above them? Or tectonic plates beneath?)
> (Armstrong & Jefferson, 2017, p 245)

This chapter functions as something akin to a literature review. We certainly do not pretend to provide some form of systematic or empirical review of the literature on islands, but rather, in the best traditions of qualitative writing, we have selected information-rich sources to provide foundations for the chapters that follow. First, we note that criminology has always had some interest in geographies, but perhaps reflecting its modernist birth in Western Europe, criminology has been largely obsessed with urban life. Rural criminologists have sought to correct this bias, but only recently has their work adopted interpretive and critical approaches that interrogate how crime problems are constructed in the countryside and who constructs such visions of crime in rural contexts. Even when accounting for this turn, islands remain largely invisible in the context of rural criminology.

We also draw on fictional accounts of islands and crime and attempt to provide some foundations for an interpretive or cultural approach to island criminologies. In doing so, we extend the concept of 'islandness', which has significantly informed island studies, to account for two broad polar visions of islands – island idylls and island horrors. These concepts, we contend, are best operationalized through the lens of power relations. We argue here for a criminological approach to small-scale and remote societies that conceptualizes both place and space.

Social sciences, space, and place

Geography is obviously important to a project of island criminologies. In particular, geographies which account for power relations are useful in charting the place of islands as produced through discursive practices. Drawing on Raewyn Connell's (2007) work, Carrington, Hogg, and Sozzo (2016) have joined others to call for a decolonization and democratization of criminological knowledge, which they argue has privileged the epistemologies of the Global North. This follows similar calls by black and Indigenous scholars to decolonize criminology and the academy more broadly (Moreton-Robinson, 2004; Tauri, 2013; Cunneen and Tauri, 2016; Agozino, 2018, 2019; Watego, 2020, 2021). Such a project, it is contended, would assist in countering universalizing tendencies in the social sciences, which present concepts, methods, and ideas as timeless, placeless, and apolitical. In what he refers to as his *Humanifesto of the Decolonization of Criminology and Justice*, for example, Nigerian-born criminologist and genocide survivor, Biko Agozino (2019, p 13), talks about marginalization of Indigenous and black scholars in Eurocentric criminology, partly because the very discipline of criminology itself is, as he sees it, 'closely tied to the project of colonization and patriarchal imperialism as a science designed for the control of Others'.

Most islands, especially those in the Pacific, are distant from the major centres of world population, including industrial and intellectual life (Connell, 2003, p 555). Yet, 'Few islands can have excited imaginations more than those of the Pacific' (Connell, 2003, p 555). Unfortunately, for better or worse, criminologists seem to have been immune to the excitement that islands might generate. Modern conceptions of crime are linked with the advent of cities and processes of urbanization. Population growth and mobility have become fundamental to understanding how crime has been interpreted in modernity and beyond. One of the more influential criminological works of the late 20th century, John Braithwaite's *Crime Shame and Reintegration* (1989, p 44), outlines 'facts a theory of crime must fit into', drawing upon the 'strongest and most consistently reported associations in empirical criminology'. Of the 13 'facts' listed, fact number four reads: 'Crime is committed disproportionately by people living in large cities' (Braithwaite, 1989, p 47). To support this contention, Braithwaite cites higher rates of urban crime reporting in official statistics, victim surveys, and self-report surveys. Of course, Braithwaite, himself a pioneer of Southern criminologies, is right: research has mostly reported on crime in urban environments. We could add to this that research has mostly occurred in the metropoles of the Global North. As we note below, the most well-known city for spatial analysis of crime is the American city of Chicago. As Connell (2007) points out, the 'developing' or 'pre-modern' peripheries of the Global South mostly served as data-mines to test or develop the theories which emerged from Northern metropoles. In this sense, knowledge is a commodity and knowledge production does not occur in a geo-political vacuum. Not only were the pioneers of classical criminology 'white' males (needless to add, now, reputedly dead) of the Global North, the places and houses from which they published were and remain (not unlike this book) situated in the Global North (Hogg, Scott, & Sozzo, 2016). In this way, the power to create global understandings of islands is arguably best appreciated through the lens of political economy and critical geography.

Criminology textbooks are wonderful artefacts for tracing discursive constructs of crime and criminality. It is not surprising that imageries of crime, including those appearing on textbook covers, often contain references to cityscapes and urbanization. Simultaneously, remote, rural, and isolated places are almost universally neglected in criminological textbooks. Similarly, political economy dictates that textbook production mostly occurs in the Global North. A country such as Australia is relatively wealthy enough to produce 'its own' texts with the aid of Northern publishing houses, but these are dependent on a criminological canon derived from the Global North. You are, for example, unlikely to find references to Australia's closest neighbours (island nations) in Australian criminology texts, or even those of its biggest trading partners (excluding the unilateral knowledge trade).

Criminology, as with the rest of the social sciences, has largely theorized by drawing on the temporal dimensions of crime. While, however, both 'place' (the social construction of crime in space) and 'space' (the objective social and geographic conditions that have criminogenic impacts) are important in criminology, the former has been relatively neglected. Indeed, *place* has mostly been an afterthought in criminology, examined occasionally with reference to fear of crime (see Loader et al, 2000) or in cultural criminology focusing on urbanity (see Hayward, 2004) or rurality (see Scott & Hogg, 2015). However, as Murray (2017, p 32) argues, humans are 'placelings' in that all action and thought is located in place.

Place sculpts the identity of peoples (for example, mountain people, coastal peoples, polar peoples, forest peoples, jungle peoples, and so on) (Hay, 2006, p 22) and, similarly, places are also dependent on people for their identity (Memmott et al, 2006, p 41). Although place is a foundational concept in geography, it was not until the 1970s that a phenomenology of space in geography emerged with an emphasis on place as 'space with meaning'. Phenomenology would argue that our personal and social experiences are embodied and are inclusive of the way in which we experience places (Murray, 2017, pp 32–5). As such, it is not just the objective or physical characteristics of space that are important; place can also be a location or repository of meaning, imbued by individuals, groups, and socio-cultural processes (Tuan, 1979; Altman & Low, 1992; Kolodziejski, 2014, pp 29–30). As Armstrong and Jefferson (2017, p 245) point out in the epigraph at the beginning of this chapter, place-making bends and flexes in response to geographic markers like water and land, but place is also a discursive construct that ranges from home to state and informs identity, such as ethnicity. It is embodied in a simple and common question asked in first encounters: where do you come from? And yet, such a common question can have a myriad of responses depending on the context of interaction. Moreover, perceptions of places, including fear of crime, can be both evocative and highly criminogenic. For example, there have long been 'bad neighbourhoods', slums, ghettos, shanty towns, and crime hot spots. In popular culture, London's East End has a strong association with the 'Ripper' murders and New York City's Central Park with muggings. Such associations can be hard to dislodge. There are also placeless locations or 'non-places', such as airports, which get stripped of character and are virtually indistinguishable from one another, being almost devoid of meaning (Kolodziejski, 2014, p 29).

People can have a conceptual attachment to place or a space-specific attachment (Kolodziejski, 2014, pp 29–30) and have a strong sense of place, either positive or negative. This perception may depend on the degree to which they have agency in regard to their location. For instance, some people are born and bred in places and others choose to relocate (Kolodziejski, 2014, pp 43–4). Place attachment can also be informed by emotion, cognition, practice, action, social relations, and temporal aspects (Altman & Low, 1992). Place attachment has been linked to pro-environmental behaviours (Scannell & Gilford, 2010), just as it could be linked to crime prevention. Place attachment might also be considered one element, albeit an important one, which informs belonging – a concept used in sociology and political-ecology in relation to in-groups and out-groups and one that is often closely associated with longevity in place. There is also a link here to the associated concepts of social capital and collective efficacy, which we elaborate on later in relation to rural and remote criminologies (Wikstrom & Sampson, 2003).

In contrast to the relatively neglected status of *place* in the social sciences, *space* has continued to be a primary focus of criminologists, notwithstanding that different spaces have received unequal attention. Space was highly visible in some of the foundational texts of criminology. For example, crime maps were among the first products of classical criminology and were created during the 19th century by Andre-Michel Guerry and Adolphe Quetelet, founders of the Cartographic School of Criminology. They tried to measure and plot delinquency and deviance across space, albeit they also laid foundations for criminology's obsession with delinquency and urban environments. In this way, tools essential to colonial projects first emerged in Northern cities. For the scientific flâneur, the slums of Europe were distant but proximate and largely invisible (Weisburd, Bernasco, & Bruinsma, 2009; Weisburd et al, 2009).

European interest in geographic and statistical analysis of crime ebbed after the 19th century, perhaps owing to a relative easing of the 'strains' associated with mass urbanization and industrialization. The early spatial works were followed by the Chicago School in the 1920–30s, which combined ecologies of crime with urban sociology to chart the spatial distribution of crime, arguing that crime was linked to social disorganization and poverty in urban settings. The analysis also shifted from a regional and comparative focus to an emphasis on crime within cities, communities, and neighbourhoods. Chicago, like many other American cities, had witnessed phenomenal growth, going from being a small village in the 1840s to a city of almost four million a century later (Weisburd et al, 2009). The Chicago School was followed by a second wave of environmental sociology in the 1970–80s, notable among which was Cohen and Felson's (1979) critique of criminology's focus on individual motivation and resistance to examining the situational influence of places (Weisburd & Eck, 2017). This work has been advanced more recently with computerized mapping devices and digitalized police records (Russo & Strazzari, 2019, p 2). Much of this research has been foundational to crime prevention and a focus on the physical, situational, and environmental factors which make crime possible. Routine activity theory, situational crime prevention, crime pattern theory, and place management theory all put great emphasis on opportunities available to offenders in specific spaces or environments (Russo & Strazzari, 2019, pp 5–6).

Another line of inquiry, pioneered by Robert Sampson, emphasizes the social characteristics of areas, such as socio-economic features of populations and their relative levels of social integration. This has conceptualized the idea of 'collective efficacy' of populations, which examines the capacity of communities to develop and administer informal social controls (Russo & Strazzari, 2019, p 6). This body of work is notable to the extent that it has been the dominant framework informing 'rural criminology', which, as we argue in this chapter, provides insights for island criminologies. 'Social disorganization theory' asserts that communities with high density of acquaintanceship (social capital) through informal and formal interaction and shared membership in local groups will exhibit comparatively lower crime, largely because density of acquaintanceship among individuals leads to greater capacity to exert informal controls, such as gossip, to control deviant and criminal activities (Bursik & Grasmick, 1993).

Generally, rural areas have been considered to have less evidence of social disorganization than metropolitan or cosmopolitan spaces. One exception has been Australia. Whereas crime is racialized in the Global North with reference to urban enclaves, in Australia law and order politics has often been played out in remote areas, where social disorganization and crime are presented as racialized problems; as Indigenous problems (something we canvass more critically in Chapter 4) (for example, Hogg & Carrington,

2006). Conversely, rural (rather than remote) Australian communities have typically been considered to have more intact families, more stable populations, greater homogeneity, and stronger social bonding (Gardner & Shoemaker, 1989). Most recently, 21st-century criminological research has drawn attention to borders and border regimes, which shift the gaze of scholarship to the possibility of Other spaces and places that exist *beyond* the borders of Empire (themes which we also return to later in this book). Recent work has also grappled with the peripheralization of poorer suburbs and the creation of fabricated zones of danger. As we discuss in Chapter 3, there has also been much work on spaces of incarceration, including prisons, detention centres, secure care units, therapeutic wards, and other carceral 'enclaves' (Turner, 2007). Moreover, contemporary policing research has drawn on 'micro' or spatially bounded sites of protection, risk management, surveillance, and investigation, which include 'hot spots' and 'secure zones' (Russo & Strazzari, 2019, pp 2–3). Nevertheless, it is still the case that aside from only relatively recently emerging rural and remote criminologies, the criminological gaze has been largely Eurocentric, Northern, and urban, severely biasing criminological scholarship and theorizing.

Researching islands

Rural spaces have long been identified as distinct from urban spaces in the social sciences. While criminology has largely neglected rural and remote places, so-called 'rural' criminology' has similarly neglected islands and other remote locations. Criminologists in the US have maintained a limited interest in rural crime since before the mid-20th century, while recent decades have seen growing interest in rural crime, as demonstrated in the development of organized groupings, journals, and book series devoted to its study. Typically, rural crime literature has been content to focus on agriculture and *gemeinschaft* relations, or insider–outsider relations. One of the earliest and most resilient means of defining and categorizing rural and urban stems from Tönnies' (1957) notion of *Gemeinschaft*, which contrasted rural community with urban society, the latter described as *Gesellschaft*.

Much of what has passed as rural criminology has been content to look at what are imagined to be relatively tightly integrated and static social networks in rural locations, particularly in terms of their social control or crime preventative effects, the idea being that tighter social integration in rural places assists in crime prevention. Indeed, early rural criminology was largely focused on how social order is created in rural settings and not concerned with how differentiation is achieved, and/or how difference is produced in social networks. This leads to a key limitation of early rural criminology, it being largely uncritical in orientation, often ignoring power relations in its analysis of crime. Rural criminology often neglected how difference and differentiation was achieved in small-scale social and remote settings and failed to examine the social construction of crime in such places. The social disorganization frameworks which have dominated rural criminology have been more concerned with problem solving than how social problems are constituted in rural places – that is, definitional activities of social groups in rural places in terms of claim-making activities associated with crime problems (Schnieder, 1985). For instance, although evidence suggests high rates of violent crimes in many rural societies, the focus of law and order is almost exclusively on property crime, young people, and public disorder (Hogg & Carrington, 2006, p 168). When rural places have been presented as criminological concerns, the focus has tended to be on farm production, service delivery, and planning, mostly to aid what might be called 'crime prevention' efforts. In this way, 'crime' has typically been constructed from the perspective of dominant social groups residing in rural settings. In much rural criminology and sociology, white male landholders/farmers have been the public symbols of rural life and, accordingly, also the victims of rural crime. The interests and economic wellbeing of such groups has been presented as fundamental for the wellbeing of other rural groups (Lockie, 2001).

Studies have observed the invisibility of women in rural research or the tendency to confine women to private spheres associated with housewifery or mothering. Since the 1970s, there have been efforts to correct this bias, especially on the part of critical and feminist scholars who have drawn attention to relations of production and gendered normative structures within small and remote communities. This has shed light on how the work women do in rural places is undervalued and made invisible in a way that further compounds their disenfranchisement under patriarchal capitalism more generally. An intersectional lens enables us to see how this is even further exacerbated for women of colour, including Indigenous women, whose labour is regularly devalued and ignored altogether (Crenshaw, 2011; McKinley, Liddell, & Lilly, 2021). More recently there have been efforts to examine gendered crime within a rural context (DeKeseredy & Schwartz, 2009) and the racialization of crime in rural contexts (Hogg & Carrington, 2006). In this way, there is a growing body of critical research that contradicts these romantic images of a crime-free rural life (La Nauze & Rutherford, 1997; Websdale,1998; Neame & Heenan, 2004; Hogg & Carrington, 2006).

Philo (1997) has pleaded with rural studies to engage with neglected 'rural Others', which he argues have been painted out of the rural landscape. In a similar vein, Murdoch and Pratt (1997) have drawn attention to 'strange ruralities' to highlight difference and division in the countryside. Rural Others are presented as illegitimate members of the rural community because of social characteristics or markings they embody. In the British experience such groups have included (but are not restricted to) those identifying as queer, single mothers, travellers/Romany, and non-white. Similarly absent are others with differing ethnic, social, or economic backgrounds, who might also have legitimate and unique claims in their own right to be representative of rural places (Carrington et al, 2009). The cultural, social, economic, and political significance of these groups has been understated in public discourses and this has translated to the research literature.

Islands have been significant in the development of the physical sciences, especially evolutionary theory, though they have been much less influential in the social sciences despite the laboratory-like environs they exemplify. Nonetheless, classical anthropology drew heavily on island research. While it is highly problematic (most notably in its depiction of islands as backwater homes to 'savage' peoples), Malinowski's work in the Trobriand Islands, which included *The Sexual Life of Savages* (1929), emphasized the sexual freedoms of islanders. This imagery was later popularized in a range of texts, from postcards to *The National Geographic* which, as with earlier texts, characterized Polynesian islands as picturesque, bountiful, exotic, and sexualized (Connell, 2003). Margaret Mead's *Coming of Age in Samoa* (1928), while also problematic, remains arguably the most famous anthropological work written. She was critical of the pseudo-liberating forces of modernity, and while presenting societies as 'primitive' and untouched, she did not necessarily equate simplicity with inferiority. Rather, she adopted a form of pluralism that allowed her to see 'simple' societies producing solutions to complex problems. Her work challenged the fashionable psychoanalysis of the period and its structural emphasis, instead appealing to an American society attracted to notions of individual freedom (Baldacchino, 2004, pp 274–5). Baldacchino (2004, p 276) argues that Mead was keen not just to learn about islands and islanders, but *from* them. 'Mead didn't go to Samoa just to study Samoa. Rather she wanted to understand the whole human race' (Pipher, 2001, p xviii). In one excerpt, Mead (2001, p 88) reflected:

> How little privacy any one has ... all of an individual's acts are public property ... there is a very general cognizance on the part of the whole village of the activity of every single inhabitant. ... The oppressive atmosphere of a small town is all about them; in an hour, children will have made a dancing song of their most secret acts.

This passage reinforces some of the arguments above regarding why crime has been largely invisible in remote and rural locations. Indeed, strong social organization networks are likely to exist in communities that exhibit stable population patterns and widespread and intimate personal bonds. Other studies have similarly demonstrated that belonging is attached to a strong sense of community, kinship, and shared heritage in island spaces, including those on the peripheries of (Northern) Empires, such as Anthony Cohen's classic study of Whalsay in the Shetland Islands and Messanger's older account of Inishere in the Aran Islands of Ireland (Dodds & Royle, 2003).

Islands have only recently appeared in criminology, though studies generally do not deeply consider the critical or constructed characteristics of island settings. For example, Stallwitz (2012) situated their empirical study on heroin use in the Shetland Islands (Scotland) within rural criminology but did not take account of the potential uniqueness the islands might hold *beyond* their mere rurality. A focus on island spaces has also arisen in the literature concerning organized crime, for example in: Corsica (mafia-like clans); the Dutch Antilles; the Canary Islands or Cape Vert (drugs); the Cayman Islands, Virgin Islands, Isle of Man, Island of Jersey (tax havens and money laundering); and Lampedusa and Zanzibar (human trafficking). In some cases, such as in The Bahamas, organized crime arguably has at times represented a form of neo-colonialism, layered upon older forms of colonial rule (Block & Klausner, 1987). Indeed, as Block and Klausner (1987) discuss, The Bahamas – which were first colonized by the Spanish in the 17th century, and then by the British until the early 1970s – have been chiefly controlled and dominated by large, organized crime syndicates since the withdrawal of British colonial rule, establishing a new form of dominion over the islands. This draws attention to the way in which islands have been enmeshed with global markets in the 19th and 20th centuries. Remoteness and proximity to international borders create conditions that challenge powerful Northern state controls of terrains and routes and thus states have been ready to support research that examines islands as havens for white-collar crime. Indeed, from the early modern period, with piracy as a challenge to vessels carrying national flags, islands provided a haven for criminal entrepreneurs (Russo & Strazzari, 2019, p 4). The legacy of colonial empires, many islands have become *zona franca*; offshore financial centres with geographic insularity (Russo & Strazzari, 2019, p 4). Small island economies frequently have diseconomies of scale, dysfunctional market structures, high transport costs, high openness to international trade, limited natural resources, small labour markets, and deficiencies in professional and institutional resources that further render them attractive sites for white-collar criminals (Russo & Strazzari, 2019, p 4). In a recent example, Little St. James in the US Virgin Islands was purchased by American financier and convicted sex offender Jeffrey Epstein in 1998 and, as late as 2019, operated as the epicentre of an international sex-trafficking ring, with underage girls continuing to be taken by him to the island (Aguirre, 2019). The island gained a reputation for depravity and decadence during this period, being dubbed 'the Island of Sin'.

Frequently, islands are also known in the Global North as tourist sites providing solid transport links and lodging services, attractive climates, and leisure facilities that are appealing to investors, bankers, and accountants alike

(Russo & Strazzari, 2019, p 4). Raineri (2019), for example, argues that Malta's structural characteristics have rendered it a haven for transnational criminal activities. It is a small island state with few natural resources, yet it is hardly 'isolated' and acts as a crossroads within the Mediterranean, with much global 'connectography'. These structural qualities combine with unit-specific features, common to so-called shadow states, which are frequently found in post-colonial settings where rulers bolster political power through patronage and criminal or pseudo-criminal 'business' dealings, creating illicit economic flows. The Cayman Islands and Jersey illustrate the development of offshore banking in spaces removed from the 'normal' practices of state sovereignty and territorial jurisdiction. Surrounded by bodies of water, they possess unique geological, geographical, and cultural histories owing to their limited populations, isolation, and resource scarcity (Dodds & Royle, 2003, p 487).

There has also been much written about crime and tourism, a large proportion of it focusing on islands, especially the Caribbean, not surprisingly situated in the Global North. It is perhaps no accident that the post- or neo-colonial period that commenced in the mid-20th century also coincided with the advent of widespread airline travel and global tourism. Tourism has become the chief industry of many former island colonies. Early accounts of tourism and crime argued that property offences, rather than violent offences, were more closely linked to tourism, and mass tourism has been closely aligned with increases in crime rates (mostly property) on islands (Albuquerque & McElroy, 1999) as well as the notion that tourists are more likely to be victims of such crime, rather than residents (Chesney-Lind & Lind, 1986). Two theories, both ecological, have dominated theorizing on island tourism and crime, these being routine activities theory and hot-spot theory (Albuquerque & McElroy, 1999). For instance, Albuquerque and McElroy (1999) examined the ways in which tourists' safety could be enhanced by drawing on hot-spot and routine activities theory, concluding that tourists are more likely to take risks abroad and are more vulnerable to victimization because of their outsider status.

Research has typically accepted the reality of the 'drug scourge' and organized gangs as being the chief problem of island tourist destinations, such as the Caribbean (Karagiannis & Madjd-Sadjadi, 2012). To protect tourists and their lucrative tourism sectors, islands have developed 'enclave tourism' which might be likened to 'gated' resorts whereby tourists are shuttled to and from airports in a fly-in-fly-out fashion, which isolates them from local island cultures and creates resentment towards foreigners among the population who work and live outside the resort compound (Albuquerque & McElroy, 1999). There are claims that enclave tourism encourages violent criminal activity directed against tourists, but data from some Caribbean nations indicate local populations continue to suffer disproportionately from violent crime, while also constructing island nations as havens for violent crime (Karagiannis & Madjd-Sadjadi, 2012, pp 77–8).

Some well-publicized violent robberies in the Caribbean during the 1980s and 1990s shook the tourism industry and views of the tropical Atlantic islands as an 'American Paradise' in a similar way in which the 2002 Bali bombings disrupted Australian constructs of Bali. The disappearance of a young, white, female American tourist on the Caribbean island of Aruba in 2005 was widely covered by US media and led to a drop in American tourism to the island in subsequent years, despite its relatively low historic crime rates. Media coverage exoticized the island and framed its criminal justice system as ineffectual and incompetent. Other Caribbean countries, such as Jamaica, have similarly been impacted economically by well-publicized violent crimes (Brown, 2015). Moreover, during the early 1990s the US Virgin Islands had the supposed and dubious distinction of having higher violent crime rates than New York City, which led tourism officials to hire a major public relations firm to improve the image of what the local police chief described as 'our islands' (Albuquerque & McElroy, 1999, pp 972–3). Tourism crime reminds us that islands are often highly racialized post-colonial settings. In tourist scenarios, the outsiders are victims of crime and the typical focus is crime prevention to improve the safety of the economically significant group (Albuquerque & McElroy, 1999). In this research the safety of the outsiders takes precedence over socio-structural factors, such as the economic exploitation of islands and their inhabitants.

In a rare and excellent critical piece on islands, Young and Woodiwiss (2019) argued that the dominant law and order focus in the Caribbean by international legal institutions (in turn influencing local institutions) has been drug trafficking as a form of organized crime. This presents a major security threat to all nations, notably the US, which has used its power to fund research and crime control, in line with its war on drugs from the 1970s onwards. There is a dearth of research that challenges this agenda in small developing island states. The authors contend that the way in which assumptions involving the war on drugs have been readily accepted by academics, policymakers, and international legal communities is underpinned by post-colonial ideologies. It would seem no accident that the war on drugs had as its primary targets black communities internal to the US and that the international policies have harshly impacted states in the Caribbean with majority black populations. The US paradigm of organized crime control policy continues to frame drug trafficking as the main problem in the Caribbean. However, the authors argue that the most significant criminal justice issue facing the Caribbean is the illegal trafficking of firearms mostly from the US, which has been ignored. They cite research that has shown Jamaican law enforcement authorities have long recognized the threat of firearm trafficking, but that this is represented internationally as a Jamaican problem. They also show that research indicates that the volume of firearms being trafficked from the US has increased in recent years, as has the rate of crime associated with firearm use. Karagiannis and Madjd-Sadjadi (2012, p 82) also observe that perhaps the biggest challenge to crime control in the Caribbean is:

> to provide the youth of the Caribbean with well-paying, full-time, permanent jobs ... [since] The lack of opportunities for constructive engagement lead wayward youth to pursue antisocial behaviours ... [They also recognize that] Corruption is an ongoing battle that makes it difficult to fight crime because the same people who are sworn to uphold the law are also breaking it ... [thereby breeding] contempt for the rule of law among the populace. (Karagiannis & Madjd-Sadjadi, 2012, p 82)

So, beyond white-collar crime and tourism crime, criminological research has rarely focused on island nations and, where it has, tends to be descriptive and empiricist in application. There are exceptions. Hodgkinson et al (2017, p 109), for example, examine fear of crime in the Maldives, noting that 'most theorizing and empirical research on fear of crime has involved large liberal Western democratic societies ... [meaning] it is not evident whether findings can be generalized to smaller, more rural indigenous island population locations'. Moreover, some work has been critical and focused on the post-colonial experience (see Pratt & Melei, 2018).

A recent study of four Nordic island societies provides some much-needed attention to islands and crime in the Global North. Although the research delves little into theory, it is notable that some of the islands in the study had been former colonies and, as in the case of the Faroe Islands and Greenland, are governed with limited autonomy by Denmark and in the case of Åland, by Finland (Lauritson, 2019). The island societies all contain small populations, although population density varies considerably in each. While Nordic countries have very low crime rates and prison populations compared with other regions in Europe, each of the island societies examined in this project experience crime that is even relatively *lower* than 'mainland' Nordic countries. For example, the Faroe Islands in 2016–18 had 12 prisoners for 100,000 inhabitants, while mainland Nordic countries had between 51 and 63 prisoners per 100,000 population; still low compared with the median Western European rate of 81 prisoners per 100,000 population. Insofar as crime reports received by the police in the Faroe Islands are concerned, there were a total of 468 crimes in 2018, of which thefts comprised the bulk.

One proposed reason for the relatively low crime rates is a high level of income equality in each of the island societies. Up until recently, traditional living in small communities meant that prison was rarely imposed on offenders and Greenland did not have a prison until an open correctional centre with low level security and an 18-person capacity was opened in 1967. The main principle of the institution was that the convicted person should maintain their affiliation with the surrounding community through employment in the city, so they could be re-socialized and supported for a future crime-free existence (which is similar to the case study of a Norwegian Prison Island we discuss in greater detail in Chapter 3). However, due to the breakdown of traditional society through 'modernization' in the 1980–90s, demand for extra prison facilities grew and what was termed 'The Great Greenlandic Incarceration' started, with the institutional capacity doubling and the number of prisoners in relation to the general population greatly surpassing anything previously known in the Nordic countries. Subsequently, Greenland's incarceration rate strongly surpasses that of the other islands in the study, which may not be surprising when considering it is the furthest of the societies from its colonial mainland and that it has the highest Indigenous population of the societies studied, which raises the potential that the criminal justice system has also been utilized as a tool of colonialism (as has been seen in many other sites globally, as discussed in Chapter 4). Today, Greenland's correctional facilities resemble other closed prison sites in Europe, where barbed wire, surveillance cameras, and locked doors have gradually come to increase control, while training, treatment, and employment resocialization is relatively limited. Just over half of reported crimes are property crime violations and about 20 per cent of crime is interpersonal violence, with about 10 per cent made up of sexual offences. The reporting frequency of sexual offences in Greenland is almost ten times higher than in Denmark. In general, the Greenlandic society appears considerably more violent than the Danish.

Aside from this focus on crime in Nordic island societies, and the sporadic appearance of islands in some criminological research concerning tourism and white-collar crime, there has been little theorizing of crime in island spaces and places. The existing research rarely delves into theory and consistently overlooks the interwoven effects of space and place when considering how crime is constructed and experienced in island contexts. Islands have instead long remained on the periphery of criminological thinking. In the remaining sections of this book, however, we aim to rectify this.

In doing this we draw on recent post-colonial theorizing. For example, as Pacific Islands transitioned to independence, then nationalism, and then nation building, identities and traditions were reviewed independent of colonial impositions. The notion of the Pacific Way allowed islanders to value those things that outsiders were considered to lack, such as attachment to place, extended kinship solidarity, reciprocal obligations, and a strong sense of community, consensus, and compromise in decision-making, appreciation of nature, and spirituality. While ideological and mythological in scope, the Pacific Way provided an alternative identity and a point from which to launch a critique of the 'modern, capitalist, community-subsuming state (Connell, 2003, p 571).

Over the last 40 years the place of islands in culture has been re-evaluated and re-imagined with respect to environment and inhabitants. In particular, 'continental island discourse' which presented 'islands as opposed to the sea, isolated, delimited, conversely paradisiacal or hellish, enclosed habitats, fragile environments, and individuated containers for archaic biologies and cultures', has been critiqued (Goldie, 2011, pp 3–4). Part of this shift relates to the spatial turn in the social sciences, sparked by Deleuze and Guattari's writings on 'deterritorialization' and the nomad, while another impetus has been post-colonial discourses. A key writer to have conceptualized islands, with reference to the Pacific in particular, is theorist and fiction writer Epeli Hau'ofa, who:

> analyses envisage islander perceptions of the sea which, unlike continental ideas, do not oppose the sea to the land or perceive the sea as a dead, threatening, or uninhabitable place. Hau'ofa's phrase 'a sea of islands' describes Oceania by taking into account the sea as much as the land. Moreover, he describes the ways in which the sea is a source of sustenance and narrative as well as a medium of communication. (Goldie, 2011, pp 7–8)

However, Hau'ofa and others' reconceptualizations have been criticized for their generalizations, idealism, and transcendent gestures, which seem to replace insularity with universal interaction. Insularity is not merely a construct that exists outside islands to be placed on them and their inhabitants but is something that is created and manipulated by islanders themselves (Goldie, 2011, pp 9–10).

Crime fiction

Islands are a central metaphor in Western discourse, informed by utopian and dystopian stereotypes. As noted in the previous chapter, not unlike rural places, discursive constructions of islands in popular culture veer between two poles, providing for diverse and contradictory meanings and narratives. The isolation and remoteness of some islands is especially evocative of what might be termed 'island-idylls' and 'island-horrors'. Both tropes are important to the criminological narrative as both speak to idealized articulations of human nature and social order. Each became prominent with Western imperial expansion. Indeed, islands were important sites at the very beginnings of Western colonization and imperialism (as per Chapter 4) and remain today among some of the last vestiges and dormant reminders of empires. Within these contexts, these analogies have been primarily (though not exclusively) constructed from the 'outside, in' by those observing and imagining island life, rather than by island locals themselves.

Islands have been popular sites for the creation of crime fiction, both dark and fanciful. A recent example is the critically acclaimed HBO series *The White Lotus* (2021). The series is set in an exclusive resort on a Hawaiian island and involves a burglary, commencing with cargo, labelled 'human remains' being loaded onto a commercial airplane. While murder and robbery form crucial aspects of the plot elements, the real victims of crime are less the tourists, presented as self-centred and materialistic, but are instead the hotel workers, many of whom are Indigenous islanders who have had their land stolen from them only to work menially in the resort. The series explores the power structures that define our world and provides a counter-narrative to the trope of tourists as crime victims, discussed in the previous chapter.

The cynicism and politics of *The White Lotus*, however, is rare in popular culture and can be contrasted with the pure escapism of the long-running and highly popular British crime drama *Death in Paradise*. Part of the attraction of *Death in Paradise* has been put down to 'meteorological escapism', airing, as it does, during winter in the UK. However, this alone cannot account for its widespread popularity which extends to the warmer regions of the world. Since first airing in 2010, the series has been one of the highest-rated dramas in the UK and has screened in 237 territories. The series follows a plot outline which would be familiar to readers of the classic age of detective fiction: a serene situation is disrupted by a murder; the lead investigator summons all suspects to a location (often the scene of the murder) and recounts through flashback the series of events which leads to the identification of the murderer and explanation of their motivation. Each episode concludes with the restoration of serenity, with the police officers celebrating the resolution to another difficult investigation. St Marie's status as an island colony of Britain is reflected in its main economy being tourism and, indeed, the victims and perpetrators of crime are often presented as tourists, living a luxurious lifestyle. The series breaks with the gritty realism of much British crime drama of preceding decades to present a post-colonial world of consumerism and escapism (Hasan, 2017).

Crime writers have long exploited both the physical space (the island) and islandness (experience of place) of small islands. Crane (2016) lists an extensive array of contemporary detective and crime literature associated with islands and demonstrates how the meanings produced and circulated by genre novels are contingent on 'placial' thinking, with island settings including the Shetland Islands (northern UK), Isle of Man (between the UK and Northern Ireland), Outer Hebrides (Scotland), Mediterranean, Artic, Falklands (south west of Argentina), Hawaiian (Pacific Ocean), Americas Atlantic coast, and the South Pacific. Islands are often provided an agency in placial discourse and, through their supposed isolation, are able to influence peoples' mindsets and actions. Islands are not passive backdrops for characters, but drive narrative and produce meanings.

The Faroe Islands, rocky islands 370 miles west of Norway with a population of just 50,000, boast the lowest crime rate in the world. Nonetheless, they have become a key site in the Nordic noir genre, acting as a focus for crime-fiction writers from Spain, Scotland, Poland, and Denmark's own best-selling crime writer, Jógvan Isaksen. Although suffering from a spree of fictional murders, the islands have in reality experienced only four murders in the last three decades. The islands' turf-roofed prison has a mini-golf course, no bars on its windows, and boasts picturesque mountain scenery. Police on the islands say that their most onerous duties are reporting deaths that result from the harsh weather the islands are often exposed to. Alongside that, there are also reportedly infrequent drunken brawls between men (Crane, 2016).

Placial elements, especially spatial restrictions, have been important in crime writing, as reflected in locked-room and country house representations, which *Death in Paradise* draws on, and islands have been a persistent setting in detective fiction from the Golden Age of the genre (see Agatha Christie and Margery Allingham) to more recent waves of Nordic and Tartan noir (see Mai Jungstedt and Peter May) (Fletcher, 2011; Crane, 2016). Indeed, the Golden Age of detective and mystery fiction, during the late 19th and early 20th centuries, had stories frequently set in claustrophobic worlds and closed stages of ships, planes, universities, libraries, and of course, the English country house. Christie, in particular, specialized in the kind of 'locked room' mystery first set out in Poe's *Murders in the Rue Morgue* (1841). *And Then There Were None* (1939) is Agatha Christie's most well-known work and, having sold over 100 million copies, is not only the world's best-selling crime fiction, but also one of the best-selling books of all time. The stage for the mystery is a mansion situated on an isolated island off the coast of Devon, inspired by actual Burgh Island Hotel frequented by Christie also off the coast of Devon, which would also provide inspiration for her later Hercule Poirot detective fiction novel, *Evil Under the Sun* (1941). In *And Then There Were None* (1939), Christie assembles a cast of ten people on a small island off the coast of Great Britain, then proceeds to have them killed off one by one. The victims are all related in that each has allegedly been responsible for the death of another person, without having received any kind of punishment from the legal system. The island, cut off from the mainland by wild seas, proves to be the perfect setting for an expanded locked-room mystery and the dénouement proves to be ingenious, if somewhat unlikely. In Christie's work, islands, not unlike a rural village, provide the natural boundedness of an enclosed chamber and are prone to gossip and eavesdropping. These settings become the locus for wider social structures and power relationships, being highly ordered – albeit exotic – worlds in the disrupted spaces of modernity. They are often hierarchical and organic communities where outsiders are not welcome.

Idyll

To understand how islands have been imagined and how islandness is reproduced, we can draw from Bell's (2006) concept of the rural idyll. Bell argues the rural idyll to be a symbolic landscape into which various meanings of rurality are condensed. 'Idyllization' involves processes that produce stylized representations of the countryside, while simultaneously rendering certain aspects of rurality marginalized or invisible. In criminological idyllization certain types of crime are highlighted and certain 'crimes' are hidden. For example, the genocide that occurred in colonies to create settler space, may be unexamined as crime. The theft of land and resources typified the colonial and now neo-colonial experience. The destruction of rural and remote environments has only recently been highlighted by green criminology, with landscape itself a victim of crimes perpetuated upon it.

For Bell (2006), the idyll is symbolically and materially an exclusive and exclusionary space. With respect to this, idyllization tends to obscure aspects of difference, fragmentation, and division in the countryside. In this way idyllization can be considered as an ideological process. What is often produced is reification of a community and social order as a bounded and sealed space. Ignored in this process are more complex social relations and social networks, notably relations of power. Representations of place in 'rural criminology' often ignore certain places which challenge a neat and bounded conception of the rural as agricultural. As per the examples in the previous section, this process may involve making island tourists visible as victims, while rendering the problems of islanders invisible or marginal. Important in Northern narratives of islands is their value as sites of consumption – a point taken for granted in *Death in Paradise* and rendered cynically in *The White Lotus*. Connell (2003, p 573) while acknowledging diverse possibilities, argues that islands are predominantly represented as utopian places 'in which to construct social and spatial ideologies, reconfiguring landscapes and peoples, as projections of outsiders', and more recently insiders', visions'.

Early precursors to island literature include Shakespeare's *The Tempest* (1611), More's *Utopia* (1516), Bacon's *New Atlantis* (1626), and Defoe's *Robinson Crusoe* (1719). Another early precursor, *Gulliver's Travels* (1719), had been inspired by Dampier's voyage across the Pacific and along the coast of New Holland (Connell, 2003, p 562). These are like early sociological writings, which use islands as a stage to present mainland visions. *Robinson Crusoe* drew on Shakespeare's *The Tempest* and was so successful that it created a genre of fiction sometimes referred to as a 'Robinsonade' or 'desert island story'. Unlike *The Tempest*, this novel and those that followed and imitated it presented a colonial undercurrent, with the island being an inhospitable place from which progress could be achieved through rationality and technology (see also, *Gulliver's Travels*). The genre can more recently be found in science fiction dealing with isolated planets (see *Lost in Space*), while its high point was perhaps R.M. Ballantyne's *The Coral Island: A Tale of the Pacific Ocean* (1858), which was immensely popular and considered a classic for English-speaking schoolchildren for much of the 20th century (other popular versions include *The Blue Lagoon* and *Castaway*). Islands captured a boyish spirit of male adventure and freedom from oppressive governments and moral norms. Escapist and *Boys' Own* story dreams were captured in a slew of imperialist-period texts in which the establishment of ideal societies played to escapist fantasies of readers (Connell, 2003, p 556).

Many of these depictions of the island-idyll drew on imperial exploration in the Pacific and fuelled images of latter-day gardens of Eden and ideas of Pacific culture as an exotic Other (Amoamo, 2011, pp 2–3). Urbanization during the 18th and 19th centuries saw Europeans pine for imagined landscapes and lands that had never existed, be they countryside Arcadias or tropical island retreats. The Romantic Movement invented isolated Arcadias (not unlike gated communities), free of the vice, disease, and pollution identified with the urban landscape. In Europe and North America, idealized visions of nature and wilderness were positioned as something that existed in the past or that were under threat – something to be preserved. In the colonial experience it was quite different. Nature and the wilderness were something to be conquered – even re-invented. Instead of people flooding into urban landscapes, the 19th century saw movement into 'empty' and remote colonial settings. The social sciences, including criminology, also briefly played a significant role in colonizing remote areas through creating constructs of space and place.

The South Sea Islands represented an escape or return to nature from the misery and drabness of the Industrial Revolution. During the first significant encounters, European philosophy proclaimed islanders 'noble savages' whose proximity to nature made them relatively morally pure (Connell, 2003, p 556). This 'discovery' also coincided with the Industrial Revolution. As (Connell, 2003, p 556) puts it, 'in cold lands under grey skies, a harsh repressive urban industrial landscape was being created, whilst on hot islands in warm blue seas, nature appeared bounteous to local people and particularly to scurvy ridden sailors'. Of course, the beneficial qualities of islands were not lost on Enlightenment penal reformers and isolation served to not only incapacitate criminals, but it could also enhance rehabilitative functions. As Hogg and Brown (2018) have observed, transportation as a penal project has been largely forgotten today. While it was characteristically 'Southern', it was also at times an island project and a global one (Hogg & Brown, 2019). As we canvass in Chapter 4, what more were the rotting hulks on the 19th-century Thames than man-made islands? What more was Australia than a series of 'punishment' islands ranging from New Holland to Tasmania and Norfolk?

Islanders were considered physically attractive and fit and apparently amorous and uninhibited (see Chapter 2). This became a foundation for a persistent feminization and eroticization of the Pacific through the gaze of outsider males (Connell, 2003, p 556). In modernity, Pacific Islands represented an erotic and permissive society which contrasted to the repressive social norms of the Victorian period (Pitt, 1980, pp 1051–9).

The explosion of the Polynesian myth can be located with Bougainville's report of his voyage to Tahiti, published in 1771, following which Rousseau popularized the idea of the 'noble savage' in Europe. Rousseau, pioneering Romanticism and its nature worship, delighted in islands. When living in Geneva he spent two months on St. Peter's Island, which he described as the happiest time of his life and an island in the Rhone, where his statue stands, is named after the philosopher (Pitt, 1980, pp 1051–9). Neo-classicism also drew on notions of islands, with islands occupying an important place in Greek antiquity. Plato, for example, saw islands as metaphors and concepts for utopian socio-political possibilities. In this way, Polynesians were aestheticized – idyllized – in classical terms (Connell, 2003, p 556). A large aspect of idyllization is the way in which island life, especially in the South Pacific, has been sexualized. While literary fiction has been central to this sexualization, so too has academic research. Perhaps the most notorious of texts has been Margaret Mead's *Coming of Age in Samoa*, which as we noted was first published in 1928. Still considered a key text in nature versus nurture debates, the book argued the primacy of culture in psychosexual development. While such idylls were to wane for reasons outlined below, following the horrors of the Pacific Theatre in World War Two, the musical *South Pacific* (1958), and James A. Michener stories, representations of an idyllic Pacific were revised, reaching a culmination with a 1980 remake of *Blue Lagoon*.

Horror

In describing how placial thinking has influenced rural studies, Bell (2006, p 151) introduced the concept of the 'rural abject' to describe 'those people and things dispelled from the [rural] idyll'. Some notable 'other rurals' include places of economic decline and decay (post-productivist places), the industrial countryside, places of resource extraction, remote places, and/or discrete Indigenous communities, all of which have also been associated with real and imagined island-scapes. Topographies of the rural have concealed topographies of power, with too much focus on powerful groups such as farmers in the countryside and lack of attention to other actors and social groups (Philo, 1997). Again, in the context of islands we might refer to the consumer-tourist and those places and peoples they consume. As we described earlier, Philo (1997) has implored rural studies to engage with neglected rural 'Others', which have been typically omitted from the rural landscape. In a similar vein, Murdoch and Pratt (1997) have drawn attention to 'strange ruralities' in order to highlight difference and division in the countryside.

These 'rural others' tend to include sexual minorities, young people, Indigenous peoples, people of colour, the destitute and poor, and itinerant groups, such as the Traveller community. When considering localized crime threats, the social groups which are subject to much crime talk are those which present as peripheral to the economic and social life of rural places. Indigenous peoples, for example, are often subject to gossip and public ridicule, which presents them as lazy, welfare dependent, violent, and alcohol or drug addicted. We would argue here that a feature these groups have in common is that they are likely also to be victims of crime because of their relative lack of power and social marginalization. As Scott and Hogg (2015) argue, a common feature of other rurals and rural others is their apparent lack of productivity. Typically these groups, as victims of crime, are subject to interpersonal violence (see, for example, Flood & Hamilton, 2005). While it is clear that anyone at any time can be a victim of crime, it is equally apparent that in order to be constructed/accepted as a genuine victim, certain social processes have to take place. Circumstances of race, class, and gender have continually been shown to be important in the construction of victimhood in relation to different types of crime.

While the island-idyll creates island space as an object of desire because it is not urban or mainland, island space may also be presented as an object of dread for the same reason. There exists in cultural texts a less than Arcadian island (Bell, 1997, p 94). In this context, the island might represent aspects of incivility that are threatening because they are wild or 'primitive', at least from the perspective of the outsider's gaze. Thus, the island can also be unsettling because it exposes the fragility of mainlands or civilization (Bell, 2006, p 152). With the dystopian island, what was normatively valued in the idyll becomes a source of the abject (Kristeva, 1982). For example, the dense social networks and organic solidarity that often characterize island communities may also produce and support violence (see Chapter 5). Bell (1997, p 106) observes, for instance, that here we see societies which seem idyllic, but which are malignant, at a dead end, and viewed in the grip of their death throes or in need of civilizing interventions. This can be clearly found in horror and crime fiction, in which we see traits which are legitimated in idyll, here being presented as exotic, uncivil, or excessive. Inbreeding, insularity, and backwardness are traits associated with island dangers.

Islands have been havens for mad scientists (*The Island of Dr Moreau*, 1896) and Bond villains (*Dr No*, 1957) and have been the setting for popular police serials (*Bergerac*, 1981–91; *Death in Paradise*, 2011–; *Shetland*, 2013–). One of the more chilling narratives, *The Wicker Man* (1973), centres on the visit of a police sergeant to an isolated British island to investigate a missing persons case, only to discover that the inhabitants have reverted to paganism and are engaged in sacrificial murder. These narratives invert the idyll and, referring to Douglas (1992), recreate islands as uncanny spaces where the prison in paradise presents as 'matter out of place'. It may be, as with *The Wicker Man*, an outsider intrudes into a space where they do not belong, or the civilization or law intrudes on the island idyll. Entering such a space produces what Freud described as the uncanny, in which the *heimlich* becomes *unheimlich*. What was normatively valued in the idyll becomes a source of the abject.

The nightmarish side to island idyllization included early accounts of cannibalism, sacrifice, infanticide, and endemic warfare (Rigby, 1997, pp 68–9). Threats to the island idyll included progress itself, at least the kind of progress that was untempered and produced what Durkheim (2006 [1897]) would term anomic conditions. Islands could also be incubators of unnatural sexual practices and passions, which variously confirmed or contrasted with readings of Mead's work. For example, Norfolk Island was intended to be the '*ne plus ultra* of punishment', a 'hell on earth', and the most dreaded place in the British Empire (Governor of New South Wales, Sir Thomas Brisbane, cited in Hughes, 1987, p 429). But such pitiless intentions gave way to its image among many observers as 'Sodom Isle' (Macklin, 2013). In places of secondary transportation, such as Norfolk Island and in Van Diemen's Land (Tasmania), 'unnatural' crimes became a major source of official and popular anxiety for British penal reformers during the 1830s and 1840s. The preoccupation, so hideous to contemporary sensibilities that it had usually to be discussed in code, was highly consequential. The preoccupation influenced the take-up of enduring practices of incarceration (such as cellular confinement) and the separation of boys and men and was also the vital, if unmentionable, ingredient in the 'convict stain'. Concerted efforts to create moral and cultural distance from the convict era in turn shaped emerging social, sexual, and national identities and the manner of their policing, as transportation came to a close and the penal colonies gained self-government (see Hogg & Scott, 2023).

Another representation of islands existed which was characterized by endemic violence and fearful superstition. Diderot had been critical of Bougainville, observing sexual licence was necessary for population growth, as labour was in short supply. The killing of Cook in Hawai'i in 1779 marked a symbolic turning point from an idyllic Pacific, the antithesis of industrial and capitalist Europe, to a Pacific that was a place of sin and violence and in need of redemption through colonial interventions, including by missionaries. Islands were perceived increasingly by established outsiders as fractious places, with existing divisions often exacerbated by colonization. New imagery emerged, perhaps no better captured in a shift of nomenclature from 'pleasant' and 'friendly' to 'danger' and 'savage' islands. So the Pacific came to serve as a negative model for the West's supposed cultural superiority. The places remained idyllic but the people were not, with islanders having lost and corrupted their paradise and now requiring civilizing interventions (Connell, 2003, p 558). One of the last utopian works on the Pacific was Byron's *The Island* (1823), following which literature increasingly emphasized diversity, tension, and change (Connell, 2003, p 562). Robert Louis Stevenson lived and died in Samoa and also spent time on the islands of the Marquesas. His novel, *The Beach of Falseá* (1892), was one of the first to adopt a realism that demystified colonial myth making and adventure by emphasizing cultural change and conflict. This realism was later adopted by writers such as Jack London and in the works of French artist Paul Gauguin (Connell, 2003, p 563).

The 19th century saw a racialized geography of the Pacific Islands replace the universal idea of the noble savage, with Melanesians being essentialized as 'Negroes' and being considered as technically primitive, hostile (cannibals and headhunters), and physically repugnant. In contrast, Polynesians were represented as closer racially to Europeans and, perhaps, a distant cousin of Aryans, owing to their relatively pale complexions. Melanesia was viewed as the converse of Polynesia (Connell, 2003, p 559).

The horror of island life was no better presented than in William Golding's dystopian *Lord of the Flies* ([1954] 1986). The book could be considered a parody of *The Coral Island*, inverting the idea of evil as an external threat to the island's inhabitants and, instead, making it present in the children themselves. The idea that islands can provide laboratories for social experimentation is a constant in popular culture. A notable, if somewhat dated, rendition of this is J.M. Barrie's *The Admirable Crichton* (1902). The play begins with the Earl of Loam, a British peer, hypothesizing that class distinctions in British society are artificial. Later, when Loam and his family and friends are shipwrecked on a remote Pacific island it is his butler, Crichton, who reluctantly leads the group, when the aristocrats fail to adapt to their new environment. After two years marooned on the island, Crichton has become known as 'the Guv' with his social superiors now serving him and life on the island being idyllic under his leadership, to the satisfaction (and survival) of all. Crichton is about to marry Loam's daughter when a rescue ship appears and Crichton chooses to signal it while resuming his status as butler. The play's final act, subtitled, 'the outer island', sees the cast back in England with Loam's family and friends embarrassed by Crichton's presence and with

Loam and his son having taken credit for leadership on the island. The play was also made into a popular 1957 film.

Conclusion

Islands are metaphorically and literally the last remnants of the Age of European Empires. Today, as Connell (2003, p 569) observes, 'centuries of colonialism were transformed [by tourism] into unspoiled cultures, whilst indigenous history was erased in favour of a legacy of western representation'. In this way, islands are not unlike rural spaces in settler societies and, as with rural societies, we need to be mindful of how crime problems are constructed and who constructs such problems. Islands, for example, remain feminized, but the masculine gaze has given over largely to tourists and discourses of Western consumption. However, islands are more than just *rural*; they are distinct spaces and places that demand further attention in criminological theorizing.

The extant literature rarely examines islands as unique ecological places or even provides an account of variations in crime on islands based on geographic dimensions such as size or demographics and social structures. Further, existing studies ignore the social construction of crime on islands, only examining its 'real' dimensions. In an era where post-colonial and Southern criminologies have alerted attention to the forgotten places and spaces of criminology and the selectiveness of the Northern gaze, it is timely to consider the place of islands in criminology. 'Idyllization' involves processes which produce stylized representations of islands, while simultaneously rendering certain aspects of islandness marginalized or invisible. For example, such processes might combine nature, romanticism, authenticity, and nostalgia to create a sense of 'tropical paradise', the contents of which vary geographically and historically. Island-idyllizations often fail to account for the fact that small, close-knit island communities, which are havens for the mainland consumer or tourist, were often created violently at the expense of other cultures and other uses of the land. This other history of island spaces is marginalized within the island-idyll; here, historical transitions and processes are smoothed over and masked. As such, the idyll is symbolically and materially an exclusive and exclusionary space – those excluded are the 'abject' or *Others*. As such, idyllization tends to obscure aspects of difference and division in island societies and how crime problems are constructed in such societies.

3

Isolation

Australian Aboriginal and Torres Strait Islander readers should be advised that this chapter contains the names of Aboriginal and Torres Strait Islander peoples who have passed away.

Islands inspire mindscapes for imagining that reality may be experienced in its entirety.

(Thomas, 2007, p 22)

The isolation of island spaces has seen them celebrated as bounded ecosystems: places where humans, animals and plants can flourish and thrive. The Galapagos, for example, have been described as a 'natural museum of geological, ecological, and evolutionary processes' – characteristics attributed to their 'extreme isolation' (Claudino-Sales, 2018). The Galapagos were also the first location to be declared as a United Nations Educational, Scientific, and Cultural Organization (UNESCO) World Heritage Site, and famously provided a backdrop to Charles Darwin's theory of evolution. The Sundarbans (Bangladesh and India) and the Rock Islands (in Palau) are similarly regarded as remote ecological paradises and are also UNESCO World Heritage Sites (UNESCO, 2021a, 2021b). Equally, islands have been important sites for human evolution. Flores (off Indonesia), for instance, is home to fossils from the earlier hominid species *homo floresiensis*, and it is the isolation of the island that has provided an axis upon which debates have arisen around this early human's origins. Those debates tend to involve two views: that *homo floresiensis* was a direct descendent of earlier human species that had been isolated and protected on the small island, or that it was a smaller more primitive cousin of modern humans that had evolved differently because of Flores' extreme isolation (van den Bergh, 2016). In both cases, island isolation inflects archaeological and anthropological theorizing about the species' origins. In this chapter, we explore how island isolation might also influence and inflect criminological theorizing.

Although to some people, 'islands are simply home' (Mountz, 2015, p 636), they have tended to be imagined through a Western lens as spaces that are both idealized and feared. As we touched on in Chapter 2, their separateness and isolation prompt visions of paradise, but also dislocation and banishment. Island isolation promises a reprieve from the pressures of 'mainstream' ('mainland') society, but for those who emigrate (or are exiled) to islands, also implies abandonment – the island-dweller either abandoning mainland society, or indeed mainland society abandoning them. Of course, concepts like isolation, separation, and abandonment are inherently relational. Just like island spaces themselves are defined (and definable) in relation to larger mainlands and surrounding seas, isolation is only definable in relation to connectedness. As Armstrong and Jefferson (2017, p 245) point out, islands are thus simultaneously discrete, isolated, *and* connected and it is this constant tension between isolation and connection that makes them so interesting. It means they can simultaneously be spaces and places of refuge as well as exile, all the while operating as sites whose possibilities are often (but not always, as we turn to in later chapters) shaped by 'mainstream'/'mainland' politics.

In the sections that follow, we focus on *isolation* as a critical and defining feature of islands and explore implications for criminology. We examine the role of island borders, which play a key role in demarcating who is 'in' ('us') and 'out' ('Other') of both island and non-island communities and consider the use of islands as sites for managing sick and polluted bodies, including through quarantine stations and lock hospitals, drawing parallels to the way that islands have been used for banishment of the criminal body (for example, islands as prisons). We draw on Mary Douglas' (1966) concept of 'pollution ideas' to think through the use of island isolation to manage and eliminate 'dirty bodies', since 'Dirt offends against order' (Douglas, 1992 [1966], p 2). We also draw and expand upon Foucault's concept of biopower to comprehend the use of island spaces as sites of isolation, banishment, and discipline (Scott, 2003; Foucault, 2004). Overall, we argue that criminology has often lacked critical engagement with public health, despite its historical and contemporary significance in regulating bodies, and despite frequent crossover in the use of isolated island spaces to prevent pollution of the body politic by 'disappearing' sick, poor, and criminal classes (Baldacchino, 2016). In this chapter, we seek to at least partially correct this.

Seeing the Other at the border

The concept of 'in' and 'out' groups, and processes of Othering, have long been a topic of interest for social scientists (Becker, 1963; Tajfel, 1974; Jenkins, 2014). Individuals (and whole communities) are 'Othered' on myriad bases, including socially constructed categories of nationality, sexuality, gender, race, and more. Who is 'in' and who is 'out' is, thus, deeply politicized and changes over time, space, and place. Nevertheless, as Jenkins (2014, p 105, emphasis in original) noted, 'Similarity and difference reflect each other across a shared boundary. At the boundary, we discover what we *are* in what we are *not*, and vice versa.' Indeed, boundaries and borders play a crucial role in Othering.

Although much of the bordering literature focuses on the boundaries of nation states, arising from Westphalian understandings of state sovereignty (Rumford, 2006; Walters, 2010),[1] globalization theorists have also argued that new mobilities have arisen as some goods and services flow in a relatively stateless and globalized economy (Castells, 2000; Urry, 2000). Building on Castells (2000), Rumford (2006, p 155) used the term 'networked borders' to describe a kind of networked/interconnected global society where 'a space of places (the territorial nation-state) is being replaced by a space of flows': similar to Bauman's (1999) liquid modernity thesis, which sees the modern as *liquid* rather than solid. In this conceptualization, the isolation and disconnectedness of pre-modernity is substituted with connection and limitless bounds. The EU was proffered by Rumford (2006, p 155) as a 'paradigm of the network state', though subsequent socio-political changes, such as the 2016 'Brexit' referendum, have seen a return to stronger reassertions of state sovereignty. More recently, the experience of the COVID-19 pandemic has also seen states re-harden their borders to keep out the virus. These shifts are described through an 'immobilities' literature, which argues that globalization has also resulted in the creation of new borders and the reinforcement of old ones (Andreas & Biersteker, 2003; Shamir, 2005; Turner, 2007), providing examples of what Walters (2010, p 146) might refer to as 'faultline[s] ... in the smooth space of globalisation' and demonstrating that borders tend to shapeshift rather than disappear.

While bordering scholars focus mainly on the peripheries of nation states, internal bordered spaces have also long been used as sites of exclusion and confinement, as per Weber's (1978 [1922]) 'social closure', Foucault's (1967, 1979) 'enclosed disciplines', or Turner's (2007) 'enclaves'. Moreover, borders are not only physical: they also exist in the non-physical realm. As carceral spaces dedicated to incapacitating and punishing deviants, prisons are an obvious example of enclosed disciplines (Foucault, 1967, 1979) that transcend the physical and non-physical. Indeed, prisons serve as sites of deliberate transformation; places where the state makes an example of those acting outside acceptable social norms, while (for most prisoners) also undertaking disciplinary and normalization work aimed at recuperating and, perhaps reintegrating, the deviant person back into society. In this sense, prisons are isolated spaces that concern 'identity, memory and internal as well as physical walls and bars' (Schliehe & Moran, 2017, p 270); as Armstrong and Jefferson (2017) argue, they might also be considered islands of sorts (something we return to later) and the 'pointy end' of what Foucault (1979) called a carceral archipelago. In prisons, the physical serves as a means of reconstructing the incorporeal, imposing both tangible and intangible constraints that affect both body and mind. The physical and non-physical borders of prisons often work in tandem: while physical borders can impose and/or reinforce mental constraints, they can also be conceptualized as tangible manifestations of mental borders – that is, borders that are first erected in the mind and which are then translated into palpable expressions of difference and exclusion. In a similar sense, non-physical borders – for instance, between understandings of the Self versus the Other – are also enacted, articulated, and made 'real' *through the landscape.*

Geography has long been harnessed and manipulated to enact and reflect borders that are first erected in the mind. Perhaps it is for this reason that islands, where the border is arguably the most visible and defining feature, have been so often imagined as spaces for the separation and exclusion of Otherness: as places where the Other can be neatly 'disappeared' to (Baldacchino, 2016) and restrained. Just as man-made borders shift and change (Borowski, 2017), island borders – typically characterized by beachscapes – are also in constant flux as a result of the erosive and modifying impacts of moving water (waves, tides). In their examination of the liminal beachscape, Breidenbach et al (2020, p 5) observed:

> Migration and climate change are among numerous conflicts, discourses and practices that manifest themselves on the beach and find their focal point there. Others are postcolonial power structures and mass tourism, environmental pollution as well as bender and burkini swimwear controversies ... [Indeed, the beach is] a cultural phenomenon that is constantly changing, transforming and diversifying in its semantic texture. (Breidenbach et al, 2020, pp 4, 5)

The dynamism of the beach (as island border) extends to island spaces on the whole and is a common theme in this chapter and, indeed, throughout the book. As we examine in the following sections, exploitation of the isolated/ isolating features of island spaces has echoed across time but has served various ends. In some instances, island spaces have been used by non-island societies to excise and banish their disenfranchised Others. At other times, they have been sites of refuge for these same groups. We explore and probe these ideas below, examining how island spaces have been used to manage both polluted and criminal bodies, with these sometimes being viewed as synonymous (Douglas, 1992 [1966]).

Island isolation of polluted bodies

For millennia, separation and isolation have served as primary strategies for dealing with infectious disease. Sehdev (2002) argues that the oldest known written references to separating sick individuals from healthy ones arise in the Old Testament (Leviticus), and concern removing those with leprosy from camps where other uninfected people were living. In *History of Madness*, Foucault (1962, p 3) discussed the use of leprosaria, which he referred to as 'cities of the damned', to isolate and manage leprosy victims, particularly from the Middle Ages to the end of the Crusades (drawing parallels to the later use of confinement, including institutionalization, for those considered 'mad' or 'insane'). During the European Middle Ages, separation and isolation were also important ways of dealing with the spread of the Black Plague. In Reggio (Italy) in 1374, for example, those with the plague had to be 'taken out of the city into the fields, [and left] there to die or to recover' (Sehdev, 2002, p 1072). The realization that the Black Plague was communicable resulted in not only isolation of the already diseased, but also requirements for those who may have been exposed, but were not yet showing symptoms of illness, to quarantine.

The word 'quarantine' arises from the Italian word '*quaranta*', relating to the typical 40 days of quarantine required of trading ships along the Mediterranean coast in the 14th century, initially in Italy and later in other parts of Europe (Sehdev, 2002; Tognotti, 2013). Ragusa (modern-day Dubrovnik, Croatia) is believed to have been the first place to legislate quarantine orders, which it did in 1377 (Ogden, 2021). The system in Ragusa was highly successful, eventually involving sophisticated contact tracing, record-keeping, and the use of a series of quarantine stations to enforce periods of isolation – techniques that have again become features of everyday life during the global COVID-19 pandemic (Ogden, 2021). With distance and isolation being desirable characteristics for quarantining and because quarantine stations of the past often needed to service those crossing borders by boat, many stations have been situated on coastal islands. For example, the Lazzaretto Vecchio, situated off the Venetian coast, guarded against the Black Plague in the 15th and 16th centuries (Tuncbilek, 2020), while Molokai Island (between Honolulu and Hawai'i) was used to isolate and quarantine those suffering from leprosy from 1866 to 1969 (Inglis, 2017). In Australia, Bruny Island (off the Tasmanian coast) was also used to manage typhoid, smallpox, and Spanish flu between 1884 and the late 1920s (Bruny Island Community Association, nd).

While the COVID-19 pandemic has again seen the deployment of quarantine 'speak', which appeals to the benevolent utilitarianism of these sorts of strict and punitive public health strategies, quarantine is far from apolitical. As Maglen (2003, p 2873) explained, 'quarantine policies are almost always a reflection of issues other than a state's desire to protect itself from the importation of infectious disease ... [indeed,] quarantine fulfill[s] ... various political and economic needs'. Quarantine has, for example, been consistently associated with stigmatization of polluted bodies, with examples including 'stigmatization of the Jewish population of Venice during the bubonic plague, of Mexicans during the swine flu, and of Chinese during SARS and COVID-19' (Ogden, 2021, p 901). Similarly, leprosy outbreaks in Australia were historically blamed on Aboriginal and Chinese populations, since it was believed that these populations were inherently inferior to those with British lineage, aside from 'the occasional throwback' among British settlers (Bashford, 2003, p 96). This commitment to framing Aboriginal and Chinese populations as diseased and contagious aligned with and reinforced settler colonial strategies of exclusion, such as White Australia policies that pursued Anglo-centric whiteness as a marker of citizenship (Moreton-Robinson, 2004; Bashford, 2003). Indeed, these examples are remnants of a far longer lineage of equating sickness of the body and mind with inferiority, impurity, and evil (Foucault, 1962). In this sense, what Douglas (1966, p 4) calls 'pollution beliefs' can also be understood as being frequently 'used in a dialogue of claims and counter-claims to status ... [with] some pollutions [being] ... used as analogies for expressing a general view of the social order'.

Foucault's (1962, pp 85–6) exploration of isolation and confinement for those with physical and mental illness showed 'a profound complicity between medicine and morality', with the two being inextricably bound in a way that creates a powerful discursive 'truth' that is repeatedly deployed to justify repression and punishment in myriad forms. As Foucault (1977, p 230) argued, 'When a judgement cannot be framed in terms of good and evil, it is stated in terms of normal and abnormal' and thus, 'Repression ... becomes doubly efficacious, as it cures the body and purifies the soul' (Foucault, 2006 [1961], p 87). This foregrounds the use of different regimes of power to manage various manifestations of Otherness. Drawing on Foucauldian Governmentality, for example, Scott (2003) explores legal and public health responses to prostitution in the Australian state of New South Wales. He uses the terms 'sanitationist' and 'hygienist' to describe two public health regimes that deploy different forms of power, which he argues are also highly relevant to criminologists. Sanitationist regimes more closely approximate Foucauldian conceptualizations of sovereign power, separating, isolating, and quarantining through the application of top-down domination. State-led enforcement of quarantine measures to segregate sick populations, as described above, is an obvious example. Alternatively, hygienist regimes tend towards producing responsibilized and self-disciplining subjects that govern their own health and wellbeing, as well as self-recuperate. Within a hygienist framework, thus, power is dispersed and diluted; akin to Foucault's (1980) notion of biopower, which involves an all-pervasive 'conduct of conduct'.[2] The ability to decide *who* and *what* abnormality/normality or good/evil look and feel like foregrounds the operation of these different regimes of power and, as Foucault repeatedly pointed out, is a site of domination in and of itself. It is this characteristic of being able to define deviance (whether medical or criminal) that unites public health and criminal justice policies, as we return to throughout this chapter. In fact sometimes, as in Scott's (2003) example of illegal and medically 'risky' prostitution, these are one and the same.

Despite being couched in objective science, medically ordained definitions of 'normality' are deeply political, reflecting the ontology and morality of the person (and profession) doing the defining. This knowledge–power nexus creates a site of both domination and resistance. The medicalization of characteristics held by oppressed groups has often resulted, for example, in their stigmatization and isolation (Foucault, 1980). The pathologization of homosexuality provides an obvious example, as does the medicalization of women's so-called 'wandering wombs' and associated 'hysteria', arising from the patriarchal understanding of women as an inferior class whose primary social function is their reproductive capacity, and whose sexual desires and needs are (unlike men's) considered deeply problematic (Deveraux, 2014). The early 20th-century theorizing of prominent New Orleans physician, Dr Samuel Cartwright, about the medical conditions of African American slaves offers a further disturbing example of how race has also been mobilized as a defining feature of 'disease' (Willoughby, 2018). Cartwright socially constructed, for example, the diseases of 'drapetomania' (which he believed caused slaves to abscond) and 'rascality' (which he believed made them commit petty offences) (Willoughby, 2018). In these examples, the medicalization of political resistance (for example, abscondment from the brutal slave trade) opened the door to oppressive regulation in the benevolent name of medicine. In Australia and Canada, medicine has been similarly deployed as an instrument of oppression, with Indigenous peoples being frequently isolated and detained by the settler state on medical grounds. Across Australia, islands have been repeatedly used to this end, creating a long history of profound trauma. A disturbing example is the use of Bernier and Dorre Islands, situated about 50 km off the Western Australian coastline, as lock hospitals to detain more than 800 Indigenous 'patients' between 1908 and 1919 (Pervan et al, 2020).

Those detained on Bernier and Dorre had been forcibly removed from their sovereign lands and transported to the hospitals under racist settler colonial policies (some of which we elaborate on in Chapter 4). Sometimes these individuals were ill, and at other times they were simply guilty of resisting settler colonial takeover of their lands, thereby being institutionalized as veritable political prisoners. Indeed, the use of these isolated island lock hospitals blurred the line between medical and criminal justice policy, with Pervan et al (2020, p 93) referring to those interred there as 'prisoner patients' (also see Barrington, 2015). Pervan et al (2020, p 93) further explain:

> The journey [to the Lock Hospitals on Bernier and Dorre Islands], … conducted on foot with 'patients' usually confined in neck chains,

was long and traumatic, and often accompanied by long periods in prisons or other lock-ups awaiting their final transport by ship to the islands. There, they were imprisoned until 'deemed' cured ... and were subjected to medical and surgical experimentation. Conservative estimates suggest more than 200 people died on the islands, and many others perished on the journey before their arrival.

As this description illustrates, the logics and practices of criminal justice can and have been readily adapted to deal with those whose Otherness is defined as sickness rather than evil (Foucault, 1977). The forms of administrative detention enabled under the guise of medicine are, however, even opaquer and more disempowering than judicial detention. Indeed:

> imprisonment [within the judicial system] occurs only after a substantial process of laying charges, trials and sentencing. In contrast, people are subject to administrative detention because they meet certain administrative criteria, without rigorous investigation into whether the detention is correct and justified, and few opportunities of review. Whole groups of people could be subject to administrative detention, not as the result of an illegal action, but because they belonged to a particular social category. ... Finally, the conditions of administrative detention are not subject to the same regulations as judicial imprisonment. Unlike prisoners in the judicial system, for example, administrative detainees are not informed of the length of their sentence before incarceration, and may be detained indefinitely. (Nethery, 2012, pp 86–7)

This exemplifies, as does much of Foucault's work, medicine as a site of extreme power and oppression. It also shows how distinct institutions can operate through very similar logics, to the point that their practices and techniques – including the use of island spaces as sites of isolation and discipline – can become almost indistinguishable. This is obvious in the conflation of disease, deviance, criminality, and evil as attributes of particular social classes. Returning briefly to the example of the Bernier lock hospital in Western Australia, the story of Jaal, who was a Yamaji senior lawman and inmate at Bernier, demonstrates this conflation, his life having been punctuated by 'violence and surveillance by scientists and government officials as a prisoner *and* suspected syphilitic' (Barrington, 2015, p 54, emphasis added). Barrington (2015, p 54) goes on to explain, 'Early policy accounts of Jaal as "perfectly civilised" were later replaced with the more enduring colonial tropes of "cannibal" and "outlaw" that were concomitant with his increasing retaliations for violence and dispossession [from his lands]'. In Jaal's case, disease and ill character/criminality were woven together in a narrative that was used to rationalize and justify his island isolation and punishment as a political prisoner. Below, we further explore the overlap between public health and criminal justice, turning our attention to how islands have also been explicitly mobilized as sites of isolation and punishment under criminal justice policy.

Island isolation of the criminal body

Islands have long been used as 'natural' prisons to pursue strategic aims of displacement, containment, seclusion, and colonization, most notably in the form of penal colonies and detention camps (Russo & Strazzari, 2019, p 2). According to Borowski (2017), because of their physical and psychological barriers, islands are ideal places of exile or imprisonment. As Thomas (2007, p 22) points out in the epigraph to this chapter, islands do indeed 'inspire mindscapes for imagining that reality may be experienced in its entirety'. As we also touched on earlier, they might be likened to what Goffman described as 'total institutions': social arrangements in modern society where no barriers exist between work, home, and leisure spheres of life. Further, while each sphere has different participants and different kinds of authority, the total institution has an all-encompassing rational plan, and is created through the construction of natural and artificial barriers (Borowski, 2017). On a broader level the control of space and individuals living in it is a guarantee and sign of power and security (Borowski, 2017, p 53). The place where barriers exist to their greatest extent is penitentiary institutions on islands, which may be found throughout history and in different cultures and political systems, including liberal democracies and totalitarian societies (Borowski, 2017, pp 53–4). Banishment to islands is almost universal in cultures where access to remote islands is possible; Japanese and Polynesia provide historic examples.

The Solovetsky Islands in the White Sea (Russia) was the first forced labour camp and '*gulag*' in the USSR, although it had been previously used by the Tsars for exiles and heretics. Prior to the revolution, only a few hundred people were detained there in 400 years, while during the Soviet period hundreds of thousands were detained in the islands, with up to 70,000 residing there at any one time. The first prisoners from 1920 were political prisoners, who were followed by clergy and common criminals (Borowski, 2017). In another famous example, the small Island of Alcatraz operated as a closed maximum-security prison between 1934 and 1963. It sits in San Francisco Bay and is clearly visible from the city, just as the city would have also been visible to its inmates. Prior to this the island accommodated a military fort and then a military prison. Its most famous inmate was Al Capone who was kept there from 1934 until 1939 (before he was transferred to the low-security Terminal Island [formerly *Isla Raza de Buena Gente*] Federal Correction Facility due to ill health). The island also formed the backdrop to the 1963 book (by J. Campbell Bruce) and 1979 film (by director Don Siegel), both named *Escape from Alcatraz*, which told the story of the 1962 escape from the island. In both cases, Alcatraz was depicted as impossible to abscond from due to its layered isolation, consisting of its man-made maximum-security prison bounds as well as the natural bounds of the island itself. Alcatraz was eventually closed because of high running costs and today serves as one of San Francisco's major tourist attractions (for an examination of Alcatraz and Robben islands as sites of Dark Tourism, see Strange & Kempa, 2003). Robben Island, situated off Cape Town in the Republic of South Africa, held Nobel Laureate and former South African President Nelson Mandela for 16 years of a 27-year sentence. Prior to 1961, incurables and lepers were sent there. More recently, Guantanamo Bay (Cuba) military prison and detention camp leased by the US after the attacks on New York of 11 September 2001, became a place for the detainment of prisoners accused of terrorism, who resided in wire-mesh cells in an area called Camp X-Ray. Torture and humiliation were alleged to have been routine, as confirmed in a subsequent Federal Bureau of Investigation (FBI) report (Borowski, 2017, p 61).

As Borowski (2017) points out, where prisons are situated *on* islands, boundedness is magnified, and multiple barriers (natural, artificial, symbolic) conflate to compound isolation. Indeed, island prisons essentially create islands *within* islands, amplifying and intensifying their separation from the mainland (Mountz, 2015). Owing to their isolation, however, islands themselves can *feel* like prisons, without the need for additional barriers or structures. As Defoe's (1719, p 1111) Robinson Crusoe reflected, 'I was a prisoner, locked up with the eternal bars and bolts of the ocean, in an uninhabited wilderness, without redemption'. Similarly, reflecting on Devil's Island, Redfield (2000, p 101) stated that:

> to run from the human prison is only to face the real prison, to go deeper into the equatorial nightmare of untracked jungle [towards the outer island]. The narrative of escape becomes that of a caged beast, driven mad by the sun, fleeing from the wilderness and fighting to survive, far more than that of a clever deviant outwitting a rational machine. Exotic nature itself is the real enemy, full of hidden traps and unknown dangers. ... Lost amid strange surroundings, lacking most rudimentary skills of survival and means of support, such a prisoner was trapped more surely by his freedom than by his imprisonment.

Norway's 'open prison islands' provide a contemporary example of how the natural barrier of the island boundary and encroaching seas can stand in for the typical walls and fences of the non-island prison. Situated on the otherwise unpopulated Bastøy Island, off the Norwegian coast, south of Oslo, Norway's Prison Island is the only Norwegian prison located on an island, and is a form of 'open prison', where inmates live with relative freedoms in units (during first transition) and then free-standing cabins (where they move after a few months) (Shammas, 2014). In this sense it has been cited as an example of Scandinavian penal exceptionalism, though Shammas (2014) challenges this. The prison houses a mixture of violent and non-violent offenders, many having been transferred to the open island prison after serving earlier parts of their sentence in closed, higher-security prisons on the mainland (James, 2013; Shammas, 2014). The island prison boasts, however, the lowest recidivism rate in Europe, at 16 per cent in 2013 (James, 2013); far lower than in most Western democracies beyond Europe as well, which often sit between 40 and 50 per cent (for example, Australia, the US, Canada, New Zealand).

In Bastøy, connectedness with the mainland again brings the isolation of the island into sharp focus and provides a 'there' from which 'here' is defined. Shammas (2014) explains that, even though there are far fewer rules and restrictions on Bastøy than in other mainland prison facilities, there are nevertheless examples of strong informal social regulation that come into being at least in part due to the ongoing *threat* of possible transfer to mainland prisons. For example:

> Violent confrontations are strongly frowned upon by inmates because violence attracts the officers' attention and can get innocent bystanders kicked off the island and sent back to less comfortable, higher-security facilities. As far as possible, inmates try to sort out conflicts that arise without involving officers. (Shammas, 2014, p 107)

This is an interesting reversal of the threats of island exile we discuss later (for example, in Chapter 4), and again demonstrates that the social construction and lived realities of island spaces are in continual conversation with non-island spaces. Indeed, one inmate described living on Bastøy as 'like living in a village, a community' ('Petter' in James, 2013, np). Another inmate, who was serving a sentence for murder, said that 'Before coming here [to Bastøy] I never really cared for other people', but he was now applying to take up a leadership and pastoral role on the island ('Sven' in James, 2013, np). For this prisoner, isolation and exclusion were experienced in his previous life on the mainland, *not* on the island prison. Instead, the island prison offered a sense of connectedness and belonging that he had not experienced *beyond* the island space (a point we build on further in Chapter 6).

On the basis of his ethnographic study with Bastøy prisoners, Shammas (2014) argues that it is this tension and push/pull between free/unfree, bounded/unbounded, isolated/connected that is experienced as a form of harm that often goes unnoticed in research concerning Scandinavian penal exceptionalism – what he calls the 'pains of freedom' (Shammas, 2014, p 208; building on Sykes' [1958] 'pains of imprisonment'). He explains: 'freedom within constraint is itself the source of experienced pain ... [and] in open prisons [such as Bastøy], it is the provision of freedom within the context of isolation and restraint that causes discomfort and anguish' (Shammas, 2014, p 109). As one prisoner in Shammas' (2014, p 114) study recounted, the freedoms of living on Bastøy Island were experienced as simultaneously liberating *and* constraining:

> You get to make phone calls out, but the problem is that at the same time you get a *contact* with freedom, you *notice* freedom without being free. You get more involved in the troubles your wife has at home, but without being able to do anything about them. ... It makes it harder because you're seeing the problems they have at home a whole lot more. In closed [prison] you can isolate yourself more. You don't *know*, you're isolated.

Thus, in this prisoner's account it is not simply the presence of isolation, but being able to *notice* that isolation, that is the cause of pain. In the case of Alcatraz, inmates similarly reported the pains of being able to sometimes hear loud celebrations on the mainland, or laughter from passing boats, both of which were agonizing reminders of the freedoms that existed beyond the island's bounds (Quillen, 2015). Referring to an earlier study of an open Norwegian women's prison by Neumann (2012), Shammas (2014, p 115) notes that 'even as the body remains relatively free ... this is an extreme case of "imprisoning the soul" and perhaps the "ultimate version of Foucauldian governmentality"'. Indeed, in this environment of the open island prison, inmates are coerced into becoming responsibilized, self-governing citizens, so much so that in a space where they are relatively free to leave, they 'have to build inner bars ... in order to return every day' (Neumann, 2012 in Shammas, 2014, p 115). Quoting Foucault, Shammas (2014, pp 118–19) states, 'in the open prison, it is instead the "submission to subjectivity" that constitutes the vector of control, that is, the remoulding of subjects into "docile bodies". ... To govern in open prison is to produce self-governing prisoners.' Thus, while mainland prisons have been likened to island spaces, in this particular case, the isolation of the *island* prison is what makes this kind of *freedom within constraint* possible, and which translates it into a form of punishment that is arguably unique from mainland prisons. As we return to throughout this book, however, islandness is a mobile concept that can 'appear and [be] ... reproduced in other forms' (Mountz, 2015, p 638). There are, indeed, numerous examples of island spaces being *created* to serve the purpose of imprisoning those considered criminally deviant, and which simultaneously make isolation more *noticeable* than in terrestrial prisons. Prison hulks provide an example.

Prison hulks were originally commissioned in 1776 as a way to house Britain's overflowing prison convict stock (McKay, 2021). As moored ships, they imitated island characteristics, separating, and isolating unwanted individuals, and might be considered as man-made 'stepping-stone' islands, since they also acted as holding bays for convicts awaiting transportation, including to Australia (Sydney Museums, nd). Conditions on these man-made islands are mostly understood to have been brutal (though some dispute this [Leunig, van Lottum, & Poulsen, 2018]). As McKay (2021) points out, punishment meted out to the hulks' convicts in Britain often extended across life and death: indeed, 'the bodies of deceased convicts were [frequently] used by surgeons for training purposes, in experiments and dissections', which sometimes contravened the (then) Anatomy Act and could be part of a gruesome spectacle for fellow convicts, with 'Entrails [at times] taken from the body, and thrown into the river [in front of prisoners], where dozens had gone before' (McKay, 2021, p 163). In one case, aired during an 1847 Inquiry into dissections of prison hulk corpses, the hulks' chief surgeon was accused of allowing convicts to die as a means of 'supply[ing] the anatomy schools', though he was never prosecuted (McKay, 2021, p 165). This practice nevertheless reaffirms that prisoners were seen as waste products to be fixed or simply discarded (whereafter at least their bodies could be made useful) – much like the ill and polluted bodies described in earlier parts of this chapter.

Hulks were partially abandoned by the French because of costs in 1852 and a range of islands were mooted as a solution to the growing convict population, until the colony of French Guiana, situated in the Atlantic Ocean, was chosen (1852–1953). For instance, the Cayenne penal colony ('*bagne*'), or 'Devil's Island', situated in the Atlantic, housed a mix of (mainly) French political prisoners and hardened thieves and murderers, and gained a gruesome reputation owing to its location, climate, and geography (solid rock protruding 40 m from the ocean). Its most famous prisoners were Alfred Dreyfus and Henri Charriére, the latter of whom told of his experiences in the semi-fictional bestselling book *Papillon* (1970), adapted into the Franklin J. Schaffner film *Papillon* (1973). *Papillon* ('butterfly'), which was in reference to the butterfly tattoo on Charriére's chest, tells the author's own story of escaping the island prison; a prison that was renowned for its brutal treatment of inmates, and from which attempted escapes had resulted in death for many.

Prison hulks were later used in Australia, including in Victoria (for example, the *Sacramento*, 1853–78), South Australia (for example, the *Fitzjames*, 1880–85), Tasmania (for example, the *Anson*, 1844–50; the *Duke of York*, 1824–43), and New South Wales (for example, the *Phoenix*, 1825–37), where unsanitary and violent conditions were also widely documented (Richards & May, 2003; Williams, 2005; Duncan, Gibbs, & Sonnemann, 2013; Wettenhall, 2015; Sydney Museums, nd). Like the British hulks, the Australian hulk system similarly encapsulated features of islandness, which were noted as a primary reason for their use. The South Australian Chairman of the Destitute Board described, for example, the *Fitzjames* (a hulk for criminal and destitute boys) as being 'preferable to a land-based [reformatory] because it allowed "safe custody" by the mooring of the vessel "some distance from shore"', which avoided the risk and costs associated with securitizing a land-based reformatory (in Richards & May, 2003, p 26). A floating fleet of five prison hulks, moored in Melbourne's Yarra River (1853–78), also housed serious and non-serious offenders, as well as women and children (Wettenhall, 2015). The so-called 'Yellow Fleet' (because they were painted yellow, to demarcate them from other ships – drawing parallels to the use of yellow flags to distinguish quarantining ships) included the *Success*, which was converted to a hulk in 1853, and the *Lysander, President, Deborah*, and *Sacramento* later converted in 1854 (Duncan et al, 2013). A total of 5,128 prisoners were stationed on the hulks in only their first five years of use (Duncan et al, 2013). The commander of the Yellow Fleet, John Price, was familiar with the use of islands as sites of imprisonment, having formerly been commander of the Norfolk Island penal colony off the Queensland coast (and to which some prisoners held on the *Phoenix* hulk in Sydney were awaiting transportation) (Harrison, 2013; Wettenhall, 2015). Price was accused of using regular violence against the hulk prisoners and met a gruesome end in 1857 when he was murdered by a group of convicts on Williamstown Beach (Victoria) (Wettenhall, 2015).

Australia's Victorian hulks were discontinued in 1878 and remaining prisoners moved into Melbourne's terrestrial Pentridge Prison (Duncan et al, 2013). This occurred after an Inquiry brought the deplorable conditions of the hulks to light. By circa 1885, all Australian prison hulks had been discontinued. Similarly, the British hulks were discontinued in 1884, after multiple inquiries and public agitation regarding the inhumane conditions on the ships, including by Jeremy Bentham (Jackson, 1988; Wettenhall, 2015). A 1798 report by the British Select Committee on Finance, which included commentary on the hulks (and which was apparently part authored by Bentham), concluded that they were 'a principal Cause of that Corruption of Morals, which is the Source of every Species of Criminality' (cited in Jackson, 1988, p 47, capitalization in original). Bentham's model of the panopticon was proposed as a more humane alternative, which would ostensibly be better aligned with the move towards pursuing rehabilitation through incarceration (Jackson, 1988). While they lasted, however, these floating, man-made prisons not only mirrored islands insofar as they were characterized by isolation and dislocation, but they also gave shape to the idea of islands as spaces that are *hidden* and *secretive*. That is, as sites of 'exception' (Agamben, 2005) where rights and laws (of the undeserving) can be easily thwarted, away from the purview of regulators. The panopticon directly addressed this, introducing the notion of an all-seeing 'eye' that would theoretically encourage the prisoners and prison guards to self-regulate their behaviour, as Foucault (1979) explored. As we turn to briefly below, however, the isolation and secretness of island spaces does not only foreground sites where horrors can go unnoticed. The island boundary can also be flipped and understood as a line of defence, particularly where island spaces provide *refuge* for Othered populations.

Island self-isolation

As discussed earlier, the isolation of islands is both alluring and dangerous; islands thus simultaneously act as a site for escapism from mainstream cultural and social standards, but also as sites of risk. In her examination of four Australian islands, Nethery (2012, p 85) states, 'The qualities that attract today's tourists ... are the same qualities that make islands well-suited for banishment, exile, segregation and control'. Sometimes, self-banishment and exile can also be a form of escape for Othered populations, and island emigration can make space for collectivization and resistance against oppression. The historical use of Fire Island (New York) provides an example of island isolation being deployed as a form of escape from discrimination and criminalization.

Fire Island is located nearby Long Island (~50 miles from New York City) and was, from the early 20th century, a popular vacation spot where homosexual men and women could find 'a refuge from the everyday, a place which each summer would play host, away from the potential hostility of the dominant culture, to the community's "awakening"' (Parlett, 2020, p 339). Fire Island emerged as a site of sanctuary at a time when homosexuality was explicitly criminalized in New York State (and many other parts of world), framed as a means of preventing homosexual males in particular from subverting Victorian sexual norms and thus 'poison[ing] society all around them' (Nelson, 1993, p 269). Although Fire Island vacationers initially set up camp at Ocean Beach in the 1930s – a small settlement that was still relatively accessible to the mainland – they eventually moved to Cherry Grove, a more remote, isolated, and thereby hidden part of the island (creating yet again an island *within* an island [Mountz, 2015]). Newton (2014, pp 21–2, emphasis in original) explains:

> While both resorts [at Ocean Beach and Cherry Grove] had hotels, Cherry Grove did *not* have police, church, or school, welcome deficits for those whose eccentricities or sexuality were on the other side of

the law. Looking back, [Grove resident] George Gibson thought that 'unconventional [city] people' were drawn to the Grove because in the 1930s 'nobody knew who anyone was here'.

Thus, the island, and particularly its remote Cherry Grove settlement, acted as a refuge of safety for groups that were considered and treated at this time as sexually deviant outlaws. This flips on its head the use of islands as prisons; spaces of banishment and horror are instead reclaimed as sites of safety. In both cases, however, islands obscure the oppressed from view. In the case of prison islands, this (ostensibly) serves to protect society from 'evil' criminals, and in the case of Fire Island, to protect persecuted individuals *from* society.

Referred to in the 1940s by poet W.H. Auden as 'Pleasure Island', however, the Grove eventually became seen as a place of risk, particularly with the advance of the AIDS pandemic from the early 1980s. The perception of AIDS as a 'male disease', and particularly a gay man's disease, saw a drop in the kind of tourism that had previously sustained Cherry Grove (Newton, 2014). While 'gay men had always had to deny and defy danger to have sex', it had now become even riskier; 'sex = death' (Newton, 2014, p 291). Hygienist approaches to AIDS (Scott, 2003), which prioritized self-regulation through chastity or condom usage, were associated with individual stigmatization of AIDS victims, driving some Fire Islanders to self-withdraw and isolate themselves *within* the island space. There were, for example, frequent incidents of '"closet AIDS", people who "just hide in their houses", who wouldn't let anyone know what was going on and who didn't or wouldn't seek help' (Newton, 2014, p 292). More generally, the island community, which had begun its life as a site of resistance against sexual oppression, grew more and more insular, with Grove 'regulars' becoming increasingly suspicious of outsiders and 'day-trippers' (Newton, 2014, p 286). Again, the place and culture of the island changed over time in response to mainland politics; the island as an inclusive site of paradise was transformed into yet another place of exclusion of the recreated Other, in the form of 'straight couples' and 'young gay day-trippers of all races' (Newton, 2014, p 286). Arguably, with increasing acceptance of homosexuality in mainland New York, the refuge of the island also became less necessary. Nevertheless, this again shows that island spaces are complex, contradictory, and in consistent flux; places where definitions of Otherness are dynamic and folded atop one another – at times being sites of oppression, and at other times sites of resistance.

Conclusion

The isolation of island spaces is arguably their most defining feature. It is this isolation, demarcated by the island border, that has enabled imaginaries of Otherness to be etched onto the landscape. Whole classes of people — the infirm, diseased, criminal, and politically disenfranchised — have been governed through the use and creation of island spaces as means of segregation and punishment. Just as medicalization of the characteristics of the oppressed has served to justify the strict governance of polluted bodies through island isolation, so has the criminalization of the behaviours and characteristics of the Other. Indeed, both public health and criminal justice operate as similar technologies along a spectrum, which sees sovereign power utilized to separate, demarcate, and punish the disenfranchised as the epitome of Otherness, while biopower is simultaneously at work on *all* bodies: both *Self* and *Other*. As Baudrillard's (1981, pp 12–13) discussion of the hyperreal and imaginary suggests, imaginary worlds serve the purpose of enacting simulation in a way that suggests life *beyond* these worlds is somehow different or more 'real':

> Disneyland is presented as imaginary in order to make us believe that the rest is real, when in fact all of Los Angeles and the America surrounding it are no longer real, but of the order of the hyperreal and of simulation. It is no longer a question of a false representation of reality (ideology), but of concealing the fact that the real is no longer real, and thus of saving the reality principle … [Extending this logic], prisons are [also] there to conceal the fact that it is the social in its entirety, in its banal omnipresence, which is carceral.

Drawing on Baudrillard's argument, Moran et al (2013, p 240) similarly state, 'Prisons give us something to stare at while distracting us from our own incarceration.' Today, many of Australia's penal settlements operate as tourist sites, and relics of the convict era litter the landscape in the form of roads, bridges, and buildings. These penal vestiges act as reminders of captivity, freedom, and pain, with some having modern traumas layered upon them. For example, the Port Arthur penal settlement, situated in modern Tasmania, was located on a peninsula connected to the mainland by an isthmus only 30 m wide, known as Eaglehawk Neck. Convicts were transported there between 1830 and 1853, before free settlers later took up residence. Much later, the site became a backdrop to Australia's worst mass shooting, when a lone gunman killed 35 people and wounded 23 more. The isolation of the site and narrow isthmus helped trap the victims there; many were unable to escape the gunman. In 1997, Port Arthur became a World Heritage Site, and is now a setting for dark tourism, with visitors drawn to the ruins of the penal settlement and penitentiary, as well as to the memorial for the massacre victims. In essence, the site has become a repository for unimaginable horrors, which are contrasted against the 'real', 'free', and 'safe' spaces beyond its boundary.

Just as prisons might be regarded as the 'hyperreal' and means of concealing the conduct of conduct that manifests in biopower relations across all societies, so too might island spaces be regarded as a kind of hyperreal version of containment that brings into existence the notion of the mainland as 'free' (and vice versa, as in the case of Fire Island). However, as we have hinted at in this chapter, and as we expand on in the chapter that follows, the concept of islands also gives shape to far broader practices that deploy *islandness* as a governing technique. This opens up a portal to thinking about islanding as a verb rather than noun, and as a key technique of invasion.

4

Invasion

> Island displacement not only physically freed up land for colonization, it also sustained the imperial project ideologically.
> (Roscoe, 2021, p 183)

Although isolation can protect islands and island spaces, it can also render them vulnerable to invasion by outside forces. In this chapter, we explore the concept of islands as locations that have been shaped, but also at times *created*, through processes of human invasion. We consider the role of colonial and neo-colonial forces in moulding the spaces and places of islands, broadening our theorizing of island spaces to incorporate islands situated on *terra firma* and bounded by desert. In respect of the latter, we focus primarily on the example of remote Indigenous communities scattered across Australia's sparsely populated 'outback' as islands in the desert. These islands have, we argue, been created and shaped as carceral reserves through ongoing colonial processes that have produced distinct crime histories and patterns. In investigating the specific case of Australia, we draw comparisons to settler colonies elsewhere, considering how invasion has worked alongside isolation (Chapter 3) to influence crime and justice practices and outcomes.

First, the chapter reflects on human invasion of islands, including through different typologies of colonialism (Feyrer & Sacerdote, 2009; Shoemaker, 2015). We then discuss the use and creation of islands as carceral spaces under Australian settler colonialism, building on themes from earlier chapters. This enables us to explore how island spaces can be created and mobilized as part of a broader array of governing techniques for dealing with deviance, which are interlinked with racialized Othering, including bordering of spaces, places, and bodies. 'Islanding' is in this case, we argue, co-opted as a socio-political technique to maintain and perpetuate the white settler state's legitimacy and claims over stolen Indigenous lands: what we call 'islanding as erasure' (building on Amoamo, 2013; and Vázquez, 2011). As a means of enabling the settler state to 'legally dispense violence' (Nielsen & Robyn, 2003, p 39), agents of the criminal justice system have been complicit in, and often spearheaded, this practice of creating and maintaining carceral islands in the Australian desert. This has ongoing implications for justice practices and outcomes in these locations today and demonstrates the importance of weaving together socio-political and spatial histories to enable a fuller understanding of how islands can inform criminological theorizing.

Island invasions

As (typically) remote and distant places, islands can be protected from, but also vulnerable to, forces of invasion. Human arrival at and settlement of islands has occurred progressively over time, with sea-level changes also creating and re-creating islands by cutting off pre-existing land bridges (for example, Japan) (Keegan & Diamond, 1987). Processes of colonization have also seen the invasion and re-invasion of islands, with expansion of Empire through the so-called 'second wave' of European colonialism during the 19th century reaching the remotest corners of the globe. Such expansion has been influenced by distance (for example, from colonizing entities), configuration (for example, ease of access through 'stepping-stone' islands), and area, while ocean currents and wind patterns can also either shrink or exacerbate geographical distance (Keegan & Diamond, 1987). Regardless, mobility has been 'the life-blood of empires' and islands have remained important sites of colonial conquest and control (Ballantyne, 2014). Indeed, 'Islands ... were the first territories to be colonized in the European Age of Discovery, [have often] suffered the colonial burden most intimately and thoroughly, and have been the last to seek and obtain independence' (Baldacchino & Royle, 2010, p 140). This has resulted in islands accounting for nearly all of the world's 17 current non-self-governing territories, according to the United Nations (2021; also see Baldacchino & Royle, 2010).

The expansion of Empire through colonialism has been facilitated and eased through concomitant practices and discourses that have socially constructed untravelled lands and unmet people through an Orientalist canon as a wild and savage Other (Said, 1978). These confected myths – which fit neatly with images of a Hobbesian state of nature – insinuate that Otherness must be tamed to be made *useful* to the colony, setting the groundwork for violent, oppressive, and assimilatory colonial rule involving, among other techniques, depopulation, genocide, legal control, and paternalism (Nielsen & Robyn, 2003). Colonial invasion and destruction have also been heavily racialized, with the notion of race itself having been imagined into existence through Western modernity's hegemonic classificatory logics, which have established powerful epistemic borders between the black racialized *Other* and the white, non-racialized *Self* (Mignolo, 2011; Moreton-Robinson, 2021). Indeed, 'generic whiteness' (Taylor, 2005, p 7) stands in the background as a default and largely unexamined 'norm' against which blackness is persistently judged as inferior (Smith, 2014) and, thus, 'race is deemed to belong to the [black] Other', not to the [white] Self (Moreton-Robinson, 2004, p 76).

Geography is also inflected by race; islands, for example, have featured strongly in techniques of colonial conquest. As Weaver-Hightower (2007, p xiv) argues for instance, racialized narratives of island castaways assisted in the interpretation of colonial expansion as 'natural' and unproblematic. Such narratives typically extended, she argues, on longer-standing metaphors that equated the English political system with the (white, masculine) human body – 'a naturally occurring organism straight from the hands of the creator' – and which by extension connected the metropole (the head, heart) with the colonies (the entrails, the digestive system) (Weaver-Hightower, 2007, pp xv, 43). The Robinsonade (see Chapter 2), for example, typically features a white, male castaway, who finds himself stranded in unruly and untamed (black) island spaces and who impulsively seeks to conquer and pacify them. And thus, the narrative seamlessly connects 'the right to authority over the colonial landscape ... to one's right and ability to command one's own flesh' (Weaver-Hightower, 2007, p xiv); that is, as innate, necessary, unproblematic, and unquestionably 'just'. These popular narratives weave together race and space; while the unruly wilderness of uncolonized spaces is typically equated with blackness, white civility is equated with neat, tamed, and conquered spaces. The regularly repeated story of the castaway who emerges victorious over wild island spaces and peoples thereby serves to validate the ideology of white superiority, setting the moral groundwork for colonial expansion to either rid the colonial 'body' of pollutants and/or discipline/normalize/tame and thereby neutralize the Other's polluting qualities (Douglas, 1992 [1966]; Staines, forthcoming).

Of course, colonialism is not a homogenous or monolithic concept. Its forms and practices are heavily heterogeneous and modulated by time, space, and place (Wolfe, 1998). Indeed, much has been written about the 'structural complexity' of colonialism (Wolfe, 2006, p 392). However, while it takes many forms, most scholars of colonial studies still tend to demarcate between two overarching typologies: 'colonialism' and 'settler colonialism'. Whyte (2018, p 283) uses the analogy of parasitism to describe these two forms as follows:

> The first [system] involves a parasite invading and living fully or partially off a host. The relationship ends when the parasite intentionally or unintentionally kills the host, the parasite runs out of what it needs to live (hence leaving), or the host repels the parasite. The second parasitism involves a parasite invading and living off a host too. But the goal of the parasite is not just to invade and live off the host, but to *become* the host – eventually reversing the two roles. The original host is either eliminated, or the new host deprives the original host

of its needs, causing rampant suffering. The first type of parasitism is similar to colonialism in which one group invades another and exploits benefits without actually permanently settling; the second type is settler colonialism.

While, therefore, colonialism is parasitic, destructive, and violent, it is time-bound (even though its ramifications frequently linger long after the colonizing entity runs out of exploitative opportunities and vacates, as we explore in Chapter 7). Settler colonialism on the other hand is a 'structure not an event … [where] The colonizers come to stay' (Wolfe, 1998, p 2) and where, in a stroke of deep irony, Indigenous peoples themselves tend to be reframed as the parasites who are consistently 'clamoring for "undeserved privilege"' from the settler state (Whyte, 2018, p 278). As Nan Seuffert (2011, p 13) explains, 'Settling involves reproducing the home country in the form of a colony that is still dominated by the home country'. Thus, in the process of settling, the 'mother' country transposes home life onto its colonies, overlaying, dismantling, undermining, and usurping existing peoples, ontologies, and epistemologies. An obvious example is the deployment of European crime and justice as a technique of settler colonialism, which has ascribed upon colonized lands and peoples legal regimes of classification and punishment that are not only foreign, but also that operate as an extension of state power under a guise of impartial scientism. Indeed, settler criminal justice systems can be understood as colonial tools (Broadfield, Dawes, & Chong, 2021); 'the most powerful short-term tool at the disposal of any government, in that it can be used to legally dispense violence' (Nielsen & Robyn, 2003, p 39). By extension, the academic discipline of criminology itself, as an export from the West that is rooted in Enlightenment scientism, can also be understood as a further colonizing institution, which has largely justified and reinforced the false 'truths' that have enabled state violence as a prop for colonial dispossession and destruction (Agozino, 2019). As Agozino (2003, p 6) points out, 'Criminology emerged as a discipline for disciplining and controlling the Other at a time when colonial administrators were imprisoning most regions of the world' and is 'closely tied to the project of colonisation and patriarchal imperialism as a science designed for the control of Others' (Agozino, 2019, p 13).

The deployment of criminology behind an intricate façade of Western science has gone hand in hand with, and served to perpetuate, the criminal justice system's false guise of neutrality. And it is behind this thinly veiled pretext that it has been consistently asserted that crime and justice are blind to race, while such systems routinely prosecute and incarcerate black colonized peoples the world over, while overwhelmingly ignoring (or worse, celebrating) the 'criminals that worked for imperialism' (Agozino, 2003, p 4). In the Australian context, for example, early white invading settlers were rarely prosecuted for violent atrocities, including massacres, against Indigenous peoples, while Indigenous peoples were 'hanged after incomprehensible trials, not whites' (Kercher in Nettelbeck, 2013, p 357). Of course, these interlinkages are becoming better understood, as critical whiteness scholarship continues to expand, turning a critical lens back onto the oppressors, rather than the oppressed (for example, Agozino, 2003, 2019). What is less well understood, however, is how island spaces have played a role in, and perhaps also mediated, the deployment of criminal justice policy and criminological empiricism/theorizing under colonialism, as well as to what effect. We turn to this below.

Crime and 'islanding as erasure' in settler colonial Australia

Islands present an interesting case when considering how colonialism has utilized criminal justice to pursue its invasive conquests. As we argue in other chapters, the isolation, boundedness, and insularity of islands can have both criminogenic and crime-protective effects. For example, if we consider the case of the Torres Strait Islands – an Australian archipelago that sits between the North-East tip of Australia and Papua New Guinea (and which we focus on in greater detail in Chapter 5) – geographical distance from initial European settlements in Australia as well as the archipelago's geographical spread complicated colonial control of these spaces. This, we argue, had the effect of diluting colonial regimes and practices, with distance, isolation, and difficult-to-navigate geography acting as a kind of protective buffer from the worst excesses of settler colonial violence and displacement (Staines & Scott, 2020). As a result, colonial governance happened at arm's length from afar, enabling the maintenance of relatively strong social capital that, we argue, has contributed to comparatively low crime rates in these communities today (see Scott et al, 2021). Of course, less intensive colonial control also presented fewer opportunities for Torres Strait Islanders to be judged as wanting against the imposed hegemonic standards of white settler colonial justice, and thereby socially constructed as criminals. That is, agents of the criminal justice system had fewer opportunities to define, treat, and punish Torres Strait Islanders as deviant Others in these spaces/places. Alternatively, colonization of other parts of Australia has occurred differently and been associated with dramatically different effects. We turn to these in this section, where we discuss 'islanding' as a technique of colonization. In doing so, we move beyond thinking about islands *in the sea* to also considering islandness as a feature of communities that can be situated *beyond the sea*, including within the vast desert of the Australian outback. First, we set some context by discussing Australian settler colonialism in greater detail, including how islands and islanding have featured in this context.

Indigenous Dreaming stories tell of First Nations peoples as having always been on the lands that are now called Australia; that is, since the Dreamtime or Creation (Lambert, 2018).[1] From the alternative perspective of Western archaeological science, the Australian land mass is thought to have been originally settled by humans around 65,000 years ago when it was still connected to New Guinea (making the larger continent of Sahul), after which point Australia was isolated by rising seawaters (Bradshaw et al, 2021). The continent of Australia itself has, thus, also been imagined as an island, bordered by the vast waters of the Pacific and Indian oceans (McMahon, 2010). Indigenous peoples thrived on the Australian continent for millennia, understood as having a population that numbered up to 5.5 million and which lived in sophisticated, pre-colonial societies (Pascoe, 2013; Bradshaw et al, 2021). European colonization of the continent from the 17th and 18th centuries onwards, however, has overseen extreme violence against Indigenous peoples and severely disrupted Indigenous ways of living and being.

Dutch ship, the *Duyfken*, travelled to the Australian mainland in 1605–06, making landfall on the western coast of Cape York (Far North Queensland) in February 1606. Months later, Spanish explorer Luis Vaz de Torres charted the islands of the Torres Strait. The Dutch made additional voyages to the Australian mainland, including in 1618 when Willem Janszoon charted much of the western coastline. It was not, however, until 1770 that the British made landfall in Australia on the *Endeavour*, commanded by Captain James Cook, who charted the Continent's Eastern Coast. Aboriginal and Torres Strait Islander peoples were looked upon by Cook and his compatriots with a sense of infantilizing intrigue; Cook himself described them in 1770 as savage 'wild beasts' whose lands were 'uncultivated' and thus, could be interpreted under British law as *terra nullius* – no man's land, awaiting discovery and settlement (Cook, [1770] 2014, p 321). This had the effect of both constructing and denying Indigenous presence on the Australian landscape. While Indigenous peoples were constructed as a (dirty, inferior) Other from which a (clean, superior) Self could be cultivated (Douglas, 1992 [1966]), they were simultaneously expunged from emerging 'Australian' life and identity, a theme that we return to later.

European settlement of Australia began with the arrival of the First Fleet in 1788, which brought a mixture of early settlers and convicts. Between 1788 and 1869, over 162,000 convicts arrived on Australian shores having been excised from the 'mother' country as an alternative punishment to execution, and as a 'means of improving and making … the colonies and plantations more useful' to Britain (National Museum of Australia, 2021, np).[2] As a penal colony, therefore, the very birth of settled Australia was made possible and articulated under British law, and through its use of island deportation as a technique for punishment. These re-settled convicts, which

Wolfe (1998, p 2) describes as Australia's 'structural counterparts to [North America's] African slaves', were simultaneously blights on British identity as well as beacons of colonization. Along with free settlers, they were to serve a crucial role in infecting the new Antipodean settlements with European morality and ontology. Australia was, thus, first viewed by the colonizing 'mother country' as a large Southern island of deportation; what Lennon (2008, p 165) refers to as a 'prison island' where 'unwanted people ... [were] sent to the "ends of the earth"'. It was constructed in the minds of the colonizers as a largely undiscovered, uninhabited, floating land mass, and a place where the worst kinds of people (convicts) could be 'disappeared' to (Baldacchino, 2016). Of course, the use of islands as sites of incarceration was not new. The British had long used islands dotted across the Atlantic and Indian oceans 'for exile of deposed monarchs and anti-colonial leaders, and as penal colonies for non-elite political rebels and "common" criminals' (Roscoe, 2021, p 173). As Roscoe (2021, p 175) described it, 'Australia's offshore islands [have also] played a distinctive role in colonial governance ... [and] displacement to islands was used to govern Indigenous people[s] who resisted frontier expansion as well as to punish recidivist convicts who did not rehabilitate into colonial society' (Roscoe, 2021, p 175).

Indeed, the typical fate of Indigenous peoples who resisted violent removal from their lands by pastoralists and agents of the state during Australia's 'forgotten war' (Reynolds, 2013) was to either be killed or relocated to islands. Islands off the coasts of Tasmania (Bass Strait) and Queensland (Norfolk and Palm islands), for example, became frequent sites of ex-communication for both Indigenous peoples and convicts – practices that reveal the extent to which Indigenous peoples have been (and, as we later argue, *continue* to be) likened with criminals in the white, settler imaginary. They were an 'evil' scourge that was to be removed; as local colonial administrator George Augustus Robinson claimed after convincing Tasmania's Big River peoples to relocate to Flinders Island, 'The work is done, the great evil is removed' (in Roscoe, 2021, p 181; also see Clements, 2014). However, while island displacements of this nature freed up lands for the colonizers and thwarted resistance efforts, they were often framed as a form of *protection* for both white and black. As Roscoe (2021, p 179) put it, 'The British government framed these islands as sites of protection [for Indigenous peoples] from frontier violence, but policies of displacement actually "protected" settlers and their property. Whether Indigenous people[s] were convicted or coerced to live on islands, surrounding waters were an effective barrier to escape.'

Nettelbeck (2012) explores how incarceration of Indigenous peoples in Western Australia, including banishment to island prisons (as was then the case under Governor John Hutt's formal 'protection through punishment' scheme), was not only conceived of as protecting them from the vigilante violence of white settlers, but also from themselves, since island prisons were sites where the disciplinary normalization and civilizing work of the colony was intensely pursued (Nettelbeck, 2012; Roscoe, 2021). This strategy was integrated into a broader intentional policy effort from the mid-19th century with the rise of what is now referred to as the 'protection era' (circa 1860s to circa 1950s), followed by an official policy of assimilation (circa 1950s to early 1970s). The protection era saw the ascension of state-based 'protection' acts, which had the explicit objective of paternalistically safeguarding Indigenous peoples, but implicit objectives of depopulating Indigenous lands. Protection was intended to 'smooth the pillow' of what was thought to be a 'dying race' (Bates, 1944; AHRC, 1997; Martin, 2014, p 146), since it was thought that the 'pure black ... [would soon be] extinct' (Queensland's *Telegraph* newspaper [1937] cited in AHRC, 1997, p 24). In practice, this involved the division of states into 'protectorates' and the appointment of white 'Protectors', who were typically (though not always) police officers (Frankland, 1994). This period oversaw diverse, interlaced strategies to segregate, separate, and 'rehabilitate' (normalize/assimilate) Indigenous peoples, which also led to the creation of island-like spaces in the continent's interior desert. This, we argue, was one example – among others – of colonial practices of invasion utilizing features of 'islandness' as a technique of separation, isolation, and punishment. That is, as we discuss below, island spaces were not only *utilized* under settler colonialism in Australia (as per the above discussion) but were also *created*.

Creating islands under Australian settler colonialism

In defining islands, Keegan and Diamond (1987, p 51) include 'true islands' (that is, bounded by sea) and exclude what they call (drawing on the biological sciences) 'habitat islands', which are 'habitat patches isolated from each other by alien habitat ... such as deserts'. They did so as a way to reduce the scope of their own study, but also noted that these 'habitat islands ... pose interesting questions' in terms of human movement and socialization (Keegan & Diamond, 1987, p 51). As we canvassed above, 'true' islands have been widely utilized under Australian settler colonialism: a tradition borrowed from the British, and also used by other settler colonies (including Canada, for example [Roscoe, 2021]). In an extension of the same logics of separation and isolation that propelled this use of true islands, however, island spaces and places have also been *created* as a governing technique of Australian settler colonialism, which has been influenced by (and in turn, had influence upon) crime and justice practices in several ways. An example of this is the emergence of apartheid-like policies in Australia's emerging cities during the protectionist era, which had the effect of establishing (invisible) lines within and around urban areas that demarcated spaces where Indigenous peoples could not travel, essentially creating urban islands of white and black. 'Boundary' streets and lanes continue to exist today as remnants of this colonial bordering (Greenop & Memmott, 2013). Man-made islands also emerged in the form of prison hulks: a technique borrowed from the British. As we discussed in Chapter 3, these man-made islands were places where horrors could be hidden: a characteristic that is also reflected in the creation of 'missions' and 'reserves' under Australian settler colonialism as islands in the desert – 'desert' islands (McMahon, 2010).

In her exploration of Australia's islandness, McMahon (2010, p 182) reflected:

> Australian colonial records indicate a shifting perception of the interior: from hopeful speculations on inland waterways and seas, as with explorers Banks and Sturt, as the endpoint of imperial adventures searching for El Dorados, and the site of undiscovered Utopias; each of these imagined centres taking the literal shape of a bounded, circumscribed core. The disappointment of these dreams recast the center as a dead heart: a desert. In this understanding, the periphery and the center are disconnected and unknown to each other. The unapproachable nature of the interior for the coastal dwellers held their gaze on the alternative center outside country, namely Britain.

This 'disconnection' between the centre and the periphery of the Australian continent established, in essence, a kind of desert island within the country's interior. This distinct interior mirrored key characteristics of islandness and established the desert outback as a site where unwanted people and things might be rendered invisible (Baldacchino, 2016): a sort of 'islanding as erasure'. Throughout the protectionist era, this included an intentional strategy to 'disappear' Indigenous peoples to these outback desert islands through the creation of missions and reserves.

Missions and reserves were carceral, bordered spaces, operated under the strict management of churches (in the case of the former) and governments (in the case of the latter). They were sometimes situated on 'true' islands in the sea (for example, Palm Island reserve [Queensland], Bathurst Island mission [Northern Territory]), but were mostly remote and isolated spaces, with hard borders, nestled amid vast, barren, and (ostensibly) uninhabitable stretches of land:[3] akin to 'habitat islands' (for example, Aurukun and Cherbourg missions [Queensland], Borroloola and Philip Creek missions [Northern Territory]) (AIATSIS, nd). These spaces operated as prisons in every way bar their names. Their borders were administered and guarded by white 'protectors', and Indigenous 'prisoners' were unable to escape without explicit permission from the state, which came in the form of an exemption pass: a 'dog tag' (Thelma McAvoy in Watson, 2010, p 43). Thousands of

Indigenous peoples were removed to these spaces; either for 'offending' (as judged against imposed colonial laws and tried within a deeply racist justice system), or for simply resisting colonization (Watson, 2016). In her account of Palm Island reserve (Queensland) Watson (2010, pp 36, 38) explains:

> Throughout the 1920s, Murris [Queensland Aboriginal peoples] and Torres Strait Islanders were shipped to the island 'like cattle' and by truckloads, some following sentencing by white courts, others after release from prison, or from other reserves where they had refused to show deference to white authorities. Others were simply 'whisked away' in periodic government round-ups on the mainland. … Many were marched in leg irons, in neck chains, or in both, and often at gunpoint.

This included women who had birthed children to white men, notwithstanding that many of these mothers were likely victims of rape – another common form of colonial violence. It also included Indigenous peoples who were unemployed or found to be 'vagrant' or destitute; 'all the blacks they [settlers] thought were troublemakers' (Bwgcolman man Fred Fulford cited in Watson, 2010). Those removed to these spaces had their freedoms stripped away in the same way as prisoners, and were subject to state-sponsored genocidal violence, including regular beatings, forced labour, theft of wages, and sexual violence (Watson, 2010; Cruickshank & Grimshaw, 2015). Watson (2010, pp 38, 158) referred to Palm Island as Australia's former Alcatraz, identified as a place where the worst of the worst arrived. This 'true' island reserve was utilized as a prison for the most 'troublesome cases' from the interior missions and reserves, showing that islanding was deployed in a stepped way, with habitat islands perhaps being slightly easier to escape than true islands bounded by water (Chief Protector J.W. Bleakley cited in Watson, 2016). The design of the Palm Island reserve was also intended to encourage horizontal violence as a way of (ironically) protecting the white 'protectors':

> Palm Island penitentiary was developed, in its early days, with the deliberate and articulated desire to allow conflict to foment between the various groups forced into exile there – 'if there is to be any letting off of steam, they would go for each other.' 'Horizontal violence', exacerbated so much by the introduction of alcohol, was widely tolerated until recent times. Moreover, at each critical point of Palm Island's history, when the violence threatens to become 'vertical' and is directed at the oppressor, the mask of benevolence falls. The 'kindly uncle boss' is consumed by his fear of 'the black man', and reacts with loathing. (Watson, 2010, pp 157–8)

Indeed, state-sanctioned violence characterized colonial governance on Palm Island, and arguably still does (Watson, 2010). This has included continued use of the criminal justice system to substantiate these acts of violence, with the island's initial superintendent, Curry, acting as 'prosecutor, clerk of court and judge with no system for appeal [and with court being] ... held in the strict privacy of Curry's office' (Watson, 2010, p 44). Other nearby islands were also used as additional penitentiaries to further exile particularly problematic Palm Island residents, further demonstrating how islanding was a layered practice of punishment.

In Queensland (as in other jurisdictions), exemption passes, which would enable travel outside the missions and reserves, were only granted on the basis that individuals would take up formal employment, and/or in cases where women were 'lawfully married to, and residing with, a husband who himself is not an aboriginal [sic.]' (ss 10, 12 of the Aboriginals Protection and Restriction of the Sale of Opium Act 1897 (Qld), from herein 'Qld Act'). Holt (2006, p 3), whose mother was removed to Cherbourg [formerly Barambah] mission in inland Queensland, described the need to 'jettison some of the "baggage of blackness"' as being necessary for enjoying freedom through exemption from these carceral spaces:

> Factors such as freedom to travel outside and whom one could marry were determined by the Protector of Aborigines who had all the power to give or take away. My mother applied three times for an Exemption Certificate, which ultimately deem her 'civilised' enough to live beyond the boundaries of ... [Cherbourg] mission to which she had been removed and relegated.
>
> I'm sure that for my parents' generation, that was part of the 'glittering prize'. That is, to be deemed 'respectable and responsible' enough to no longer be considered an Aborigine under the Native Affairs Act. To attain the certificate must have been a real relief. For the first time one could travel anywhere one wanted to and marry anyone one wanted to. ... To the day she died [my mother] ... never lost her fear of authority; be it in the form of the police or their equivalent who could, for whatever reason (real or imaginary), take away one's freedom.

But just as exemption came at the price of a level of assimilatory obedience, assimilation was also actively pursued *within* the boundaries of these desert island spaces. Indeed, those forced to live in missions and reserves were prevented from and punished for speaking their ancestral languages and practising their cultures (AHRC, 1997). In Aurukun mission, which was established as an isolated penitentiary on western Cape York (Queensland) in 1904, strict authoritarianism was combined with an emphasis on

Christianizing; 'on establishing what were seen to be self-evidently morally superior forms such as domestic units based on the nuclear family and the values of work, self-reliance, and economic independence' (Martin, 1993, p 2). Moreover, mission and reserve residents were forced into a sedentary lifestyle that was in keeping with white, Western norms. As Roscoe (2021, pp 179–80) describes:

> Many British scientists believed Aboriginal Australians to be an inferior hunter-gatherer race who were behind Caucasians in the hierarchy of human development. Islands were ideal spaces to enforce sedentariness on Indigenous people, encouraging farming and living indoors, twin pillars of European 'civilization' ... [Indeed], the bounded island [was] an ideal 'laboratory for civilization'.

Thus, just as those incarcerated in regular prisons are simultaneously incapacitated and immobilized, while maintaining a possibility of *rehabilitation and release*, this also characterized the lives of those existing on these missions and reserves. This brings into view the concept of islands as 'relative spaces: bounded but porous; isolated, connected, colonized' (Stratford, 2003, p 495). Indeed, as we canvassed in Chapter 3, the isolation of islands sits in tension with their connectedness, because it is in relation to this connection (to other people, places, spaces) that islandness is defined and comes into being, much like the Other is only definable in relation to the Self.

As we also discussed in Chapter 3 in relation to the isolation of prison hulks, those trapped within the bounds of missions and reserves were not only unfree, but also hidden and *unseen*. In this sense, islanding again served to not only depopulate lands, but also to remove uncouth blackness from the purview of the nation's (white) identity, while only 'rehabilitated' Indigenous peoples were made visible (Staines, forthcoming). This fits with the notion of 'translation as erasure', whereby translation of systems of meaning, languages, and more to fit with conventions of Western modernity can 'perform ... a border-keeping role', being enacted and experienced as a form of both epistemic and physical violence that erases aspects of the Other that do not 'fit' (Vázquez, 2011, p 27). The physical and imagined isolation of island spaces shows how they can also be mobilized as 'places where persons, but also states, get erased and rendered absent' (Baldacchino, 2016, p 97). Deploying island as a verb, Baldacchino (2016, p 98) recognizes interlinkages between politics, erasure, and islandness, stating that history is littered with 'islanding performances of people, and states, "going missing"'. This centres the notion of erasure as a key technique in the politics of colonialism, and in this case, settler colonialism, and the 'making [of] a national body [which is] ... inevitably a process of loss and denial', *facilitated* through islanding performances (Anderson, 2005, p 257). As Amoamo (2013, p 234) describes it, 'erasure is tied to any appreciation of identity; it is largely the act of neglect, looking past, and minimizing, ignoring, or rendering invisible an *other*'.

In the case of Australian settler colonialism, only 'seeing' the white self (or the convalesced black Other as a near-enough approximation to whiteness, at least enough to be made visible but not necessarily ascribed equal access to rights and other social goods), and *disappearing* the black Other, has been frequently undertaken through islanding, deploying a mixture of both 'true' and man-made or 'habitat' islands. These practices have continued to shape contemporary governance of these (now former) remote spaces, relabelled 'remote' or 'discrete' Indigenous communities since the state handed local governance over to Indigenous peoples (via Indigenous councils) from the late 1970s. This renaming and 'opening up' of these remote desert island spaces occurred around the same time that, as McMahon (2010, p 178) argues, Australia 'discovered' the centre of the continent, collapsing the 'connection between the *desert [interior]* and the *island [periphery]*'. In part, this was spurred by increased economic interest in the centre, with it being (re)imagined in the mind of the colonizer – as the margins of the continent had already wholeheartedly been imagined – as an 'object ... of possible possession' (McMahon, 2010, p 182; Moreton-Robinson, 2015). However, although this has involved a debordering of the island-like spaces of the (now former) remote missions and reserves, they have still retained echoes of their carceral characteristics; a carcerality intimately connected with and arising from colonial islanding practices, and which has continued to reverberate across time.

Echoes of island carcerality in remote Australia

From 1972, Australian federal policy officially moved away from 'assimilation' to support Indigenous self-determination. As noted above, this involved local governance of the remote island spaces of former missions and reserves transferring to newly established Aboriginal and Torres Strait Islander councils. In relation to Aurukun (Queensland), Martin (1993, pp 4–5) explained that after a local Aboriginal council was formally established in 1978, the mission:

> was no longer isolated ... [instead being increasingly] exposed ever more directly to the forms and institutions of the wider state; the full introduction of a cash-based economy, alcohol, consumer goods, telephones and television, vehicles, ever greater numbers of outsiders living there or passing through, the courts and legal system.

In sum, this meant that even though Aurukun remained technically remote, its isolation was dramatically reduced (Martin, 1993, p 5). The borders of these spaces were subsequently made more porous and permeable, particularly since exemption passes were no longer needed. Freedom of movement onto ancestral Country beyond these communities, including to practise culture, as well as mobility in and out of (now) urban areas, was restored and enacted through the 'Homelands' or 'return-to-Country' movement (Altman, 2018). Moreover, a new sort of border was erected in the form of a sort of 'usurpatory [social] closure' (Trigger, 1986, p 100), with these island spaces being rearticulated *by* Indigenous peoples as areas where Indigenous practices and organizations dominated (Taylor, 2013). Islanding in part, thereby, fulfilled its promise of protection when definitions of boundary were *self-determined* by Indigenous peoples. However, as Australia marched towards the 21st century, colonial politics took a regressive step, overseeing a return to assimilationist intent and practices. Even though the islandness that had previously defined these spaces was at first diminished, it was arguably later reinforced, with the borders of these spaces again being re-hardened and their administration returned to the state.

Arguably, a catalyst for this change was a series of important legal decisions in the early to mid-1990s, including *Mabo and Others v The State of Queensland* (1992) and *Wik Peoples v Queensland* (1996), which were perceived as threatening white possessive identity, particularly since the *Mabo* decision overturned the doctrine of *terra nullius* upon which white Australian nationhood had been built. *Seeing* the previously unseen/ignored sovereignty of Indigenous peoples shook the very foundations of whiteness and prompted fear campaigns by politicians, white pastoralists, and the mining industry, which (re)stoked colonial undercurrents of Othering and islanding. The Australia Mining Council took out advertisements in state and national newspapers that framed *Mabo* as a significant threat to business and jobs (Gelder & Jacobs, 1995), while then Prime Minister John Howard (1997, p 7) claimed that 'The pendulum has swung too far in the direction of Aborigines in the argument', the subtext being that it was time to swing the pendulum *back*. Subsequent policymaking has represented a return to islanding on the terms of hegemonic whiteness, with assimilation being again revitalized as a pre-requisite for exemption/freedom (Altman, 2018). A range of overlapping measures and policies have been introduced to survey and govern the behaviours of the Other in remote Indigenous communities, and these have arguably had the combined effect of again turning these spaces into carceral island enclaves.

One example is the Northern Territory Emergency Response (NTER), which was implemented in 2007 on the (contested) basis that child abuse was rampant in remote Northern Territory Indigenous communities: sentiments that involved the rearticulation of these remote spaces as unregulated and lawless, and of Otherness as an ominous threat to an imagined Australian way of life (Howard & Brough, 2007). The NTER involved a wide package of measures, including a five-year federal government lease scheme and removal of a permit system that enabled Aboriginal communities to decide who could enter Aboriginal lands; that is, a transferral of control over the borders of these island spaces from Indigenous hands, back to the state (Howard & Brough, 2007). A more recent policy, the Community Development Programme (CDP), has also (re)hardened the borders of these remote island spaces. The CDP is a 'welfare to work' or 'workfare' policy that operates only in remote Australia (across 1,000 remote communities, most of which are Indigenous communities) and carries a caseload that is ~80 per cent Indigenous (despite only ~3 per cent of the Australian population identifying as Indigenous). Under the policy, unemployed peoples must undertake mutual obligations, like work for the dole activities, in order to qualify for social security unemployment benefits; if they fail to comply, they lose their benefits for up to eight weeks at a time. The stated policy goal is to transition people into waged work, but this is an often-difficult (if not impossible) task in remote Australia, because there are few to no jobs available. Thus, participants have little option but to remain in the programme, where they churn for sometimes years or decades at a time. This creates a situation where participants are also, however, prevented from moving beyond the (re)congealed borders of these remote communities and onto Country, because they must remain close to their job service provider in order to complete their obligations and maintain their incomes. Permeation of the borders of these island spaces (that is, freedom to move back and forth between community and Country) again only becomes possible via entry into the workforce; a situation that is reminiscent of the exemption permits of the protectionist era.

The combination of these (and other) policies means that surveillance and discipline of Indigenous peoples living in remote communities, by both the penal and welfare states, is ever increasing. Indeed, alongside these kinds of social policies, policing has been deliberately intensified. Under the NTER, for instance, an ongoing police presence was established for the first time in 18 remote Indigenous communities, and night patrols were also significantly increased (from 23 to 80 communities). The CDP is also, like other social policies that target Indigenous communities (for example, 'income management', see Marston et al, 2022) animated through crime metaphors that stigmatize community members as being predisposed to crime (Staines et al, 2020). This results in further calls for increased policing resources, producing a situation where policing in remote Indigenous communities today is generally more intensive than elsewhere, with police-to-person ratios being consistently higher (for example, Valentin, 2007). As in the past, the large majority of sworn police working in these remote spaces are non-Indigenous, which has significant implications for their relations with local communities, what they might judge to be antisocial behaviour worthy of police investigation, and for potential racism and racial profiling (Cunneen &

Tauri, 2016; Dwyer et al, 2020). This must of course be understood within the context set out earlier, where state police have been historically mobilized to enact violent colonial policies, including disappearing Indigenous peoples to these remote island spaces in the first place. This history is echoed in police–Indigenous relations in remote Indigenous communities today. As a non-Indigenous Constable (cited in Dwyer et al, 2020, p 8), working in one of Queensland's remote Indigenous communities, recently stated: 'At best we are tolerated; generally speaking, most people here would be happy if we were not here.' Various forms of resistance against continued colonial occupation also characterize these remote spaces:

> We ... find in our regular interactions we get called 'Captain Cook cunt', 'bully man' and other sort of derogative names. (Constable, cited in Dwyer et al, 2020, p 9)

> Every other night we have stuff thrown on our roof. ... As soon as we showed up we will just be subject to abuse, 'what the fuck you doing here, fuck off, you have no right to be here'. (Constable, cited in Dwyer et al, 2020, p 9)

These tensions and acts of resistance produce higher crime rates and are used to justify even further calls to strengthen surveillance and policing of these spaces, which has the effect of creating a self-perpetuating loop (Staines et al, 2020).

In combination with deeply rooted intergenerational traumas, which are a product of past and present colonial violence, intensive surveillance of Indigenous peoples in remote communities has driven crime rates in these spaces up. Indeed, rates of incarceration for Australian Indigenous peoples increased by 41 per cent between 2006 and 2016 (ALRC, 2018) with the incarceration rate for Indigenous peoples being 13.3 times higher than for non-Indigenous peoples in 2020 and with this gap continuing to grow (that is, 2,081 per 100,000 adult population versus 156.3 per 100,000 adult population, respectively) (Productivity Commission, 2021). In Queensland's remote Indigenous communities in 2016–17 in particular, crimes against the person were between 2.8 and 30.7 times higher than the Queensland average (DATSIP, 2017). Former 'true island' reserve, Palm Island now records consistently high rates of reported crime; in 2016–17, for example, rates of reported offences against the person were 89.9 per 1,000 persons, which is 12.7 times higher than the average Queensland rate (DATSIP, 2017). Similarly, the former 'habitat island' mission of Aurukun now consistently records among the highest crime rates in Queensland, if not the country, and has also been identified as the *most* disadvantaged location in Queensland (DATSIP, 2017; Tanton et al, 2021).

Both spaces are consistently identified in national media as being particularly violent and 'problematic'. Aurukun, for instance, frequently garners media attention because of community-wide outbreaks of violence, which have recently involved deaths of community members and administration buildings being burnt down (Grant, 2007; Archibald-Binge & Wyman, 2020) and which are typically discussed in ways that are heavily decontextualized, laying blame solely with Indigenous peoples themselves who are repeatedly framed as 'thugs' and criminals (Carden, 2017). Similarly, Palm Island was the backdrop to the 2004 death of Mulrunji, a 36-year-old Bwgcolman man who died in police custody shortly after being arrested under a public nuisance charge, triggering an island-wide protest and string of government inquiries (Watson, 2010). Although a coronial inquiry found a (white) police officer responsible for Mulrunji's fatal injuries, and the officer was later charged with manslaughter, he was subsequently acquitted. Thereafter, a government inquiry recommended that police numbers across all remote Indigenous communities, including Palm Island, be intensified to improve security and safety; little was made of the fact that intensive state surveillance and policing was what had led to this situation in the first place, and would be unlikely to therefore 'fix' the challenges created by colonial invasion (Staines et al, 2020). This case offers an analogy for what is generally perceived to be the continually racialized nature of policing in this island space, echoing historical practices. This is encapsulated in a short narrative, which Watson (2010, p 160) deploys as a powerful end to her book:

> In April 2008, a Palm Island police officer fell from the balcony of the police barracks on Palm, after circumventing alcohol restrictions by partying on nearby Orpheus Island – a five-star glamour resort offering seven course meals, positioned across the channel from this 'Third World' community like a parallel universe. The wasteful consumption of medical and emergency services that this incident caused seems to have brought no condemnation.
>
> Less than a month later, the Police Department's Ethical Standards Command delivered its findings in a case lodged by Palm Islander, Charlie Gibson. Gibson complained that he had been strip searched by Palm Island police who were looking for alcohol or drugs. The 26-year-old was made to disrobe and expose his genitals, in public and in front of nearby women friends and children. No intoxicants were found. Gibson's complaint was dismissed as 'unsubstantiated'. Just business as usual, on this 'certain paradise for certain people'.

Overall, these remote, desert-locked communities experience crime rates that are on average far higher than other parts of Queensland (Staines & Scott, 2020); a situation that is repeated across other Australian states and territories, and which has led to Australian Indigenous peoples being identified as the most incarcerated peoples on the planet (Anthony & Baldry, 2017). In many ways, these remote island spaces arguably continue to act as assimilatory enclaves, much as they did when first created during the islanding practices of the protectionist era. They exist as remote, isolated, and (still relatively) unseen spaces, with re-hardened borders that trap and seek to discipline the non-conforming Other. Conformity is enacted by submitting one's labour to the institutions of the settler state – either by taking up employment or having one's labour extracted through policies such as the CDP – strategies that have the concurrent (implicit) impact of keeping Indigenous peoples off their ancestral lands. The 'choice' of disengaging with these sorts of social policies is largely illusory, since it also means being cut off from social security income and likely thrust into dire poverty. Although these remote island spaces have changed and morphed over time, they continue to either lock people in, or simply lock them out (for example, most obviously via ever-increasing incarceration) (Povinelli, 2019; Staines et al, 2020). As Baldacchino's (2016, p 97) description of morphing island spaces indicates:

> The nature of an island morphs into shady and fuzzy layers of stricture. ... Specific groups of 'undesirables' – detainees, terrorists, irregular migrants – can be physically rounded up while enjoying mobilities that transcend those denied by, or available through, conventional carceration.

Indeed, choice and freedom are illusory in these still highly regulated island spaces – mere desert mirages – demonstrating how islanding as erasure has not only been a technique of historical settler colonial policies in Australia but also remains a core technique of invasion and discipline still today.

Conclusion

History is littered with stories of island invasions. However, just as they were viewed as sites of possible invasion and settlement, features of islandness have also been repeatedly adapted by invaders themselves and re-assigned as *techniques of invasion*. The conceptualization of remote Indigenous communities as islands in the desert helps to illuminate this mobilization of islanding as a technique of settler colonial invasion. To use Baldacchino's (2016, p 97) words, this demonstrates 'how people are managed via their im/mobility on island spaces, with or without necessarily being locked in a prison cell'. In settler colonial Australia, islands have not only been adapted to be used as 'natural prisons', mimicry of islandness has also informed the creation of new spaces and places to displace, segregate, erase, and discipline deviant Others. Islanding as erasure, thus, becomes another colonial strategy of punishment, silencing, and discipline – techniques that produce echoes which ripple across time, seeping into and informing contemporary experiences of crime and justice.

Australia is, of course, only one example of how islands have been utilized in settler colonial contexts; similarities can be drawn to settler colonies elsewhere. In Canada, for example, islands were regularly used to resettle and restrain Indigenous peoples. The Odawa and Ojibway peoples were resettled on Manitoulin Island from 1836, with commissary general Randolph Routh (in Roscoe, 2021, p 181) describing the island 'as a "desirable asylum" where their [Indigenous peoples'] wandering impulses could be "restrain[ed]" enabling a "natural progress" towards civilization'. Meanwhile, the creation of Indigenous reserves was also a central feature of colonial governance in Canada. As Harris (2004, p 167) explained, 'Native people were in the way, their land was coveted, and settlers took it. ... Native people had been placed in compartments by an aggressive settler society that, like others of its kind, was far more interested in native land than the surplus value of native labor' (also see Lea, 2020). These (and likely also other) examples thereby demonstrate how deeply embedded social phenomena, like Othering, can be ascribed upon and expressed through geographical means. In a broader sense, this also demonstrates how physical geographies are integrated into the imaginations of settlers: indicative of a mutual, symbiotic relationship between humans and nature, with settlers' thoughts and ideas being expressed *through* the land, as well as ascribed *upon* the land. This proffers a deeply relational understanding that runs counter to Western notions of humans as being disconnected from, and conquering of, lands and seas; a relationality that is ironically more akin to Indigenous ontologies, which tend to see humans as being in a symbiotic and reciprocal relationship with the lands that nurture them (Dudgeon & Bray, 2019; Yunkaporta, 2019). As Indigenous scholar, Irene Watson (2008, p 99) describes it:

> Our bodies and the land are connected. Our health and wellbeing are tied together ... though I am dispossessed and assimilated, I am still a resisting Tanganekald Meintangk *mimini* [woman[4]]. I still belong to country. It is bred into me and it is an old idea and it is one that still lives.

Islands have provided a backdrop to invasion but have also seeped into the imaginaries of the invaders, shaping and informing their colonial toolkits. While, therefore, invaders have used island spaces and imaginaries primarily for their abilities to *isolate*, *separate*, and *hide*, islands can also be sites of intensive integration. The forms of resistance that have cropped up in remote Indigenous communities offer one example, such as the case of Palm Island residents forming a united Bwgcolman identity, despite the community being a culmination of displaced individuals from numerous clan groups spread across Queensland (Watson, 2010). In the next chapter, we further explore the notion of integration in island spaces through additional case studies that demonstrate how intense integration and strong social capital can be both crime preventative *and* criminogenic.

5

Integration

> ... we are all islands – in a common sea.
> (Anne Morrow Lindbergh, 1955)

Although much has been written about rural policing, accounts of policing islands in the Global North are rare (see Souhami, 2020). One exception is a light-hearted account of policing the Isles of Scilly (population 2,200) off the south-west coast of England. The longest serving police officer on the Scilly Islands presented them as sleepy, crime-free backwaters, with crime mostly consisting of bicycle thefts and people stealing petrol from cars. What might have been a bust on a 'drug smuggling ring' proved disappointing when the 2 kg of cocaine turned out to be a bag of mozzarella cheese (Taylor, 2016). Research in the Global North has presented policing in remote and small-scale societies as community focused, owing to low crime rates in such societies. But is there actually less crime or less reportage of crimes such as domestic violence, which recent research has found to be endemic in all social contexts? Is there really less violence in the Scilly Isles than on the mainland, or is crime reportage a response of how police do their work and is how police do their work influenced by specific environments and social networks?

In this chapter, we examine the issue of integration in relation to policing in the Pacific, where most research on policing islands has been conducted. The Pacific Islands are loosely sub-divided into cultural and geographic groupings of Polynesia, Micronesia, and Melanesia. Most Pacific Island communities (PICs) are microstates with small, geographically dispersed populations. Approximately 90 per cent of the region's population of approximately 11 million people live in four independent Melanesian states, with the largest in size and population (8 million) being Papua New Guinea, and the others including Fiji, the Solomon Islands, and Vanuatu (Watson & Dinnen, 2020). These nations are often spread over wide geographic areas of small islands, contrasting the influential neighbouring countries of Australia and New Zealand. PICs also have a relatively high police-to-population ratio (Newton, 1998). All the countries in the region may be classified as 'developing nations' with limited public sector resources, lack of infrastructure, and relatively poor communications (Newton, 1998). We draw on these examples to show that, contrary to popular, largely idealized accounts of policing in remote and small societies, islands demonstrate the need for caution about valorizing specific models of policing as universally appropriate and functional. Indeed, policing within opaque and densely integrated networks can create difficult-to-navigate tensions, which can hinder the pursuit of justice for some victims, particularly those belonging to marginalized groups.

Localistic versus legalistic policing

In both popular culture and the research literature, policing in rural and isolated places has highlighted the often quaint and community-focused aspects of the work. A consistent aspect of research into policing in remote and small societies has been the observation that police adopt a generalist style or community-oriented approach, grounded in close associations with residents (Thurman & McGarrell, 1997). The police officer is able to respond to an assortment of departmental and community needs, only a few of which are statutorily defined as law enforcement responsibilities. Payne et al (2005) found the most common type of case described in police reports in a 'small town' in Pennsylvania involved animals. Other problems commonly dealt with involved drunkenness, dysfunctional interpersonal relationships, and public disorder involving traffic violations, vandalism, assault, and disorderly conduct (see also Maguire et al, 1991). In their study of the relatively homogenous New South Wales (Australia) community of Walcha, O'Connor and Gray (1989) classified rural police work under four headings: (1) bureaucratic (for example, granting licences and permits); (2) service-welfare work (for example, peace-keeping, assisting the public, and offering advice on a wide variety of issues, which was important in building positive community rapport); (3) order maintenance (for example, liaison with schools and media, managing a youth disco, and regular patrols of hotels at night); and (4) law enforcement, which despite being a central aspect of their job, constituted a minor part of an officer's day-to-day activities. Police in this small town regarded formal law enforcement as a last resort measure, avoiding such action where possible.

Indeed, law enforcement is only one function of policing, particularly in remote and small societies (Swanson, Territo, & Taylor, 1988). It seems that lower crime rates, actual or perceived, have resulted in officers spending greater amounts of time providing community services. Whereas police generally assume specialist roles in metropolitan environments, both rural police and their constituents undertake multiple functions (Pennings, 1999). Officers tend to be generalist police who handle all varieties of crime, often spending more time in service roles than law enforcement. Commensurate with community expectations, officers are as likely to administer to tragedies and accidents as they are to 'serious' crime. These 'welfare' or 'humanitarian' duties establish officers as good citizens and indirectly facilitate law enforcement and reduce crime (Wilkins, 1982). Greater importance is accorded to establishing and maintaining public tranquillity or 'the peace', as opposed to imposing law and order at any cost. Most police enjoy and readily adapt to this role (see Jobes, 2002). Given the emphasis on generalist service provision, what develops is a 'localistic', as opposed to 'legalistic', approach to policing.

With a localistic model of policing, the public influences how policing is carried out, defining important aspects of the role of the police, including police discretion. In contrast to metropolitan policing, where discretion is solely influenced by the organizational structure of a department, rural police discretion is likely to be influenced by the way in which the community is organized. What little theoretical work has been done on policing in small-scale societies has highlighted the issue of integration and how it might enable and limit the task of policing. In remote and small-scale societies, police typically reside within communities, their private lives being closely intertwined with their public role.

Colonial transition in the Pacific

Historically, while colonial rule in the Pacific entailed the introduction of selected Western laws and legal institutions, these were poorly resourced and Western-style courts were restricted to small expatriate enclaves, while so-called 'native courts' were designated for Indigenous peoples and were much less formal in character (Dinnen et al, 2003, p 10). In many places the colonial administrator could fulfil several justice roles and functions, including police and magistrate. While Indigenous justice was considered by colonizers as largely inadequate, Western practices had limited influence and most Indigenous communities continued to deal with conflicts, disputes, and infractions according to local 'kastom'. Colonial administrators, unfamiliar with local customs and often unable to speak local languages, were dependent on local justice structures given the limited reach of colonial mechanisms and the ability of Indigenous practices to resolve disputes in a holistic fashion.

Centralized policing in many PICs was part of a wider process of colonization and, as independence approached, colonial forces became more paramilitary in character and, in some cases, increased in size (Dinnen & Braithwaite, 2009). The colonial systems were imposed and were often in conflict with informal systems that had existed throughout the history of islands, the aim of such systems to maintain stability and order among island subjects rather than create elaborate and durable investment in expensive systems of state justice. As a result, the social penetration of the colonial system of justice could be shallow, with subjects continuing to rely upon informal and localized forms of dispute resolution for security (Dinnen & McLeod, 2009).

When independence dawned for Pacific states during the 1970s, colonial practices were deemed discriminatory and paternalistic, and institutions such as police and courts were transformed into professional and neutral, modern arms of justice. This transition was difficult in former colonies that had been politically fragmented in their administration or had been controlled by weak and under-resourced colonial regimes. Dissatisfaction with the process resulted in a revival of older forms of self-help, including violent forms of dispute resolution (Dinnen et al, 2003, pp 11–13). In the postcolonial Pacific, localized practices have also been favoured over state-based policing. In some islands, especially rural regions, there is strong resistance to state-based policing and communities consider themselves subject only to customary law (Newton, 1998, p 350). The architects of independence tried to accommodate as much as possible both the state and traditional forms of authority (Dinnen et al, 2003, pp 15–17).

The effectiveness of state-based law enforcement has been challenged in the Pacific by lack of resources. For example, at the time of Papua New Guinea's independence (1975), the coverage provided by the 'national' police force, which included 5,000 officers, extended to only 10 per cent of the total land area and 40 per cent of the population, of 4.6 million people (Dinnen et al, 2003, p 17). Papua New Guinea's larger urban centres have become associated with high rates of violence, especially sexual assaults and gangs. This has provided a disincentive to tourism and other forms of economic investment in the Nation, while extreme law and order responses have seemed to worsen such problems. Such issues, especially youth gang violence, are also evident in other Melanesian nations, including the Solomon Islands, Fiji, and Vanuatu. A major issue driving growth in violence is thought to be youth unemployment and general lack of economic opportunities for young people, many of whom have migrated to urban centres from rural areas (Dinnen et al, 2003, pp 19–20). The situation is comparable to mainland rural areas experiencing economic decline.

Throughout the region there has long been a strong reliance on foreign aid, which can include assistance in the form of training from foreign police (Newton, 1998, p 350). In Papua New Guinea, decades of Australian development assistance have had little impact on police performance, and failures include incompetence, brutalization, nepotism, corruption, politicization, and poor responsiveness to community needs (Dinnen & Braithwaite, 2009). Failures of policing were traditionally blamed on imposed models drawn from colonial and later doner interventions, and it is often argued that policing will be more communitarian when it is in harmony with local sources of socio-cultural authority (Bull et al, 2019, pp 157–8). Among the failures of doner programmes has been the imposition of an urban-centric policing model, including the location of most infrastructure in urban centres, despite 85 per cent of the population living in rural and remote villages, surviving on subsistence agriculture and cash-cropping. Transport and communications infrastructure for most of the population is rudimentary with bonds of kinship, shared language, ties to ancestral lands, and Christianity providing the basis for communal interactions. The modern state, Christianity, local customs, and commercial enterprise all inform social relations and articulate authority and legitimacy, although in many cases the modern state and its systems of governance have limited influence with individual identity and obligation being tied to kinship affiliations. Violent forms of self-help, including vendettas and warfare, remain legitimate response to grievances in many isolated communities (Dinnen & McLeod, 2009; Dinnen & Braithwaite, 2009). In PICs, the state has generally failed in the monopolization of the legitimate use of force and social orders, which are inclusive of normative violence, have flourished (Dinnen & McLeod, 2009).

Recent research, which has associated violence with modernity and urbanization, can romanticize heritage and gloss over history (Chandler, 2014). As Watson and Dinnen (2020, p 167) observe, policing:

> can be oppressive and discriminatory towards particular groups and individuals, just as others can be respectful and empowering. Kastom is by definition conservative in orientation and can obscure significant imbalances in power and divisions along lines of gender, ethnicity, age or religion. The problematic treatment of women in particular is a widely recognised problem with traditional or kastom-based approaches to justice and policing in the Pacific ... customary practices can become corrupted when detached from their traditional social moorings. Informal policing initiatives that are inadequately regulated or supervised can be captured by partisan interests and become instruments of oppression. Likewise, church-led approaches that place a singular emphasis on forgiveness and reconciliation, can promote immunity for offenders and injustice for victims.
>
> Plural policing, with its implied options and choices, can also confuse those seeking clear pathways for the processing and resolution of their cases. At the same time, it is important not to allow such challenges to obscure the potential and opportunities presented by plural policing and legal pluralism. Many of the same concerns raised in respect of non-state policing providers are also aired regularly in relation to government police organisations: for example, corruption, lack of accountability, brutality, discrimination against vulnerable groups

Papua New Guinea, for example, has a hybrid system of introduced and Indigenous justice in which traditional village courts sit within the formal system. Under Papua New Guinean law, village courts do not, however, determine criminal matters such as rape and murder, which are referred to the district and national courts. Yet the reality is that for remote villages the police may be a five-day walk or 1,000 km boat trip away, making local intervention the reality (Dinnen & Braithwaite, 2009; Chandler, 2014). In Papua New Guinea there has also been a return of less centralized, less paramilitary policing that in some respects resembles the old colonial system (Dinnen & Braithwaite, 2009). In Bougainville, a community policing philosophy has been adopted and police often live and work in local villages (Dinnen & Braithwaite, 2009). Given the diverse sources of authority, people in Melanesia often 'forum shop' for justice among the various regulatory structures available to them within the constraint imposed by individual status and wealth (Dinnen & McLeod, 2009).

However, this recent hybrid turn in critical security analysis aligns with global neo-liberal orthodoxy of public sector retreat from security provisions and outsourcing of security agency work to private entities. Ideas about culture and tradition in PICs have been subject to local and national processes of contestation, highlighting a complex interplay of colonization, missionization, and recently, globalization and neo-liberalism. It raises issues around how authority is defined and understood in local contexts and whose voices are deemed authoritative (Bull et al, 2019, pp 158–9). Women have highlighted gendered failings of the state and failings of customary forms of justice (Bull et al, 2019, p 159). One question that may be posed here is the extent to which policing strategies such as community policing represent a response to the failure of penal welfarism in the final decades of the twentieth century (see, for example, Garland, 1996). For example, are these strategies part of what Garland described as 'the new criminologies of everyday life', which involve increasing commercialization and rationalization of criminal justice functions, utilizing the actors and agencies of civil society to manage crime? This model of policing has been described as a 'pluralisation' of policing or 'neoliberal strategy of governing at a distance' (Cherney & Chui, 2010). Weber (2007) observes that community policing (not unlike restorative justice) assumes the existence of a recognizable and relatively homogenous community. Sarre (2005, p 311) recognized that the key to implementing community-policing principles lies in the ability of police officers to 'interweave and coordinate policing "networks", to mobilise the community sector, and to integrate police alliances into existing community structures'.

Gendered violence

Rapid globalization and institutional fragility have made regional security and stability priorities for Australia and New Zealand in the South Pacific. Since 2001 these countries have adopted a more interventionist approach in the region, especially with regard to transnational crime and internal conflict and political instability in several Melanesian countries, including Papua New Guinea, the Solomon Islands, and Fiji. Part of the response has been to strengthen law enforcement (Watson & Dinnen, 2020).

Until recent years, gendered violence was less a focus of these interventions, which can in part be explained by privileging the security/policing priorities of the metropolitan countries/donors over those of the recipient countries where they are assumed to be the same (Watson & Dinnen, 2020). Recent studies conducted in the South Pacific (including Samoa, the Solomon Islands, Kiribati, Fiji, Vanuatu, Tonga, and New Caledonia) suggest that between 40 and 70 per cent of women experience violence at the hands of intimate partners and family during their lifetimes. In the Solomon Islands, for example, nearly two in three women (aged 15–49) have experienced physical or, more commonly, sexual violence (Bull et al, 2019, p 155). There has been much work to reduce gendered violence in the region, including new legislation, prevention programmes, police training, foreign aid, and prioritization of the issue at the Pacific Island Forum Leaders meeting (Bull et al, 2019, p 156). Amin, Girard and Watson (2020) have also highlighted how gender non-conformity is regulated through a hybrid model of regulation in the Kingdom of Tonga. The Tongan system draws on English Common Law, Indigenous culture, and Christianity.

Naviti (2003) examines the failure of state responses to violence against women and children and argues that restorative justice, if it can be inclusive of women and empower them in its processes, might provide a better response in island societies. Watson and Dinnen (2020, pp 170–1) show how solutions to domestic violence are often borrowed from Western nations and simply imposed in diverse and foreign contexts. However, in both Vanuatu and Papua New Guinea (PNG), research has suggested that customary forms of justice have also often been faulted for laying undue stress on reconciliation and the harmony of the 'community' at the expense of individual survivors/victims of domestic and family violence (DFV). When women have turned to a legal response police have also been inclined to see DFV as a private matter to be reconciled, rather than a legal matter. Village courts in cases of adultery and sexual violence have also been criticized for victim blaming and silencing women's voices (Jolly, 2003).

Prevailing international conceptions of law and order assume the social desirability of violence suppression, yet disputation and violence may be considered normative features of many small-scale island societies. Violence can be viewed not as conflict, but a form of conflict resolution (Dinnen & McLeod, 2009). It has been argued that in some island communities, including much of Papua New Guinea, the position of women has deteriorated rather than improved in recent years (Chandler, 2014). Bull et al (2019) note that there has been much criticism of centralized state policing authority in the Pacific and its marginalization of local regulatory functions and forms of authority. As an alternative, there is advocacy of a hybrid paradigm of state security agencies and informal sources of regulatory authority (see, for example, Dinnen & Braithwaite, 2009).

Further, research in PNG has found that 'wife beating' was condoned by a large portion of the population: both men and women. Tolerance is also mediated by geography, with great variations between tolerance levels in differing regions. This may be a result of traditional and Christian values being co-opted into colonial political and economic systems, which have been described as deeply patriarchal (Chandler, 2014). In Fiji, where locals developed a punitive 'zero-tolerance' approach to DFV, there is evidence that women were placed under pressure by customary and religious leaders in their community not to report violence, as this may rupture the integrity of their marriage and to not report would spare perpetrators from punitive policing responses (Bull et al, 2019, p 156). In most Melanesian countries authority resides in the state, kastom, and the churches, so that national legal systems and agencies, such as the police, intermingle with older forms of authority and social organization. Extended kinship networks still provide an important basis for social relations (Watson & Dinnen, 2020, p 201).

The distinction between state and localized notions of social order which exists in much of the Pacific challenges local police, whose primary allegiance is to kin and local custom as opposed to the state and the universal values it seeks to promote. This can result in charges of corruption, nepotism, and failure to act impartially (Dinnen & McLeod, 2009). Some groups in society may receive benefits when regulatory authority is hybridized in ways that service their interests (Bull et al, 2019, pp 158–9). For example, customary courts no longer hold the same authority and deference they had in the past and power holders in the community, typically older men who dominate decision-making processes, no longer command the same levels of respect and deference. However, participation of women and children in these forums can be limited (Bull et al, 2019, p 159). It is notable, for example, that the South Pacific has the lowest rates of female political participation in the world (Chandler, 2014). Religious sources of authority can also function to discourage women from making complaints of gendered violence public, for instance by reporting to authorities. Often church leaders are the first to be approached regarding violence, but advice offered is informed by religious doctrine, which tends to favour feminine obedience and docility (Bull et al, 2019, p 159). Restorative processes may also present complaints as the product of personal circumstances and prioritize peace between tribes or the defendant making amends to the broader community (Bull et al, 2019, p 161).

Case study: policing in the Torres Strait Islands

> On one of the [Torres Strait] islands, I took instructions from a client regarding a private DV application. The client was a lady from a neighbouring island who had married into the largest family group on this island. The client's husband would beat her regularly. On one weekend, the client's husband had beaten her particularly badly. She left the matrimonial house and sought shelter with her in-laws (who made up most of the island's population), but they were of little assistance. She sought further assistance from the unsworn Torres police officers who have limited powers in the community, but as I'm sure you already know, act as the first line of law enforcement and assisting communities [to] keep the peace, in circumstances where assistance from sworn police officers is as much as 24 hours away. But the one on duty was also her in-law and convinced her to return home and take no further action. The incident was not reported by the unsworn police officer. (Female Solicitor interviewee)[1]

The Torres Strait is a body of water that stretches for 150 km between the northern most tip of Queensland, Australia (from Australia's Cape York Region) and the coast of PNG. There are more than 100 islands in the region, which are spread over 48,000 km². Islanders live in 18 permanent communities located on 17 of the region's islands but continue to visit traditionally owned islands for fishing, gardening, food collection, and recreation. All of the Torres Strait Region is classified by the Australian Bureau of Statistics (ABS) as 'very remote Australia'. This compares with the rest of Queensland where only 1.3 per cent of the population lives in very remote conditions (QGSO, 2016b, p 35). In terms of proximity to Queensland's capital, Brisbane, the Torres Strait Region is located further away than all of Queensland's other discrete Aboriginal communities. In 2018–19, we conducted a study of crime in the region, which included 27 in-depth interviews with Torres Strait Islander service providers. The following section draws on that research (see Scott et al, 2021).

The Queensland Police Service (QPS) operates police stations on Waiben (Thursday) and Ngurupai (Horn) Island, and there is currently a staff of 33 QPS officers in the Torres Strait Region, servicing a population of about 5,000 people (Commonwealth of Australia, 2010). A 2010 Queensland government report cited overall positive relations between Torres Strait communities and the police (Commonwealth of Australia, 2010). There is a history of communities, especially in the outer islands, arguing for a stronger police presence, with calls for more proactive and preventative measures rather than just reacting to incidents. In a recent report, police relations with the community were universally cited as being strong and positive (Scott et al, 2021). An important aspect of policing was doing regular visits and stays on the various islands, as these helped to build relations and trust with communities. The most successful officers integrated well into the local community by engaging in community events and networks.

The QPS Police Liaison Officer (PLO) programme was also developed to address social and cultural barriers between sworn police and Indigenous communities. Key features of the early programme were to assist communication and to divert persons from police custody. Police services across Australia have sought to increase the number of Indigenous employees, including in sworn and unsworn positions. As a result, in 2012 the QPS increased the involvement of Indigenous peoples in policing roles. During 2013–14, 31 Torres Strait Island Police Liaison Officers (TSIPLOs) were appointed to support QPS sworn police to deliver a range of policing activities aimed at stopping crime and enhancing safety in the region. For example, in Queensland, Indigenous PLOs provide a link between the police and Indigenous communities. This work involves the deployment of auxiliaries to enhance community engagement, the delivery of police services, and augment traditional policing functions (Cherney & Chui, 2010). While large numbers of police are based in the Torres Strait Region, many outer islands, which are highly isolated have no sworn police presence, despite some having populations numbering around 1,000 people.

The small size and isolation of the communities in the Torres Strait Region increase opportunity for intimate and informal interactions between police and local communities. Police (sworn and unsworn) typically reside within the community, their private lives being more closely intertwined with their public roles. Good policing practice in the region adopted a localistic as opposed to a legalistic approach (Scott & Jobes, 2007) and this included making use of informal social control networks that existed in the islands, capitalizing on the tight-knit social structures and networks on the islands.

In 2010 the main offences in the Torres Strait Region consisted of offences against the person, firearm regulations, domestic violence, and illicit drug trafficking [and] intelligence involving Papua New Guinean nationals visiting treaty islands (Commonwealth of Australia, 2010). Statistical analysis suggests that while rates of property crime in the region are relatively low, domestic violence is relatively high (Scott et al, 2021). Generally low property crime rates were considered to be caused by a mix of factors, including potential underreporting. For instance, it was argued that in a 'sharing culture', lots of property crime does not get reported to protect social networks, such as family and friends. Interviews we conducted with police and islanders in the region also suggest that domestic violence is the main justice issue. In general, the causes of DFV were hard to define; it might be best considered multi-causal. Many interviewees linked the incidence of DFV (and other offences against the person) to the introduction of alcohol and alcohol culture to the islands.

DFV was also viewed by some participants as a result of families having been displaced and trauma based around unemployment, both of which it was thought lead to alcohol abuse and then rage, anger, and frustration.

Yet, some areas were also considered to have cultural attitudes that were less responsive to DFV prevention and education. In the past, people were considered very reluctant to give statements, so DFV was 'written off' and infrequently reported or responded to, whereas now people more willing to give statements and more likely to make charges. The so-called 'shame culture' which could encourage public order, could also be linked to a lack of reporting in DFV and might even be considered a progenitor of it to the extent that perceived infractions against island norms might be best dealt with through informal and private forms of social control.

Community policing responses to DFV were also considered to be inconsistent throughout the region and cultural roles and kinship or other communal affiliations could take precedence when responding to incidents. This issue was thought to be particularly acute in the outer islands. Isolation of the islands and the inevitable slow response in attending to an incident by police also meant that there were incentives to resolve incidents informally on the island without reporting to police or for incidents to have been 'resolved' by the time police responded.

TSIPLOs could be seen as an extension of the social capital networks on the islands. This noted, being embedded in communities could also prevent TSIPLOs from dealing with serious and minor matters and prevent responses in some instances, particularly when matters involved close kin or families. In this way, there could be strain between lore and law and this was acknowledged. The (then) Queensland Police Commissioner indicated in 2010 that an additional challenge arises in the Torres Strait because of the:

> unique culture that exists for each island in terms of its own traditions and values as well as the clans and family groups. ... In that context the clan family thing is very difficult. One of the challenges for community police [now TSIPLOs] is the sensitivity of going to someone's home and saying, 'Look, you're having a domestic violence incident here. I'm going to help you and get involved in this because the neighbours have phoned', and the degree of sensitivity on an island in the Torres Strait would be greater than it is in the mainstream Australian community in that regard. (Commonwealth of Australia, 2010, p 108)

A TSILPO's story

Peter [not real name] is an active member of his community, who besides involvement as a TSIPLO, is involved in several volunteer and community activities on his island. In his words, 'I like helping people.' Peter's participation in volunteer work accords with generally high rates in the region, (QGSO, 2016a, pp 14–15). This may be a product of the relative 'smallness' of island communities and their geographic boundedness and isolation. However, it is a clear indication, along with other measures of the region's rich resources, of social capital.

Economic capital is another story. The index of relative socio-economic advantage and disadvantage indicates that the Torres Strait Region places lower than Queensland in terms of economic resources. Distance and cost can make policing difficult, requiring special equipment such as a fixed-wing plane and fast boat and, very often, access to a helicopter. Peter says that he appreciates the need for improved services to the outer islands.

But more than crime, Peter worries about the challenges posed to island life by the incursion of globalization and, with it, new technologies which can draw young islanders away from traditional forms of island life and learning. On the small islands there is only primary schooling and high school children will either travel to the main island or to the mainland as boarders. This means that for five formative years, young people leave the community and are exposed to diverse cultural influences, some of which run counter to island traditions. Still, young islanders have a strong attachment to their homes, Peter noting that kids would often misbehave at boarding school so that they could be returned home. Peter considered it to be a cultural responsibility to care for children, not a police responsibility:

> Our culture is very different. We eat together. From one plate. And we sleep together. Everything we do together and then the time comes for them to go away to school. When my first son went to high school, part of me was taken away from me. Something was missing from me. … Torres Strait people are spiritual people.

Torres Strait Islanders have a strong sense of themselves as composed of distinct peoples and cultures different from the mainland. Individual islands possess highly homogenous cultures and close-knit communities. 'Culture' is very strong, especially so in the outer islands where populations are small and bounded into small land areas by the sea. People on the outer islands are also bound by blood and kinship networks and everywhere in the region, locals are known to one another inter-generationally through clan and kinship systems. These community links present much the same problems for people policing small and/or isolated communities on the mainland, where there could be strain between roles as a community member and as an officer of the law. Peter observes: '[There are] Cultural protocols and cultural lores. Then we have L-A-W, where you are stuck before the magistrate in court.' He notes that the best way to deal with problems is through mediation. Yet he concludes that sometimes police interventions in island life are necessary. To this extent, he and other TSIPLOs are the 'eyes and ears' of the police.

A large part of Peter's work involves DFV: 'We take [it] seriously' he noted, and every incident is reported. As noted earlier, DFV is widely considered to be the most serious criminal justice issue in the region, and was closely associated with the introduction of alcohol to the islands. Indeed, alcohol had not been a traditional aspect of islander life but was considered a relatively new introduction, especially to the remote islands, primarily during the post-war period. Peter believes he knows where the DFV problem exists on his small island, locating it typically with several specific families and linked to alcohol and drugs.

Some areas are considered to have cultural attitudes that are less responsive to DFV prevention and education. In the past, people were considered very reluctant to give statements, so DFV was 'written off' and infrequently reported or responded to, whereas now people were considered to be more willing to give statements and more likely to pursue charges. The local 'shame culture' of the islands, which could encourage public order, could also be linked to a lack of reporting of DFV and might even be considered a progenitor of it to the extent that perceived infractions against island norms might be best dealt with through informal and private forms of social control. As Peter reflected:

> Because we are on a small island, everybody looks after everybody and the culture, because we are small, we look out for one another. We have nowhere to walkabout. You can't walk on water, like Jesus Christ [laughs].

This noted, being embedded in communities could also prevent TSIPSOs from dealing with serious and minor maters and prevented responses in some instances, notably matters involving close kin or families. In this way, there could be strain between lore and law and this was acknowledged: 'Without uniform I am a community member, uncle, brother, granddad.'

Integration, crime, and island settings

Much of the research literature on social capital assumes a consensus perspective that aligns 'the common good' with mainstream or official functions. However, just as social capital and dense social networks have been theorized in criminology as being crime protective, they can also be crime productive when the norms adopted by networks are criminogenic. Alternatively, the kind of thick trust involved in dense social networks may also serve to make them opaque. While opaque networks may not be crime *productive* per se, they may indeed enable conditions where crime can remain hidden and be left unaddressed.

In our Torres Strait Island research, there were several indications that some forms of crime – particularly DFV, but also some property crime – were not always brought to the attention of the criminal justice system because of the dense social capital and opaque networks present in the region. For example, TSIPSOs could be placed in difficult positions when they needed to respond to offences committed by family and kin; sometimes this meant crimes, including serious physical violence, went unreported. In a similar way, to be a successful sworn police officer in the region involved practicing a high degree of discretion.

In Australia, police who are stationed in rural and remote communities also typically live there, at least during their tenure. This means their private lives are closely intertwined with their public roles. According to existing studies of policing in rural Australian spaces (though not discrete Indigenous spaces), accomplished officers tend to integrate into their local communities and make effective use of established local social networks (Jobes, 2002). In this respect, existing research tends to demonstrate that officers take a 'localistic' approach, as described at the start of this chapter, where they consider the needs and expectations of the community they work in, as opposed to the 'legalistic' approach generally adopted in urban settings, where adherence to laws was at the forefront of their policing style (Jobes, 2002; Scott & Jobes, 2007). This relates to Bayley's (1989) observation that, while *crimes* are policed in the city, *people* are policed in the country.

Social fragmentation has been closely associated with highly urbanized environments where there is greater anonymity, population transience, and a general weakening of social control institutions. In communities characterized by fragmentation and conflict, police are likely to develop strong ties of mutual dependence. Police may adopt a 'closed shop', avoiding criticism and harassment by isolating and insulating themselves from the communities they serve (Jobes, 2002). As a result, police develop distinctive police-centred cultures with unique normative structures. In the extreme, interaction with the public may be reduced to confrontational associations, typified by an 'us and them' mentality, which defines community as the 'outsiders' and locates officers on 'the inside'. Consultation between community and police is viewed as interference and interactions are based on a client–server relationship in which the public are passively dependent on the police.

In contrast, the small size and isolation of the communities in the Torres Strait Region increased opportunities for intimate and informal interaction between police and local communities. A local officer can be well known to the community and connected to the community through informal social networks. An accomplished police officer will be able to integrate into a local community and make effective use of established local social networks, adopting a 'peace keeping' role commensurate with community expectations regarding the proper duties of a police officer. Successful integration with a community can indirectly reduce crime and accelerate law enforcement responses as an officer becomes increasingly sensitive to and familiar with the vagaries of a local environment, local population, and local social organization. Consequently, clearance rates in these areas are typically higher than in cities. The more integrated an officer is within a community, the more likely residents are to confide information that leads to apprehending a suspect. What develops is a 'localistic', as opposed to 'legalistic', approach to policing. Greater importance is accorded to establishing and maintaining public tranquillity or 'the peace' as opposed to imposing law and order at any cost (Jobes, 2002).

As indicated, with a localistic model of policing, the public can exert influence over how police work is done; the community has more input into defining the role of the police. This may influence important aspects of police work, particularly regarding police discretion. Police discretion is not influenced by the organizational structure of a department but is likely to be influenced by the way in which the community is organized. However, immersion into the community can also exacerbate the problematic aspects of police work, as police are expected to become part of the community, even where it has the potential to compromise objectivity. This may produce strain between roles of an officer as law enforcer and local resident. Yet, the reward is community support, which can improve quality of life and allow police to carry out their work more effectively (Jobes, 2002).

The localistic model does not necessarily translate to an idealized form of community policing. A problem may be that powerful groups in the community come to exert a significant influence over police and determine who is and is not subject to surveillance. The outcome may be the over policing or under policing of specific interest communities. While policing is a partnership for some members of the community, for others it is experienced as something imposed.

Not all socially marginal populations in remote and small-scale communities are subject to over-policing, at least not when considering formal responses. Women, for example, do not so much constitute a criminal concern, but sub-groups of women clearly breach gendered norms (whether defined in terms of 'tradition' or religion) and may, therefore, be considered deviant. The breaching of such norms may not be responded to formally, but responses are typically informal and policed by men. High levels of domestic violence need be considered in terms of how small-scale social networks produce higher levels of informal policing, especially in places where rigid gendered hierarchies exist. In a similar way, violence against LGBTQIA+ populations in such places, also reported to be high (Flood & Hamilton,

2005), may be considered a product of the policing and maintenance of specific gendered and sexual boundaries. Of course, the policing of these less visible populations is not always conducted in a physical and/or violent manner, with much social control being of an informal nature through intimidation, gossip, ridicule, and ostracism. Indeed, those who have spoken about social capital in rural places have noted that it can produce forms of 'closure' when members of groups adhere closely to local norms without recourse to legal contracts and, indeed, one of the 'positive' elements of social capital is considered to be rendering formal social controls unnecessary by strengthening informal controls associated with familial or communal structures (Bursik & Grasmick, 1993).

The integration of police, sworn and unsworn, should not be viewed as inherently 'bad'. For example, the deep relationships that TSIPSOs have with their communities is vital to their being able to carry out their roles and enables – to some extent – a continuation of the kinds of locally led policing approaches that have been present in the region for more than a hundred years. The discretion held by TSIPSOs may also be conceived of as an ability to uphold and enforce cultural norms in the 'space' between traditional methods and the formal (settler-imposed) justice system. However, it may equally mean that access to justice may be difficult, or impossible, for some victims of crime. As some of our participants pointed out, this may be particularly acute where inter-marriage between islands means that some women move to locations where they leave their family and kin, as well as any support these might be able to provide, behind.

The sociologist George Simmel (1971) believed that in smaller groups (such as a two-person dyad) a person might retain their individuality, but as groups grew (for example a three-person group) there is danger the individual may be subordinated to the majority. So it is that as societies increase in size they also become increasingly fragmented. Bull et al (2019) argue that Simmel's concept of the stranger may be helpful in understanding the dynamics of tight-knit island societies. The stranger is a member of a group in a spatial sense, but still not a member in a social sense: a person in the group, but not of it. The stranger is capable of adopting a perspective of an outsider and insider simultaneously. Simmel's focus is space, not culture per se, the stranger's identity being built on dynamic relationships of proximity and distance and can be considered distinct from Park's (1928) 'marginal man', who is an outsider to the group seeking assimilation, but has no status of equal membership. The stranger indicates space is a physical realm, but also a site constituted by political and social relations. Distance includes remoteness and proximity as a basic feature of human life, because spatial and temporal gaps indicate that we exist in states of being in-between. Highlighting distance and movement, Simmel describes how social life is not composed of static structures. Distance is not opposed to proximity and is not a negative condition, but can allow for capacities such as objectivity and mobility, as the stranger is not bound to the group through established ties, such as kinship, locality, or occupation (Bull et al, 2019, pp 161–3). For Simmel 'the cosmopolitan' is a personality type that expresses an awareness of what is common to all, seeing the universal within the particular and the particular within the universal, being able to once construct and transcend social boundaries (Marotta, 2017). The stranger bears a certain objectivity created through their distance. Further, they can carry out special tasks that other members of a group are unable or unwilling to do.

The stranger's status allows them to perform special tasks for a group, such as being an arbitrator, as they have an understanding of the system of beliefs and standards by which a group operates, but no deep commitment or investment in such and thus have the potential to question or counter local custom and belief (Bull et al, 2019, pp 162–3). The social category of stranger may also pose a danger or threat to social systems as they offer the possibility of different patterns of thought and, with it, social change (Bull et al, 2019, p 166). For example, state-based rule of law can challenge informal cultures by upholding professional ethical standards (Bull et al, 2019, p 166).

These qualities challenge the notion that institutionalized police are compromised by being a distant presence in tight-knit cultures and suggests instead that their role as regulators of social order may be enhanced (Bull et al, 2019, p 163). Bull et al (2019) provide examples from Pacific states where local officers can be relieved from cultural presence or communal integration with support of an institutionalized police force made up of external (state or international police) regulators (Bull et al, 2019). They also cite historical examples of police and other colonial officials who were able to exercise autonomy in dealings with local leaders because they were foreigners (Bull et al, 2019, p 165). Nonetheless, in many island nations of the Pacific, police are severely under-resourced (Chandler, 2014).

Conclusion

Policing islands demonstrates the need for caution about valorizing specific models of policing as universally appropriate and functional. Popular culture has provided a largely idealized account of policing in remote and small societies – characterized as homogenous if slightly eccentric communities. Indeed, the impacts of colonization are diverse, as are the solutions to ongoing social problems caused by colonization. Bull et al (2019) argue that customary systems and 'familiar' police actors have failed women when it comes to gendered violence and suggest that policing could be enhanced through improved state-based systems of policing that draw on strengths of state or non-local authority and regulation (Bull et al, 2019, p 157). International scholarship has shown that interventions by formal police in remote and small societies can result in increased reporting of family violence, increased safety for women and children, and increased community awareness of women's rights and safety because they are viewed as outsiders; a status that allows them to transcend local norms and question local assumptions, which can result in their sometimes disregarding systems which their local counterparts are invested in. This noted, local practices cannot simply be ignored either (Bull et al, 2019, pp 157–8).

Criminology has only recently recognized the diversity of communities and the complex relationship between community structure, crime, and policing. Despite the organizational differences in policing between Australian and other jurisdictions such as the US and the UK, their situation with regard to remote and rural policing is similar, which clearly points towards a conclusion that it is social networks that primarily influence policing styles, as exhibited in remote and smaller societies. The organization and structure of communities helps to define the conditions of rural police work. A fragmented community encourages local police to take on a more legalistic interpretation of their job, while an integrated community encourages a more localistic interpretation, adopting local norms and values. The more homogeneous a rural community, the greater the consensus regarding crime and conflict. However, the more fragmented the social structure of a rural community, the greater the potential conflict between the roles of law enforcer and good neighbour or citizen. Officers in polarized communities are excluded from becoming part of an integrated community and must deal with issues between community groups and toward the police as well; in turn, they tend to operate as 'islands … in a common sea' (Lindbergh, 1955). Although compromising objectivity and creating tensions and strains for officers, to be a successful police officer in a homogeneous community often requires immersion, allowing for an officer to become increasingly sensitive to and familiar with the vagaries of a local environment, local population, and local social organization. However, integration may also present difficulties, especially regarding police impartiality.

6

Insularity

This chapter contains references to sexual abuse of minors that readers may find upsetting or disturbing.

> The reader must remember that all these people are the descendants of half a dozen men; that the first children intermarried together and bore grandchildren to the mutineers; that these grandchildren intermarried; after them, great and great-great-grandchildren intermarried; so that to-day everybody is blood kin to everybody. Moreover, the relationships are wonderfully, even astoundingly, mixed up and complicated. A stranger, for instance, says to an islander: 'You speak of that young woman as your cousin; a while ago you called her your aunt.'
>
> 'Well, she is my aunt, and my cousin, too. And also my stepsister, my niece, my fourth cousin, my thirty-third cousin, my forty-second cousin, my great-aunt, my grandmother, my widowed sister-in-law – and next week she will be my wife.'
>
> (Twain, 1879)

Islands have been a wonderful stage for political satire and Mark Twain was quick to see the potential of Pitcairn Island, which had become a mythological place a century after mutineers had founded it. Pitcairn Island is Britain's smallest colony (1 mile long and 2 miles wide) and is also the last British territory in the Pacific. It is ideal for our purposes in this chapter, in the sense that its isolation and size, measured in geography and population, render it a stereotype of an island. Pitcairn has also been described as a 'site of textual overload' (Fletcher, 2011, p 58), which situates it well in terms of place. In addition to Twain's contribution, its story inspired a novel by Jules Verne and a myriad of Hollywood movies.

Social integration as much produces crime as it prevents it, just as crime may also facilitate social integration. This is hardly a new insight, having been famously proposed by the French sociologist, Emile Durkheim. In a similar vein, the 'social glue' of Pitcairn has been a source of both idyllization and horror. As we discussed in Chapter 2, a key aspect of the island-idyll is the notion that islands embody 'communitarian' qualities. Communities are seen as collections of people sharing certain interests, sentiments, behaviours, and objects by virtue of their membership of a social group (Amoamo, 2012, p 427). Community has often been equated with simple social structures, but rural and island spaces are not necessarily simpler, and management of intimate relationships in such places can often be complex and require significant resources.

The case of Pitcairn demonstrates a strong sense of island communitarianism, illustrated for instance in the interdependency of the island's families and the role of local gossip and surveillance in encouraging compliance with local norms.[1] This type of communitarianism embodies what sociologists have described as *gemeinschaft* qualities (also discussed in earlier chapters). These qualities, so often considered elements of small rural communities, might also be perceived as features of islandness. And while the concept of *gemeinschaft* has been relatively forgotten in the social sciences, the qualities it evoked have recently been captured by the concept of social capital, which has been theorized in various ways, but generally describes features of social organization, such as relations of honesty, cooperation, reciprocity, engagement, and mutuality that exist between people within social networks of varying density (Bourdieu, 1986; Coleman, 1988; Putnam, 1993; Portes, 2000; Rostila, 2011).

Much of the research literature on social capital assumes a consensus perspective that aligns 'the common good' with mainstream or official functions. However, just as social capital and dense social networks have been theorized in criminology as being crime protective, they can also be crime productive when the norms adopted by networks are criminogenic. Integration may also breed a kind of insularity. While insularity, may not be crime *productive* per se, it may indeed enable conditions where crime can remain hidden and be left unaddressed. For example, in rural areas, such features have recently been linked to hate crimes, such as domestic and homophobic violence or the failure to report or police such activity, as we touched on in the previous chapter.

The case of Pitcairn Island

Geography – particularly the vastness of the Pacific Ocean – is central to the Pitcairn narrative. The defining characteristic of these islands is their remoteness. Situated in the South Pacific, Pitcairn is not much larger than New York City's Central Park (Pochnau & Parker, 2007), with the nearest large nation being New Zealand, situated 3,000 miles away. Media typically describe it as 'the world's most remote inhabited island', 'tiny rock', 'outcrop', or 'speck' in the 'middle of the Pacific' (Pochnau & Parker, 2007). The technology of the airplane, which has most challenged the concept of the island as fortress defended by the sea, does not apply to Pitcairn, because it is only accessible by the sea (Fletcher, 2011 p 67). Indeed, no airplane has ever landed on Pitcairn and no ship has ever moored there (Pochnau & Parker, 2007). Landing on the island requires skilled boating by locals to take people from ships anchored 200–300 m from the rocky and cliff-faced shores (Pochnau & Parker, 2007). The entire population of the island (50 people) lives in one settlement, Adamstown. For 130 years the only method of communication with the outside world was a lantern waved at passing ships (Farran, 2007; Pochnau & Parker, 2007).

The recorded story of Pitcairn Island begins with the mutiny on the *Bounty* in 1789. Of 25 mutineers, 16 remained in Tahiti. The others sailed to the uncharted and uninhabited Pitcairn Island accompanied by 12 Tahitian women and 6 Polynesian men. The treatment of the Polynesian men on the island and rivalry for the women soon led to infighting and murder. One of the mutineers, who had worked at a distillery in his youth and discovered the intoxicating qualities of a local plant, died an accidental death, the result of intoxication. Another died a natural death. The others were murdered and, by 1808, when the island was discovered by an American whaler, only one of the original adult men, a mutineer named John Adams, remained. However, the remaining Tahitian women and their children increased the island's population to 50 and it continued to grow steadily thereafter.

Adams had turned to Christianity and tales of the idyllic existence of the children of the mutineers became a staple in Victorian texts on virtue (Shapiro, 1928). Pitcairn was transformed into a key text for the island idyll. However, eventual overcrowding on Pitcairn led all to vacate in 1856 to the then recently abandoned penal colony of Norfolk Island, which occupied a considerably larger land mass. While most stayed on Norfolk, some of the families got homesick and returned to Pitcairn where their descendants remain to his day (Shapiro, 1928). The population has fluctuated ever since, peaking at 250 in 1936. Perhaps owing to its unique isolation, the hybrid Polynesian/English society has only been studied a handful of times and for early anthropologists it represented a unique microcosm of social structure (Amoamo, 2012, p 422).

Idyllic accounts of life on the island were numerous in the 19th and 20th centuries: women had an equal share to men in election of officials and governance; property was inherited by all children regardless of sex; education was compulsory until 16 years of age; and there was a communal fund for food, to which all contributed (Shapiro, 1928). An article from the late 1920s has the islanders playing sport and as board game devotees, while cooking exotic dishes and engaging in whaling and the production of lemon juice. Selling postage stamps had sustained the island's economy until stamp collecting became unfashionable in the 21st century. In 1928, Shapiro reported:

> The social life of the islanders is very hearty and informal. Moonlight picnics, garden parties, and other gatherings of a social nature are always hilarious. A strong love of music is common, and one of the most generally attended organizations is the choral society.

The island provided something of a laboratory for anthropologists interested in hybridity of race. One observed, ominously, the population to be physically strong and not degenerate, despite 'inbreeding'.

> From necessity islanders have inbred from the beginning, so that now after five or six generations, everyone is related to the rest of the community. In some cases the degree of blood relationship between husband and wife is extremely close. Yet there are no evidences of deterioration. On the contrary, Norfolk islanders are tall, muscular, and health[y]. ... Among the Norfolk Islanders we have another example that inbreeding in sound stock is not attended by the traditional stigmata of degeneratio. (Shapiro, 1928)

The islanders have been represented as deeply religious and most had converted as Seventh-Day Adventists during the 19th century. If there is a focal point that draws and holds the islanders together, it is their religion. As an integrating force it is far stronger and more important in their lives than their political union (Ferdon, 1958, p 71).

The mythologized view of the island as an idyll, in terms of both place and space, is captured by a traveller in the late 1950s:

> But if Pitcairn homes reflect a disinterest in general comfort and spick-and-span shelter, the people themselves demonstrate the fundamental character of the town. This is, like the islander himself, clear and simple: the Lord has provided all the necessary material goods of life, and the most important thing left is to get along with one another. No doors have locks, and no one is ever turned away. ... For us Pitcairn Island was a succession of lovely pictures, and it was made more delightful by what are probably the friendliest people in the world. (Ferdon, 1958, p 71)

It would take another half-century before the representation of the island emerged which recast it in terms of place and space, suggesting a more nightmarish vision emerging from the isolation and insularity of Pitcairn.

Insularity brings forth monsters

For most of its history, Pitcairn lived with a secret sex culture that defined island life. Adultery was not just routine but pervasive, as well as the sexual fondling of infants and socially approved sex games among young children. Incest and prostitution were not unknown. Despite being a British territory, for much of its history, Pitcairn Island had its own legal code. English law books only arrived in 1997 when the Foreign Office shipped a 56-volume set of *Halsbury's Laws of England*, which the locals stored in the one-cell jail, which had been used to store life preservers (Pochnau & Parker, 2007). Most island statutes were designed to address property disputes and island peculiarities. There was no reference to rape and 'carnal knowledge' (sex with a minor) was disputed, with ages ranging from 12 to 15. The statute of limitations for any crime was six months. Pitcairn law also precluded charges of assault or the holding of private property (Pochnau & Parker, 2007). The then island police officer (paid US$780 per year) and the magistrate (her brother-in-law) had never made an arrest or held court (Pochnau & Parker, 2007).

Sexual promiscuity with underage girls had been tolerated as being part of traditional values (New Zealand Herald, 2004). One local councillor told a visiting pastor at the turn of the century that the age of consent had been 12 on the island, and evidence indicates that most girls bore children between the ages of 12 to 15. By the time of WW2, one pastor complained that the island's youth were without ambition and boys sought to 'break in' young girls on the island, with the most ambitious seeking to break in all the young girls on the island (Pochnau & Parker, 2007).

From 1997, London dispatched a police officer for nine weeks a year to train the local Pitcairn officer. At this time, allegations of sexual assault emerged. Immediately there was conflict between the two officers as to the interpretation of the law, with the local officer reluctant to act (Pochnau & Parker, 2007). A social worker sent to the island also 'began to untangle a society in which sex permeated everything: childhood sex games were commonplace, as were pregnancies and abortions among young, unmarried girls' (Pochnau & Parker, 2007). The social worker shocked London officials with reports that the sexual manipulation of babies was — much as other societies might use a pacifier — 'a feature of life for many years' (Pochnau & Parker, 2007).

Further concerns were raised in 1999 by a UK officer on temporary assignment in the island and, over two years, officers from UK, Australia, and New Zealand interviewed every woman who had lived on the island in the previous 20 years, as well as the accused men (Pochnau & Parker, 2007). As a result of investigations, islanders faced 55 charges and those living abroad 41 charges, which were heard in a separate trial in New Zealand (2005).

The Pitcairn Island sexual assault trials (2004) involved seven men living on Pitcairn Island and six men living abroad. The population totalled 47 in 2004, so the charges represented a third of the island's male population. The charges related to sexual offences against children and young people; more than 30 of the complaints made in Pitcairn could be defined as rape under English laws, with all against girls who were underage at the time (Farran, 2007; Pochnau & Parker, 2007). Details of the crimes included horrific sexual assaults, including gang rape of an 11-year-old (Pochnau & Parker, 2007). Sexual incidents were often attended by violence. One victim of rape stated 'I have seen some of the fights. All I've associated with sex on Pitcairn is violence' (Pochnau & Parker, 2007). A British social worker (in Pochnau & Parker, 2007) visiting the island in early 2000 stated, 'It's the most dysfunctional community on the face of the planet.' According to Poachnau and Parker (2007), the social worker reported that:

> Many were in a state of denial, and many of the women, even mothers, blamed the girls. At first the men were confused and terrified. They were weepy, and some appeared depressed and withdrawn. ... One feared he would be murdered in jail. A mother feared the British would hang her son – Mutineers' justice.

Pitcairn had always been notorious because of mutineers, but the trial reinvested in this notoriety and was reported in places as far away as Kazakhstan and Bahrain (Fletcher, 2008, p 60). International headlines were lurid, with an Australian newspaper reporting 'Where underage sex is "like food"' (Harvey, 2004, p 1). Dea Brickett, in her book *Serpent in Paradise* (1998), claimed that all the islanders cared about were 'the three F's – fishing, food and fucking' (Pochnau & Parker, 2007).

The scandal showed that Britain had known about the 'moral degeneracy' on Pitcairn for more than a century, but colonial administrators had failed to act on numerous complaints, showing more concern with the failure to fly the imperial flag daily (Pochnau & Parker, 2007). The trial was marked by legal challenges to the island's status as a British colony, with the defendants claiming that their ancestors, all descended from *Bounty* mutineers, had renounced their citizenship by committing a capital offence in the burning of the *Bounty* in 1790 (Farran, 2007). Pitcairners were unified by the time of the trial in mutual contempt for the British who had 'occupied' their territory, and some islanders saw the trial as a plot to de-populate their island (Marks, 2004; Pochnau & Parker, 2007). However, while the islanders blamed the intervention on outsiders, there were signs that internal conflict and pressure was placed on local women to withdraw charges, some of whom did. Moreover, meetings of 13 island women endorsed the idea that underage sex was normalized and participants had been willing.

The trials had a major impact on island life, as the accused consisted of a large proportion of the island's population. Sons and partners of women living on the island were among the accused, most drawn from four interrelated Pitcairn families who had long been interdependent on each other for survival. Notably, the most able-bodied islanders, the seamen, were jailed (Pochnau & Parker, 2007). Some women claimed the trial was a plot to jail the able-bodied men and close the island. The famed Australian author Colleen McCulloch, wife of a Pitcairn descendant, defended the customs, stating 'It's Polynesian to break our girls in at 12' (Pochnau & Parker, 2007).

Geography was important to constructing the trial narrative. In particular, the vastness of the Pacific was at the heart of the narratives and the island was positioned as 'isolated' both by its geography and its 'culture of secrets' (Fletcher, 2008, p 63). The fact the trial took place on the island and involved a flotilla of outsiders, including journalists, added to the interest in the story (Fletcher, 2008, p 60). The trial was described as 'one of the strangest in British legal history' and it has been argued that the guiding terms of the news discourse were 'strangeness' and 'isolation' (Fletcher, 2008, p 62). In the media discourse, 'isolation' became an anti-idyll – 'Pitcairn is simply too far away for safety', as one Australian journalist put it (Fletcher, 2008, p 63).

The islanders were reported to indulge in lots of gossip, fuelled and intensified by sexual habits (Pochnau & Parker, 2007). An Australian reporter was quoted as saying: 'You are never, ever alone. In that remote place, in the middle of nowhere, you'd think your problem is loneliness, but actually your problem is trying to get away from everyone. There's nowhere to go' (Pochnau & Parker, 2007). The Mayor, also charged, stated that sex preoccupied the island and sexual 'shenanigans' occupied island gossip:

> Mrs Darralyn Griffiths, 28, said she started having sex at 13, 'and I felt hot shit about it, too'. Meralda Warren, 45, said her sex life began at 12. Nadine Christian, 32, said: 'It was just the way it was. It goes way back. It's been happening for generations. You have to remember the kids here don't have any entertainment.' But others hinted at cracks in this image of carefree sexual precocity. Carol Warren, 51, said a Pitcairn man tried to rape her when she was 10. She also said she complained to police about her daughter's relationship with an older married man, which began when she was 13. (Marks, 2004)

Despite her own experience, Mrs Warren said she was certain no girl on the island had ever had sex against her will. She said it was 'sick' to have sex with a girl before she reached puberty, and she could not believe any islander could have done that. Mrs Christian added: 'There are no secrets on Pitcairn, I can tell you' (Marks, 2004).

One witness stated on trial in Auckland, 'I don't know any married people on Pitcairn who have been faithful to each other'. Her husband, the former magistrate, also charged, retold how sex education was where he had seen a schoolteacher having sex with a student when he was young, and his friends had witnessed one of their parents in bed with the parent of another (Pochnau & Parker, 2007).

All but one of the defendants were convicted of at least some of the charges they were facing. Two, who showed remorse, were sentenced to community service and the remaining islanders to prison terms from two to six years. One got six years for four rapes (Pochnau & Parker, 2007). The penalties were reported by the British High Commission in New Zealand to have been tailored to Pitcairn, and accounted for its unique isolation and population size.

Island insularity and crime

Pitcairn constitutes a small, tight-knit and kin-related grouping. It is intensely insular, due not only to its isolated and inhospitable location but also because, for nearly two centuries, the islanders have fiercely regulated who may visit (and live on) the island. Indeed, insularity, governed by strong religious doctrine and its own practice of self-government, has in part formed the social 'glue' that continues to bind the community (Amoamo, 2012, p 423).

The physical geography of Pitcairn – particularly its remoteness – reinforced the culture of the island and rendered it resistant to external and/or disruptive incursions. This geography also informs what has been referred to here as 'islandness', a way of thinking about identity and culture that is informed by place (see Chapter 2). Our research in the Torres Strait Islands in the remote northern tip of Australia (see Chapter 3) similarly found that the distinct geography of the islands and region had also made it relatively resistant to external incursions, here, namely, colonization. Indeed, available evidence indicates that levels of frontier violence and dispossession experienced by most of Queensland's Aboriginal populations did not occur to the same extent in the Torres Strait Region (Passi, 1986). This appears to be because of the remoteness of much of the region, its general unsuitability for land-based agriculture, and different approaches by early colonial administrators (Robertson, 2010; Shnukal, 2015). Torres Strait Islanders 'were not driven from their lands or exposed to unstemmed violence' of the same nature and magnitude as that experienced in Queensland's other Aboriginal communities (Singe, 1979; Sharp, 1992, p 25). Passi (1986, p 1) noted, '[colonial] contact was not as catastrophic as in other parts of Australia since Islanders were not displaced from their ancestral lands as were the mainland Aborigines ... much of Islander traditional culture was retained' (see, also, Beckett, 1977;

Sharp, 1992; ALRC, 2018). The identity of Torres Strait Islanders remains strongly informed by an understanding of themselves as a distinct peoples, both dissimilar to mainland cultures and other Indigenous cultures. One islander, for example, spoke about the first time they visited 'mainland Australia'. (The mainland/islands distinction will be familiar to anyone who has visited the much larger island of Tasmania.)

The relative maintenance of formal and informal social controls throughout the colonial period, including through state-sanctioned forms of local governance, is a key distinguishing factor of the Torres Strait Islands' history, providing a contrast to other Aboriginal communities where traditional authority structures were actively weakened and/or destroyed. Torres Strait local authority structures have also been intimately involved in the administration of justice in the region, including through the management of local community police and courts, which provides another point of departure from many other mainland Aboriginal communities. In contrast to Pitcairn, tight social integration in the Torres Straits has had a different effect on crime, with most forms of crime being relatively low, as we outlined in Chapter 5.

Place has deeply informed local identity and a strong sense of belonging in the Torres Strait Region; Torres Strait Islanders have a strong sense of attachment to place and this is celebrated in the history and culture of the islands. Place can be linked to social capital, which is particularly important in relation to social disorganization perspectives in criminology. The social disorganization model of crime control suggests that communities with low crime rates have integrated, dense social networks and include high levels of civic participation (Bursik & Grasmick, 1993; Sampson, Raudenbush, & Earls, 1997). Thus, 'strong' communities might be defined in terms of social capital, and can include such elements as strong leadership, cohesiveness, inclusivity, capacity building, and resources. Subjective elements such as attachment to place and belonging also inform the strength of a community. When considered through the lens of social disorganization theory, it is possible that this different history of colonization ensured the continuation of informal modes of social control, including strong social networks, which have thereby resulted in relative cultural continuity and high levels of social control. While this may be the case, dense social capital can also serve alternative ends, as we discuss below.

Putnam (2000) and others have supported the view that high rates of interpersonal violence suggest the absence of strong social capital (Woodhouse, 2006). The idea of social capital has been much deployed in analyses of rural crime, especially regarding social disorganization theory, where it functions as a form of social control by supporting social norms that limit anti-social behaviour. Social capital describes features of social organization, such as relations of honesty, cooperation, reciprocity, engagement, and mutual obligation that exist between people within social networks, social structures, and social institutional arrangements. Portes (2000) describes social capital as the ability of actors to receive benefits by virtue of membership within networks and other social structures. Thus, social capital is not something that resides in actors themselves but is a product of relations between them, and facilitates coordinated, mutually beneficial outcomes for the collective (Rostila, 2011).

Putnam (1993) has discussed the relative density of social networks with reference to bonding and bridging ties. Bonding ties are evident in closed and intimate groups in which all members are connected and interact exclusively with one another. These ties are inward looking and occur among people who see themselves as homogenous and coming from the same social network (Rostila, 2010). In contrast, bridging capital is outward looking and represents the links between different groups of people. It has been posited that a lack of both types of ties results in alienation and loneliness and what Durkheim referred to as anomie, often viewed as a condition of urbanized settings (Woodhouse, 2006).

Closed social networks with strong bonding capital facilitate submission to norms by rewarding or punishing behaviours (Rostila, 2011). While Putnam (1993) focuses on social relationships, on a more individual level, social control theory emphasizes social bonding and notes that when such bonds fail to develop or are strained or broken, individuals will be motivated to engage in forms of deviance or criminal activities which 'reward' them. There are four elements of social boding: (1) attachment (emotional connection to others); (2) commitment (accumulated relationships which provide a stake in conformity); (3) involvement (participation in legitimate activities; and (4) belief (the acceptance of the existing normative order). Braithwaite (1989) observed that, in control theory, the most significant social bonds are to family, school, and occasionally church. There is, for instance, overwhelming evidence in criminology to indicate that young people who are attached to school and family are less likely to engage in delinquency. This noted, such bonding can be criminogenic relative to the norms of a community. If a community, for example, is patriarchal in its norms, then bonding may involve attachment and compliance with structures and networks which encourage or reward practices that regulate and oppress women, including violence.

This may not be the case with regard to all crime. Carrington's (2007) research for example found property crime in rural and remote settings to be relatively low, while interpersonal violence was relatively high. Certainly, the ecology of an isolated and geographically bounded setting might provide a formal degree of natural surveillance not afforded elsewhere, which might prevent certain highly visible crimes (for example, property offences), but the very same surveillance can increase regulation and with it forms of social control. An excess of bonding capital can produce intolerance and insularity. For example, crime in remote areas is often blamed on newcomers or temporary visitors to closed communities. The revelations of sexual assault at Pitcairn appeared to increase some sense of solidarity among islanders while producing hostility to outsiders, seen in terms of the media, but especially in terms of the British government. But while this might explain aspects of the social integration on the island, it hardly explains the normative structure in which sexual violence became commonplace.

The fact remains that sexual violence was for a long time tolerated in the Pitcairn community and had become normative. This was despite the mutineers being British subjects (presumably somewhat aware of British laws) and also despite the influence of Christianity. During the trials, some of the accused argued that, because sexual violence had become custom on the island (and was not considered a crime), they should escape culpability. As Farran (2007, pp 142, 150) explains:

> Even if the mutineers had taken with them this invisible mantle of the common law, it has been recognized ... that common law transplanted to a foreign soil may develop differently. To hold that present day Pitcairners had the same common law as the Bounty settlers seems to ignore the passage of over two hundred years of living in a small and very isolated community. ... Can a legal system and its representatives, nurtured in such a totally different context even begin to understand or experience the life and values of people living in such an isolated environment?

The relative isolation of the island is, thus, posed as providing fertile soil for the subversion of British constructions of crime, as well as Christian constructions of faith. In this way, it might be said that integration to the point of insularity, in this context, can both *prevent* and *generate* crime, making the very concept of integration so fluid and ambiguous as to render it problematic as a variable in the analysis of crime. Similarly, as also noted by others (for example, Liu, 2004; Villalonga-Olives & Kawachi, 2017), social capital might be considered neutral or even negative, rather than being associated with beneficial or positive outcomes, since it may equally relate to both. Furthermore, membership of any community will come at a price of conforming to the values of the community and repression of individual expression (Woodhouse, 2006). Thus, the strong ties that bind a group together and enable it to succeed can also exclude other members of society, especially those in marginalized groups.

This is an important point in how we might understand isolated and socially integrated places, such as islands. The question of import to criminologists thus shifts from *whether* and to *what extent* people are integrated into the normative structures of communities, to *the nature* of those normative structures. Pitcairn, from its earliest years, was a patriarchal society where sex was not highly regulated because of an apparent need to procreate and maintain the island's population. This was especially the case during the 20th century, when the population declined because of outward migration. It was an exotic and imaginative place to the outside world, but for locals, islandness was expressed in determination to remain on the island and live as an economically self-sustaining community, despite population and economic decline (Amoamo, 2012, p 422). Constructs of 'community' vital to islandness and the romanticism of the *Bounty* was invoked in frequent references to 'mutiny' in news coverage, so that it as impossible to separate the past from the present (Fletcher, 2008, p 64). Pitcairners viewed themselves as a distinct culture with their own normative values and practices that were rationalized with reference to the island's geographic and demographic vulnerability and with appeal to 'tradition'.

Modern forms of structuration, in the form of wealth and classes, for example, were less evident in the Pitcairn environment than in mainland environments and larger islands. Status symbols, such as the motor car, had no place in Pitcairn life. As early observers concluded, Pitcairn was a relatively classless environment. But in the absence of class what other normative orders took precedence to structure and define the community? Biological markers based on sex, generation, and kinship were highly prevalent on the island. It was these markers that informed power on the island and, with it, a normative order which was like glue, yet criminogenic when British legal structures ultimately superseded it.

Conclusion

Braithwaite (1989) argued that communitarian societies, which combine a dense network of individual interdependencies with strong cultural commitments of mutuality and obligation, have a significant capacity to deliver potent forms of shaming, which produce social integration and lower levels of crime. He concluded that cultural homogeneity is a precondition for effective social control, including reintegrative shaming (Braithwaite, 1989, p 94). Sampson, Raudenbush, and Earls (1997) described social cohesion among community residents combined with their willingness to intervene for the common good to prevent crime and disorder, as 'collective efficacy'. Combined, social capital and collective efficacy facilitates crime control, and has been linked to crime prevention, especially with respect to violent crime (Sampson, Raudenbush, & Earls, 1997).

Much research in criminology has suggested that smaller, often rural communities, have an abundance of bonding capital and are cohesive and friendly places with low levels of crime. It appears that Pitcairn has strong bonding capital within what might be described as a closed social network. However, Pitcairn's high-density social network and associated social capital was *supportive* of crime. This marries with a body of research, still emerging, which has presented a different picture of crime in small-scale settings, suggesting high rates of interpersonal violence, especially domestic violence (see Chapters 2 and 5). This research suggests that the ecology of rural places and, more broadly, remote and isolated places, including islands, can be criminogenic.

As a final note, recent newspaper reports have cited how Pitcairn Island's recent history has discouraged people from moving there, even with offers of free land. With an ageing population and declining birth rate, fears have been renewed that the island may soon be uninhabited with an official population target of 80 seemingly impossible to achieve. A population growth policy was introduced in 2012 and had only achieved one newcomer to the island by 2015. What the future holds for Pitcairn is yet to be seen.

7

Industry

> While islands may be used for negative, hidden activities such as imprisonment, they are also sites utilized for development, investment, profit and 'dream making'.
>
> (Mountz, 2015, p 642)

In Chapter 3, we discussed the importance of island borders in defining who is in and out. As we noted there, however, and notwithstanding the concomitant rise of certain immobilities, globalization has seen the transcendence and shifting of borders, primarily in the interest of forging a transnational (relatively) borderless capitalist economy. This has roots in second-wave colonialism (see Chapter 4), which saw colonial powers utilizing global sea travel to conquer and extract value from faraway colonies. This current chapter builds on these and several other themes introduced in preceding sections of the book, including the role of islands in colonial and neo-colonial enterprise. We focus on the extraction of natural and human resources as part of the economic 'development' of small islands, spurred by colonial and commercial interests. Drawing on green criminology and its broadening of 'crime' to include harm to both people and environment (Shearing, 2015), we explore the cases of Nauru and Bougainville islands in the Pacific, which illustrate the role of 'extractivism' (Klein, 2015) in increasing the vulnerability of islands, damaging health and environment, causing instability and conflict, contributing to global climate change, and leaving many islands uninhabitable and economically dependent.

We interpret the impacts of extractivism in these two cases through a critical lens, returning to our earlier arguments about how colonialism socially constructs crime in the image of undesirable Others (for example, by criminalizing political resistance), while the crimes of the powerful (for example, corporations, governments) are ignored (Pearce, 1976). In regard of the latter, the case of Nauru enables us to extend our earlier arguments about islands as exceptional spaces within (neo-)colonial relations: faraway, isolated and 'ambiguous zone[s]' where legality is indistinct and accountability opaque

(Agamben, 2005, p 2). This is evident in the devastation caused by phosphate mining on the island for most of the 20th century, as well as the more recent transition to an alternative extractivist industry with the commodification of asylum seekers now becoming Nauru's main industrial enterprise (Morris, 2019). In both cases, Nauru is put to work by colonial powers at the expense of the small nation's social, economic, and environmental wellbeing, while the island's isolation serves to largely hide the Australian government's actions from its constituents' view. Alternatively, the case of Bougainville helps us to tease out the sometimes-intimate relationships between violence and extractivist mining as a form of corporate (neo-)colonialism. Indeed, as we discuss later, violence was extreme and widespread not only during the Bougainville conflict (1988–98), which erupted at least partly in response to the Panguna copper mine, but also long after the mine had shut down operations. This violence, which began as political resistance, was responded to by the Papua New Guinean government with heavy-handed and sometimes 'criminal' tactics (Adamo, 2018, p 171).

Both cases raise important questions about social justice and demonstrate how extractivism has ultimately threatened the very existence of these (and other) islands, thereby re-emphasizing island spaces as 'powerful geographic trope[s] for disappearance, both literally and figuratively' (Baldacchino, 2016, p 98; also Bambrick, 2018). The island communities we discuss in this chapter have been irreparably damaged, while longer-term climate change effects of extractive industries also leave them quite literally at risk of disappearing as seawaters rise. Although the social disorganization and strain impacts of mining in these communities are in some ways similar to those found in non-island spaces and places, islandness – including the relative scarcity of space and resources that islandness infers – means these strains are amplified. In this sense, the spatial characteristics of islands play an important role in pushing communities to the limit, leaving them economically dependent (as in Nauru) and/or damaging local culture and custom to the point of social collapse and conflict. We argue that this finiteness, produced through island boundedness and isolation, should be more closely considered within a future green (island) criminology. To conclude the chapter, we briefly consider alternatives to extractivism that are health promoting, community building, and, we argue, crime preventative. Drawing on Indigenous philosophies, we examine the notion of stewardship, which stands in contrast to extractivism, involving an emphasis on regeneration and ensuring future life continues as we continue to the move through the Age of Anthropocene.

Green criminology and extractivist capitalism

The term 'green criminology' was first coined in 1990 (Lynch, 1990; Mahabir, 1990) and sought to draw attention to crimes committed against the physical and cultural environment. More than this, though, green criminology tends to expand the notion of 'crime' to include a kind of 'harm-ology' – that is, to consider not only harms to humans that may or may not be socially constructed as crimes, but also harm to the environment, to other species, and more (Shearing, 2015). It is only relatively recently, however, that green criminology has turned its attention more wholeheartedly towards the effects of environmental destruction on Indigenous peoples, including under colonization (Lynch, Stretesky, & Long, 2018). Lynch et al (2018), for example, explore how Indigenous peoples have been caught up in a globalized, capitalist, and corporatized treadmill of production, and been subject to the exploitative extraction of natural resources from their territories (also see Bunker, 2005). Drawing on Klein (2015), Morris (2019, p 1123) explains:

> Extractivism is the form of accumulation, associated with colonialism and imperialism, whereby territories, populations, and animal and plant life were rendered into commodities for the taking so as to enrich the world economic centres. It is also an ideological mindset of removing resources under the guise of 'development', ultimately benefiting wealthy countries at the expense of poorer ones. What is new about extractivism today is the expansion of corporations and non-government organizations into ever-growing resource frontiers globally.

Lynch et al (2018, p 320) describe these as 'attacks on ... [Indigenous peoples] and ecosystems ... [often involving] partnerships between ToP [treadmill of production] organizations and state governments that facilitate treadmill access to [Indigenous] ... lands and resources'. Such attacks, they argue, have also regularly been met with strong resistance by Indigenous peoples, which have subsequently resulted in counterattacks by colonial forces, often in the form of genocide (Lynch et al, 2018). As Crook et al (2018) and Lynch et al (2018) point out, this demonstrates the interrelatedness of genocide, 'ecocide', capitalism, and colonialism. How island spaces and places might also be interwoven into this stream of green criminological research remains, however, a gap in the criminological corpus. In the sections that follow, we seek to explore this question, considering how ecocide is bound up with colonialism in island spaces. First, we return to the relationship between extraction and colonialism in island spaces and places, including the use of Othered populations as sources of plentiful labour: a kind of human-oriented extractivism.

Extractive colonialism in island spaces and places

During second-wave colonialism, the Antipodes were regularly treated as sites of consumption and extraction for Empire, with the first examples of globalized companies emerging during this time. The British East India Company (EIC, 1600–1858), for example, explicitly sought out trade opportunities across the British East Indies, primarily relating to importation of spices (Roukis, 2004). The Dutch East India Company (1602–1799) also emerged as a fierce trade competitor of the EIC, establishing 'settlements and commercial activities on several of the islands of the East Indies Archipelago (modern-day Indonesia)' (Roukis, 2004, p 942; Gelderblom, de Jong, & Jonker, 2013). Both companies forged long histories of colonial exploitation, including by participating in the international slave trade (Vink, 2003; Major, 2012). The EIC and Dutch East India Company also frequently used islands for tactical purposes, as strategic trading posts. For example, European settlement of Norfolk Island (Australia) in 1787 was undertaken because of its 'utility ... as a strategic site to tap into the China trade, linked by the South Equatorial current at the heart of the EIC's [British East India Company's] trading grounds' (Roscoe, 2021, p 176). As Sartre (2011 [1956]) pointed out in his examination of colonialism in Algeria, however, capital tends to remain invested in the colonizing country with colonial outposts acting as satellites from which the colonizer can recruit *more* capital and power. Norfolk, for example, had potential to also improve Britain's supply of flax, which was used to manufacture rope for ships:

> Norfolk Island had large flax plants which, Captain Phillip reported to the Colonial Office, could be cultivated by convicts who were, after all, on a remote island from which they would 'very seldom be able to escape'. The *Supply* sailed from Port Jackson on 15 February 1788, carrying twenty-three people (including nine male and six female convicts) to colonize Norfolk Island. Male convicts performed the manual labour of cutting timber and clearing land that, in Captain Phillip's words, 'render'd the island a resource'. (Roscoe, 2021, p 177)

This ultimately proved to be a failed project, with the eventual abandonment of the original Norfolk settlement in 1829. However, it draws attention to the use of Othered populations, including prisoners, as a ready supply of labour for colonial enterprise expansion (Anderson, 2018). In the case of Norfolk, the island's bounded isolation enabled it to double as a site of convict punishment, as well as a forced-labour camp (labour forming *part* of that punishment). This occurred off the back of a far longer history of exploiting Othered populations for labour[1] and can be understood through what Anderson (2018, p 13) describes as 'penal satellites' under colonialism, which were sites of punishment and forced labour enabled through colonial convict transportation. She explains, 'convict transportation as a form of punishment was always explicitly intertwined with both political economy and metropolitan and imperial governmentality' (Anderson, 2018, p 3).

Indeed, 'Convicts moved in and out of and circulated around penal spaces, according to the exigencies of labour needs and other social or penal considerations' (Anderson, 2018, p 13). Thus, exploitation of labour, but also land under colonial expansion, has been central to the exponential growth of capitalism. Indeed, colonization was integral to the birth and growth of capitalism and, according to Karl Marx, the excesses of capitalism were most obvious in the colonies, 'where it [capitalism] goes naked' (cited in Young, 2016, p 101). Extractive capitalism has also, as green criminology has more recently drawn attention to, long been associated with environmental degradation, regularly at the expense of Indigenous peoples whose land and labour it exploits (Lynch et al, 2018). This is well illustrated in the example of the island nation of Nauru.

Extractive (neo-)colonialism and the island nation of Nauru

Nauru is situated in Micronesia, north-east of Australia, has a population of around 10,800 people and is about 21 km^2 in size (World Bank, 2021). The island's isolation and remoteness meant that it was protected from colonization for a longer period than many other Pacific islands, though the late 1800s saw interest in fertilizer trade 'catapult ... [Nauru] onto the international trading scene' (Morris, 2019, p 1125). The island of Nauru, initially a German colony (from 1888, after Germany was gifted the island in the Anglo-German Declaration), became a League of Nations mandated territory in 1914, and was subsequently administered by Australia until it achieved independence in 1968 (Bray, 1930; Morris, 2019). Having been identified as a rich site of phosphorous in the late 1800s, it later became what Morris (2019, p 1125) refers to as an 'Australian-run British Phosphate Commission Control', with mining rights jointly held by Australia, New Zealand, and Britain (with the two former countries being settler colonies of the latter) (Bray, 1930). The Pacific Islands Company (later Pacific Phosphate Company [PPC]) began mining on the small island from 1906 (Pollock, 2014), and extractive mining soon became Nauru's main industry, with the Australian, New Zealand, and British governments buying out the PPC in 1920 to establish in its place the British Phosphate Commissioners (BPC).

Nauru's isolation and remoteness supported the monopolization of its resources by these powers, and particularly Australia as administrator. As one Australian public servant, P. Deane, cited in Firth (1978, p 36), explained, it was 'impossible ... to estimate the enormous value of the island [of Nauru] to Australia. ... It not only ensures to the farmer, free of all outside interference and control, his full requirements of phosphates – but does so at cost price.' Early representations of the role of mining in the small island nation were overwhelmingly positive, depicting residents as having been 'saved' and made rich through industrial development (Morris, 2019). For example: '[Pleasant Island, or Nauru] is ... self-supporting and the natives [*sic.*], grouped for administrative purposes into fourteen districts, each presided over by a chief, play the role of rich land-owners, receiving both rents for their lands and royalties on each ton of phosphate shipped' (Bray, 1930, p 1371).

As we turn to below, however, the reality was far different. A similar scene played out during the 20th century on Ocean Island – now part of the nation state of Kiribati, and Nauru's closest neighbour being situated nearly 300 km to the east. Phosphate mining began on Ocean Island from 1900 and continued until 1980 (Teaiwa, 2015a), originally being enabled through what Firth (1978, pp 36–7) describes as a 'scandal', since 'Albert F Ellis of the Pacific Islands Company persuaded two [Indigenous Banaba] chiefs to put their marks on a document giving the company the right to take Ocean Island phosphate for 999 years for the trifling sum of £50 a year'. As mining expanded on Ocean Island, the British administration acquired further land and eventually, in 1945, forcibly exiled the local Banabans to Fiji's Rabi Island (Firth, 1978). Drawing on the examples of both Nauru and Ocean islands, Firth (1978, p 37) argues that at the time these mining industries were established, 'governments were merely the agents of private companies, providing legality for whatever the companies wished to do'. And in contrast to the often-positive portrayals of industrial expansion on the islands, the influx of people and trade has instead wrought numerous devastating effects, while providing few if any returns.

In Nauru, new influxes of people, including indentured labourers, to support local mining brought previously unknown diseases, including leprosy from 1911 onwards (Bray, 1930). As a further example of islanding *within* islands (Mountz, 2015), lepers in Nauru were subject to the kinds of isolation practices described in earlier chapters, including being exiled to a Nauruan lazaret and for the most severe of cases, on a 'strip of the coastline, consisting of coral reef and foreshore [which] has been isolated, ... well supplied with water and food-bearing trees ... [and where] Discipline is maintained by two chiefs' (Bray, 1930, p 1373). Nauru claimed independence in 1968 and subsequently nationalized the island's phosphate mining operations, which resulted in the nation briefly claiming the second-highest Gross Domestic Product in the world during the 1970s (that is, after Saudi Arabia). Nevertheless, the phosphate reserves soon diminished and mining-related income dried up (Bambrick, 2018). Thus, in addition to the introduction of disease, phosphate extraction also failed to deliver promised wealth to Nauruans; instead, mining channelled extreme wealth *away* from Nauru and into the hands of administering states and corporations. Meanwhile,

Nauruans received little to nothing in the way of income or compensation for the pillaging of their island's finite natural resources, and the country subsequently found itself in bankruptcy, while also needing to deal with significant environmental destruction. As Pollock (2014, p 109) puts it, Nauruans have been left:

> with little land to live on, no local resources, limited finances, and a high level of dependency on outside agencies. They must import all necessities, including food and water, using whatever returns their resource has provided throughout the XXth century. Today, they have become dependent on outside aid to replace their denuded island's wealth.

Bambrick (2018, p 273) explains that 'Most of the island is [now] missing, leaving just a coastal ring, and pollution from mining has also devastated surrounding fisheries from polluted run-off.' However, neither Nauru nor Ocean Island have received just compensation for the devastation caused by the histories of extractive mining that took place there. In Nauru's case, a compensation claim was made to the International Court of Justice in relation to damage caused by phosphate mining while the nation was under Australian administration (1914–68), but no legal finding was made and the matter was instead settled out of court in 1993, with Australia agreeing to pay Nauru a mere $107 million total in compensation – about half in a lump sum, and the remaining portion over a 20-year period (Maclellan, 2013). While the payment was intended to finance the island's environmental rehabilitation, this has not occurred (Gale, 2016). Moreover, the final remaining reserves of phosphate continue to be mined on the island, with ongoing involvement by Australian mining companies. The operations of one Australian mining company on Nauru also recently attracted the attention of the Australian Federal Police, who found it had used inducements to secure political support for its continued mining operations (Dinnen & Walton, 2016). Meanwhile, Nauru's position as a severely depleted remote island, in need of external aid for survival, has been used to explain its subsequent take up of the Australian government's 'most recent industrial package', which has seen it shift to a new industry of refugee detention from 2001 onwards, beginning with the Australian government's 'Pacific Solution' policy (Morris, 2019, p 1126; also McClellan, 2013).

The primary industry on the island has subsequently pivoted in a relatively short space of time, from mining to refugee processing – again on behalf of and benefiting Australia, and arguably representing a kind of neo-colonial extractivism (Morris, 2019). The 2001 Australia–Nauru agreement resulted in an immediate influx of funding into the small island to create a new 'industry', which – Morris (2019) argues – saw asylum seekers replacing phosphate as the commodity of interest. Morris' (2019, p 1122) description of the physical legacies of this shift is palpable:

> Nauru's phosphate cantilevers went unrepaired, testament to the residues of a past resource economy in phosphate extraction. Piles of fertilizer component lay in loading warehouses, unfeasible for export to earmarked Australian and Asian destinations due to long-overdue repairs to Nauru's loading bay. The country's landscapes lay pockmarked, mined in a panic of dwindling availability. But three refugee processing centres [now] crowned the country, gleaming from in between dilapidated phosphate extraction fields.

The impacts of these dovetailing extractive industries are arguably amplified in Nauru because of the limited local resources available to those living on the small island; that is, the size and isolation of the island, coupled with the devastating impacts of colonialism, arguably worked together to seal its fate. Moreover, the isolation and small size of Nauru enables its border to be more carefully administered, while also creating a site of exception where lines of legality are blurred (Agamben, 2005). In some instances, the exceptionalism of this island space has protected Australian political and commercial interests, while at other times it has fostered and protected those engaged in corruption within Nauru itself, including Australian businesses and Nauruan nationals. In the case of refugee detention, Nauru's relative isolation is also helpful in keeping most of the horrors of Australian asylum seeker policy hidden from view, and – because they are detained offshore – these asylum seekers also have no official recourse to appeal decisions on their refugee status determinations under Australian law. This essentially enables Australia to openly contravene its obligations under multiple international conventions,[2] which has resulted in widespread criticism on the international stage. For example, the United Nations High Commissioner for Refugees (UNHCR) has repeatedly drawn attention to the poor conditions of Australia's offshore detention centres, including in Nauru, Christmas, and Manus islands, and called for an end to Australia's offshore processing policies (UNHCR, 2018), with other national and international advocacy groups doing the same (Amnesty International, 2016; Human Rights Watch, 2021; Refugee Council of Australia, 2021). Meanwhile, the Nauruan government has staunchly protected Australian political interests by frequently disallowing visas to journalists and researchers who are unsympathetic to the operation of its detention centres (Davidson, 2018). The few stories that *have* emerged, however, indicate that asylum seekers' human rights are frequently violated in Nauruan detention, with Amnesty International referring to Nauru in its 2016 report as an 'island of despair' and documenting multiple horrific stories of actual and attempted suicides, including by children. According to Walton and Dinnen (2020, p 530), Nauru not only benefits from this arrangement by maintaining Australian funding to run the detention centre, but also in terms of gaining leverage in its relations with Australia. The authors argue that this has subsequently 'constrain[ed] … critical responses [by Australian authorities] to the alleged involvement of local [Nauruan] political actors in organised crime' (Walton & Dinnen, 2020, p 530). In multiple senses, therefore, Nauru's island isolation establishes it as an exceptional site where the horrors of Australia's layered extractivism go relatively unnoticed, and whereby Australia can thus escape accountability for its actions.

Since 2015, refugees have no longer been officially 'detained' within the Nauru detention facility, but are instead able to experience a level of freedom (within island containment) in an 'open centre'. Thus, like the Norwegian Prison Island described in Chapter 3, Nauru has been similarly described as an 'open air prison that people cannot leave [due to its isolation], even when they have been officially recognised as refugees' (Amnesty International, 2016, p 5). Even worse, though, than Norway's Prison Island (Shammas, 2014), the detention of refugees under administrative (rather than judicial) arrangements means that they have no certainty about time frames for when their cases might be finalized, or when they might be able to leave the island. One Iranian refugee (in Amnesty International, 2016, p 22) who had been granted refugee status, and released to live 'freely' on Nauru, stated:

> Now, the walls have changed, but nothing else. The situation is worse than in the camp [at the Refugee Processing Centre]. Before we were at least waiting, hoping that once we have the refugee status things will change, but now we understand that it doesn't give us any freedom either. It is worse than a prison, because we have no idea how long we are in for and when we can get released.

The walls of the detention centre prison had been merely swapped out, in this refugee's view, for the boundaries of the isolated island itself, which was experienced as dangerous and threatening. Similar to the prisoners in Shammas' (2014) Norwegian Prison Island study, refugees on Nauru appear to experience the 'pains of freedom' in the form of uncertainty and (limited) exposure to freedom, without actually being free. They are trapped in a state of island-bound limbo; essentially stateless and homeless (Amnesty International, 2016).

The case of Nauru raises significant questions about social and distributive justice and, as noted above, yet again draws attention to islands as sites of exception. The 'exceptionality' of Nauru is enabled through the isolation of its borders, which are able to be carefully policed as natural exclusion/inclusion zones. Although Nauru demonstrates the devastating impacts of extractivist industry on the lands and survival of islands, as well as the ways that islands can be sites where the harmful and sometimes criminal behaviours of powerful states and corporations can go unchecked, we have not focused here on the social and economic upheaval these industries can also cause. We turn to this in the following section, using the case of Bougainville Island as an example of the relationships between island extractivism, social disorganization, and violent crime.

Extractive mining, social disorganization, and violence on Bougainville Island

Located to the north-east of Australia, Bougainville is an autonomous region of the nation state of PNG, and its main island – Bougainville Island — is about 9,000 m^2 in size. The region also consists of the smaller Buka Island and several smaller outer islands. Prior to the 20th century, Bougainville Island's relative isolation (along with other islands in the Melanesian region) was considered to have 'preserved ... typical features of traditional societies', with close-knit familial and kinship bonds nurtured by local custom and lore that governed reciprocity and community labour (Adamo, 2018, p 167). This made Bougainville a site of interest and 'authentic laboratory for several generations of anthropologists' (Adamo, 2018, pp 168–9). Although contested by some, Adamo (2018, p 168) argues that pre-colonial Bougainville was also relatively egalitarian and classless (in a Marxist sense), with land ownership and use being shared according to local rules of descent, exchange, and residency. However, the subsequent impacts of colonization, as well as extractive mining from the 1960s to 1980s, have been sudden and disastrous.

Until 1886, Bougainville (and PNG on the whole) was brought under control of Dutch colonizers, while it subsequently came under Australian rule until 1946 and then under formal Australian control in 1962 (Adamo, 2018). PNG, including Bougainville, was subsequently awarded independence in 1975 (Adamo, 2018). Rich deposits of copper were discovered on Bougainville in the 1960s, leading to the opening of the Panguna copper mine in 1972, which operated until 1989 and employed more than 4,000 people during its operation (mainly immigrants rather than locals). The mine created significant wealth for Bougainville Copper Limited (BCL), an Australian firm and subsidiary of Rio Tinto – Zinc, based in London (Adamo, 2018). The growth of mining on the island also resulted in a significant change to the population:

> between 1968 and 1972, about 10,000 foreigners out of a population of fewer than 80,000 inhabitants poured on to the island to build roads, ports, and new towns with hospitals and infrastructures conceived for copper exploitation and trade. ... Although the attachment to a traditional lifestyle and resistance to social change were still strong,

rural people were forced to move to towns and started to work in mining-related roles. (Adamo, 2018, p 169)

The mine and labour it attracted resulted in a significant breakdown of local lore and custom, as well as traditional roles of men and women, with women being sidelined in negotiations with Australian mining executives (Jewkes, Jama-Shai, & Sikweyiya, 2017; Adamo, 2018). Landowners in Bougainville received compensation, but this was insignificant when compared with the wealth that the mine exported to the BCL, with landowner royalties estimated at about 0.625 per cent of the value of all copper mined on the island (Adamo, 2018, p 169). Thus, the mining enterprise not only resulted in significant social disorganization, but also caused a significant cleavage between rich (miners) and poor (others, often locals).

Significant violence erupted on Bougainville in 1988. The violence tends to be attributed to a mixture of factors, though the operation of the mine and the social changes it caused are regularly regarded as a primary instigator. Adamo (2018, p 169) explains:

> The loss of land, the limited and unfair compensation policies, and the deterioration of living conditions in the villages re-located after the opening of the mine were ultimately followed by a huge environmental disaster [in the form of contaminated water] caused by mining activities in a biodiversity-rich virgin forest. The interaction of these factors and a widespread desire to avenge the historical-political fate of the people of Bougainville can be regarded as the basis of the conflict that broke out in 1988–89.

In April 1988, a former BCL employee and young leader in the Panguna Landowners Association requested compensation of 10 bn kina (~US$10 bn) from BCL, though this was denied, and a subsequent report commissioned by the PNG government downplayed the environmental impacts of the mining (thus, also downplaying the need for compensation) (Adamo, 2018). Not long after, the BCL's mining equipment began to be sabotaged and the Bougainville Revolution Army (BRA) was established by individuals who were Indigenous to the Panguna area (Adamo, 2018). The BRA initially attracted international support of environmental protection movements, being seen as an 'environmentalist guerrilla group' (Adamo, 2018, p 170). Its objectives soon, however, expanded to include demands for secession from PNG: 'hatred toward the national government, the BCL, Australians, and the "white mafia" at the head of the PNG economy was the main issue' (Adamo, 2018, p 171).

The Panguna mine closed in mid-1989 as a result of the subsequent violence and the Papua New Guinean Defence Force also withdrew in mid-1990, imposing 'a total blockade of the island', starving the island's residents of essential goods including medicines (Adamo, 2018, p 171). A Bougainville interim government was thereafter established by the BRA, but disillusioned (non-BRA) Bougainvilleans requested the return of the Papua New Guinean Defence Force to the island, with some newly emerging anti-BRA resistance groups subsequently fighting the BRA alongside the Papua New Guinean Army. While the BRA's separatist demands were rooted in longer-standing dissatisfaction by some locals at having been annexed to PNG rather than the Solomon Islands (with whom Bougainvilleans share language and culture) in the late 19th century, these ethnic divisions were layered upon divisions within Bougainville itself (for example, between Nagovisi and Nasioi peoples), which though they had been downplayed in the construction of a kind of Bougainvillean nationalism from the 1950s, are also thought to have re-emerged and been exacerbated through the subsequent conflict (Ogan, 1999; Adamo, 2018). Meanwhile, the embargo over the island resulted in deteriorating living conditions and 'was responsible for thousands of civilian deaths – many more than those provoked by the struggles themselves' (Adamo, 2018, p 171). In order to disrupt the BRA, the Papua New Guinea Defence Force is reported to have subsequently 'adopted criminal kinds of tactics, including the systematic burning down of villages' (Adamo, 2018, p 171). In 1997, the PNG government turned to the use of private military company, Sandline International, which provided equipment, arms, and a group of private mercenaries in an attempt to bring the Bougainville conflict under control, though this strategy also failed and attracted significant international condemnation. Overall, around 10,000–15,000 people are thought to have died during the Bougainville conflict (Jewkes et al, 2017).

The conflict officially ended in 1998, though an autonomous Bougainville government was not established until 2005 and peacebuilding has continued for some time (Jewkes et al, 2017). Adamo (2018, p 174) argues that the Bougainville conflict can be explained through the 'resource curse' hypothesis, whereby 'the presence of valuable and concentrated natural resources (copper wealth), rather than fostering economic growth and development, has a destabilizing effect on society, making it more prone to conflict'. The conflict erupts, thus, as a result of social disorganization – a state of anomie created through severe disruption to (perhaps already fragile) social bonds and capital, and which exacerbates old cleavages, as well as creating new ones, particularly between those with access to extractivist wealth and those without. The specificities of cultural differences between Bougainvilleans and Papua New Guinean nationals, many of whom moved to Bougainville to work at the mine or as families of miners, provides a further explanation. Adamo (2018, p 179) explains:

Clans in Bougainville were often matrilineal: there were Papua New Guinean women (daughters, sisters, cousins) who arrived as, or with, the miners, and who later married Bougainvillean men. Since most clans in PNG [Papua New Guinea] are patrilineal, these Bougainvillean men found themselves without land and thus without long-term financial security. Personal compensation from BCL or the PNG Government was [thereby] one of a very few limited options for guaranteeing an independent livelihood [for these men].

One focus of the post-conflict reconciliation efforts was reintegration of these disenfranchised men, many of whom had instigated the war and, thus, the aim was to at least partially rebuild social capital on the island (Jewkes et al, 2017). The conflict has, however, resulted in significant experiences of trauma, with criminal violence – particularly against women – apparently being widely tolerated in the post-conflict context (Jewkes et al, 2017). A survey of 1,743 men and women living in post-conflict Bougainville, conducted by Jewkes et al (2017) in 2014, revealed that mental ill health, including high rates of post-traumatic stress disorder and continued experiences of violence, were widespread. Gendered interpersonal crime in Bougainville is considered by Jewkes et al (2014, 2017) as one of many layers of violence that continue on the island, and which have been exacerbated by the social disorganization caused by the mining and subsequent conflict. They explain:

> Perpetration of violence against women is extremely highly prevalent on Bougainville, and we have shown that what is perceived as the enduring social, emotional and physical (disability) impact of conflict is associated with a higher likelihood of rape and partner violence perpetration, as well as the indicators of mental ill-health: high levels of depressive symptoms, drug use and alcohol abuse. (Jewkes et al, 2017, p 12)

Bougainville is not the only case where extractive mining has resulted in extreme conflict and violence; the Ok Tedi mine (PNG Western Province) and Freeport mine (Indonesia) provide further examples where 'resource wars' have raged (Ballard & Banks, 2003). Similarly, the discovery and subsequent mining of fossil fuels in Timor-Leste (East Timor) to the north of Australia has dramatically exacerbated longer-standing tensions, resulting in significant bouts of violent conflict (John, Papyrakis, & Tasciotti, 2020). The social disorganization that arises from the influx of different populations to service mining operations, as well as disruption to culture that occurs from environmental and social changes, have also been found to be criminogenic elsewhere (Garvin et al, 2009; Nguyen, Boruff, & Tonts, 2018).[3] While, however, this scenario has been repeated across several studies (Kumah, 2006;

Garvin et al, 2009; Chuhan-Pole, Dabalen, & Land, 2017; Nguyen, Boruff, & Tonts, 2018), the experiences of Nauru and Bougainville – understood through a prism of islandness – are also distinct, as we discuss below.

Understanding extractivism and crime through a prism of islandness

As Adamo (2018, p 174) points out, there are similarities and differences in the experiences of Bougainville and Nauru:

> they are both islands ... and share the challenges of their small size, limited resource base, and remoteness from market centres, etc. However, the outcome of the resource-curse-induced state failure is rather different on these two islands: Nauru suffered an economic collapse and needed external donors to recover – accepting inter alia the establishment of a detention centre for asylum seekers in Australia – while the resource curse led to a tragedy with thousands of deaths in Bougainville.

The answer perhaps most obviously lies in the different status of the two islands, one being an autonomous region while the other is a sovereign state. Indeed, the non-sovereign status of Bougainville enabled the Papua New Guinean Army to intervene in its efforts to violently suppress the BRA, which triggered and exacerbated significant violence, rooted in longer-standing tensions. The conflict can be contextualized, thus, within Bougainville's enduring pursuit of secession from PNG, which distinguishes it from Nauru. Adamo (2018) argues that weak institutions and a lack of democracy, which were more apparent in Bougainville than Nauru, were an additional factor that led to disparate outcomes. In Nauru, however, the presence of extractive mining and refugee processing has also in some ways fostered local corruption: as per the case of the Australian mining company found to have bribed local Nauru officials, and in the case of Nauru having political leverage to prevent Australian officials from demanding Nauruan political corruption be investigated.

Although the levels of violence experienced on these two islands differ greatly, both have nonetheless witnessed significant social collapse as a result of extractive mining. In both cases, extractivist industry has produced substantial wealth for external states and corporations, while causing significant environmental and social degradation for the islands themselves. Moreover, island isolation has provided a level of secrecy around harmful and potentially illegal activities carried out by Australian corporations and governments. In both Bougainville and Nauru, the corporate actions that precipitated extreme violence and environmental devastation have not been successfully challenged, nor accountability achieved. In this sense, both islands might be understood as backdrops to a kind of legal exceptionalism. Island boundedness has, however, also meant that the strains of extractive industries have been amplified on these islands. Indeed, in both cases, islandness meant that the mining industries largely monopolized the local economies, resulting in a level of economic and social dependence that might not have otherwise been seen in larger non-island societies, where there is more space and capacity to support multiple competing forms of commerce. Most of the island of Nauru has been eaten away by mining, pushing its people and government to the brink of economic collapse, and making the country nearly wholly reliant on imported foods and other goods. The subsequent 'choice' of the Nauruan government to take on a further extractivist industry in the form of refugee processing was, thus, arguably more illusory than real; this decision was a matter of survival. In the case of Bougainville:

> Industrial exploitation ... altered pre-modern social, economic and political schemes, while social stratification and further traditional features of an indigenous society were increasingly eroded (matrilineal succession, a view of ancestral land as a common asset as opposed to the increasing trend towards capitalist land use, etc.). These trends turned out to be even more destructive in the case under study, given the insularity and isolation context of Bougainvilleans. (Adamo, 2018, p 180)

Thus, not only did extractivist industry result in significant social fragmentation and disorganization, it also contributed to a state of anomie, where access to formerly shared/communal space and resources was dramatically reduced thereby producing significant social strain. In both cases, the spatial characteristics of islands play an important role in pushing communities to the limit, leaving them economically dependent (as in Nauru) and damaging local culture and custom to the point of social collapse, fomenting extreme conflict around division of scarce remaining resources (as in Bougainville). This finiteness, produced through island boundedness and isolation, should be more closely considered within a future green (island) criminology. The urgency to pay greater attention to island spaces within green criminological research and theorizing is starkly apparent when we consider not only the history of islands (such as those discussed here), but also their precarious futures.

Conclusion: turning towards justice and stewardship

The sum of the past few centuries of ever-intensified industrialization and extractivism, especially the burning of extracted coal, has been to create the looming disaster of climate change. It has repeatedly been pointed out that this event is far more likely to negatively impact the world's poorest peoples and countries before anyone else. In particular, it is island states (and non-governing island entities) that are consistently at greatest threat from rising seawaters (Mountz, 2015). These are sites 'where the impacts of climate change will be experienced early and dramatically' (Mountz, 2015, p 643); 'Sovereign archipelago atoll states – Tuvalu, Marshall Islands, Kiribati [for example] – face comprehensive drowning with even a modest rise in sea level' (Baldacchino, 2016, p 98). As Pacific islands located nearby these archipelago atoll states, Nauru and Bougainville will also be significantly affected as climate change predictions come to fruition. While these (and other) islands bear the brunt of a warming planet, the negative social and economic impacts of resource extraction discussed in this chapter will be layered upon the negative effects of climate change, significantly lowering resilience and affecting long-term health, wellbeing, security, and survival (Bambrick, 2018; Holley et al, 2018). For many other islands, too, warming seas are layered upon multiple other incursions by larger and more powerful states: the Marshall Islands, for instance, are facing climate change impacts after already surviving a traumatic history as a site for nuclear testing by the US Navy, with 67 detonations of atomic weapons in the islands between 1946 and 1958, obliterating the local environment and exposing locals to nuclear fallout (Dvorak, 2020).

Bambrick (2018) argues that, in relation to Pacific Island communities, (re)building resilience to climate change should entail a series of first- and second-order strategies that would see healthcare systems and other critical institutions strengthened, as well as promoting a shift away from extractivist capitalism and towards 'climate compatible' development that is community-led and promotes economic inclusion and security (also see Holley et al, 2018). For instance, she argues that sustainable tourism and carbon capture (for example, regeneration of forest regions to construct global carbon sinks) are potential alternatives that could be pursued (Bambrick, 2018). Some islands, such as Christmas Island (located in the Indian Ocean, a territory of Australia, and also site of a phosphate mine *and* refugee detention centre), *are* looking to establish large marine parks and zones to encourage eco-tourism (McCutcheon, 2021). A large number of former prison islands have also been (and are still being) converted into nature reserves (Mega, 2019). In contrast to the islands described in this chapter, however, these former prison islands, such as Isla Maria Madre (Pacific Ocean, off Mexico), contain relatively untouched reefs and seas, which have remained beyond the reach of industry and private fisherpersons as prison security patrol these waters to keep people out and prevent prison breaks (Mega, 2019). Thus, these island ecologies have been 'indirectly protected ... [by] prison[s]' (Aburto in Mega, 2019, p 288) and their subsequent transformation has been described by conservation biologist, Joe Roman, as providing 'hope for the future in areas that are often seen as a stain on human history' (Roman in Mega, 2019, p 288).

Nevertheless, although alternative industries like tourism and carbon offsets offer different avenues for island economies, they do not address the capitalist and consumptive structures and mindsets that continue to underlie the global climate change crisis in the Age of Anthropocene. In particular, carbon capture has been critiqued as a means of simply underwriting the continuation of extractive capitalism, while making it more politically palatable – a form of greenwashing (Klein, 2015). In contrast, a more fundamental change is arguably needed to avert the climate disaster, which would see a dramatic shift in the way that Western capitalism engages with and commodifies both people and the environment. In this regard, there is much to learn from Indigenous philosophies and practices. As Holley et al (2018, p 191, emphasis added) point out, during the Holocene (about 12,000 years after the last Ice Age), many Indigenous peoples across the globe lived with 'conceptions and rules that recognized our *interconnectedness* with the natural world', while 'many in the Global North barely glimpsed, or did not fully understand or acknowledge ... that Nature constituted our biophysical security'. An initial step towards a more ecologically 'just' future might entail, for example, re-engaging with Western notions of time and space, which are typically conceived of as linear and fixed: signalling a beginning and (inevitable) end. For some Indigenous cultures, however, time is non-linear and not even circular. As Apalech (Wik) man from northern Australia, Tyson Yunkaporta (2019, pp 44–6), explains in relation to what he refers to as 'First Law':

> It all comes out from that central point of impact, that big bang expanding and contracting, breathing out and in, no start and finish but a constant state where past, present and future are all one thing, one time, one place. Every breath ever taken is still in the air to breathe. I breathe the breaths of the Ancestors, and everybody else's too. ... This is a sustainable system. Nothing is created or destroyed; it just moves and changes, and this is the First Law. Creation is in a constant state of motion, and we must move with it as the custodial species or we will damage the system and doom ourselves.

Arguably, a dramatic shift would arise if the planet were to be viewed through this lens by the colonizing and corporate powers that have been primary architects of its destruction. Indeed, this kind of 'long' time represents a break from the short-termism that so often characterizes extractivist mindsets and endeavours. Surely also, human interaction with the lands and seas would change if all understood that, as a 'custodial species', we are nevertheless inseparable from (and thus, not in a position to dominate or commodify) the lands, seas, skies, and living organisms that reside within (Yunkaporta, 2019). In the broader research literature, these views are most often described as forms of environmental stewardship, which seek to protect, restore, and sustainably manage/utilize lands, seas, and the resources they hold, either explicitly or implicitly building on Indigenous ontologies and knowledges (Ens et al, 2016; Bennett et al, 2018). As radical (and subsequently, critical) criminology has long argued, a different valuing of natural and human resources would also perhaps contribute to reducing poverty, increasing social cohesion, and reducing *crime*. More than this, though, Holley et al (2018, p 186) ask how legal, security, and criminological scholarship in the Age of the Anthropocene can grapple with the question: 'how [can] humanity secure itself from itself?'

By breaking down the socially constructed boundaries between humans, other species, and the planet – that is, (re-)embracing Indigenous ontologies that see this inseparability as simply part of life – legal scholars, criminologists, and others might conceive of the environment and other species that live within as additional 'beings' that are also deserving of respect and protection, possibly through conferral of legal rights (Holley et al, 2018). This also potentially paves the way for a green criminology that focuses on the interwoven security of both people *and* planet (Cao & Wyatt, 2016). As this chapter has shown, the actions of colonial and corporate extractivism have had disastrous effects for both island environments and peoples. Conversely, the world's islands will be (and are) among the earliest and most significant beneficiaries of stewardship alternatives. In this respect, the places and spaces of islands in this emerging green criminology demand ongoing consideration.

8

Conclusion

I

It is debatable whether criminology is a 'discipline'. Historically it has drawn on many disciplines, most notably sociology. This sociological preoccupation has perhaps given it a temporal character. This noted, and as we have argued throughout this book, geography has always informed criminology. Most of this 'geographic' work, perhaps owing to the dominance of Northern criminologies, has been what we have referred to here as spatial in character and empirical. Of less influence have been interpretive approaches looking at place-based characteristics of criminological issues. We have attempted to compensate for this here and have been less concerned with how criminology might solve social problems, including crime, instead largely focusing on how such problems are generated and, indeed, how criminology itself has constructed such problems. In this way we view island criminologies as being as much about problem analysis as they are about problem solving (Schneider, 1985). At any rate, we have endeavoured here to draw upon a broad range of disciplines in the humanities and social sciences to map island criminologies. It is our intention in this book to situate island criminologies within these existing criminological lines of inquiry, while also taking an interdisciplinary, global, and critical approach to exploring how islandness might further inflect extant criminological theorizing. As Thomas (2007, p 22) draws attention to:

> Current island studies literature strongly suggests the importance of studying islands, supports the need for gathering islanders together, and asserts the significance of expanding island studies as a 'nissological interdisciplinarity'.

A distinction which echoes that of problem analysis and problem solving has been made between a vocational (sometimes referred to as administrative or professional) approach to criminology and that of a critical approach. The vocational approach is often empirical and is associated with improving the practices of the criminal justice system in order to reform it. The critical approach tends to be more theoretical and philosophical and is less concerned with improving criminal justice institutions than it is with questioning their existence. The distinction has been an enduring one with appeal to criminologists themselves, especially those who consider themselves part of the critical tradition. But dig deeper, and beneath all this is another distinction which informs criminological traditions and those more broadly in the social sciences, involving human nature.

In *Leviathan* (2010 [1651]), Thomas Hobbes famously characterized social life devoid of state-based institutions as 'solitary, poor, nasty, brutish and short', his point being that people are self-interested and driven to compete over scarce resources. We are not naturally inclined to cooperate for a common good. If we were in some simplistic way to subscribe to this view, the institutions of the criminal justice system, and authority more generally, should be maintained. By extension, we would believe for example that, should the 'thin blue line' of policing falter or implode, what would likely ensue would be incivility and crime. Around a hundred years after Hobbes, Jean-Jacques Rousseau developed a counter image of human nature, in which it is social institutions and structures that corrupt humans. The increasing division of labour in society has produced numerous forms of inequality, which have countered communal sentiment. Institutions, such as modern criminal justice systems, reproduce and maintain social divisions, including capitalism, patriarchy, and racism.

As we noted earlier, Rousseau's thinking was informed by accounts of 'savage' peoples in both North America and the Pacific, including islanders. It has been characterized as romantic. As we have seen here, islands, with their relatively 'flat' economic structures, preservation of traditional norms and values, and relative 'distance' from (mainland) state authority and structures, would present as ideal settings to test Rousseau's views and often they have seemingly confirmed them. Island life is regularly characterized as communal and 'islandness' seems to draw on and confirm communal qualities. Moreover, the very little research that has been conducted around crime in small-scale societies suggests that they often demonstrate relatively high levels of social integration because they maintain strong normative boundaries through the control, exclusion, and marginalization of internal and external Others. The core difference between the small-scale society and more metropolitan or cosmopolitan settings seems to be the degree to which social control takes an informal or formal character. And even here, as we argue in Chapter 5, it is not simply a matter of informal controls being *better* or providing greater justice to people, as the social value of the stranger demonstrates.

II

If there were one core fact that approximately 200 years of criminology has produced, it is the idea that social integration, in its various forms, reduces crime and bolsters social order. If we were to capture the concept of social integration with reference to belonging, it might better capture group dynamics and what Norbert Elias referred to as 'social figurations'; what is often referred to in contemporary social science as social networks. Belonging can be a resource for integration and minimization of conflict, but it can also be a source of tensions between individuals and group and provide a basis for marginalization and exclusion. Islands may assist in understanding different ways of 'doing belonging'. Despite being much used or alluded to, belonging remains an elusive concept in the social sciences. But how is it achieved in different contexts? To take one example, relevant here, belonging is often associated with longevity in place. We all belong to social relations, cultures, and groups. However, there may be differential intensity of belonging and pressure to belong, meaning that choice, integration, and embeddedness are important factors to consider in belonging. The absence of place-based belongingness produces feelings of isolation, alienation, loneliness, and displacement (Antonisch, 2010, p 649).

Yuval-Davis (2006, p 197) argues that we need to distinguish between belonging and the politics of belonging. Belonging is about emotional attachment, feeling 'at home' and feeling 'safe and secure'. When it is threatened it is prone to naturalization and can be politicized. The politics of belonging refers to specific political projects that articulate particular ways of belonging for specific groups, which are themselves constructed through such projects. Belonging as such is not just about individual social location and identity, but also how persons are valued and judged. Belonging is a political project which involves 'boundary maintenance'. It divides the world's population into categories, which are articulated in terms of 'us and them'. Communities in early rural social science were viewed as homogenous and stable units. As noted here, a post-colonial response has been to present islands as harmonious or homogenous places. Yet, as we have shown here, communities are not a natural set of relations, but constructed on broad terrains of history and politics. There is no such thing as a universal community – no community includes everybody. It is meaningless if it does. Always, communities have members and non-members; insiders and outsiders. To deny this is to deny the existence of power relations. Community, like place, is a mental and experiential construct, but is also a contested space constructed through practices of power. Finally, by working from images of small-scale societies as places, to quote Liepins' (2000, p 30), which are 'temporally and geographically specific terrains of power and discourse', we recognize the simultaneity of social organization to both constrain and enable varieties of crime in the same localities and among the same actors.

Of course, the policing of who belongs is not always conducted in a physical and/or violent manner, with much social control being of an informal nature through intimidation, gossip, ridicule, and ostracism. Indeed, those who have spoken about social capital in small places have noted that it can produce forms of 'closure' when members of groups adhere closely to local norms without recourse to legal contracts and, indeed, one of the 'positive' elements of social capital is considered to be rendering formal social controls unnecessary by strengthening informal controls associated with familial or communal structures (Scott & Hogg, 2015). Portes (2000), for example, has identified 'negative' aspects of social capital, which include exclusion of 'outsiders', excess claims of group members, restrictions on individual freedoms, and downward levelling norms. Social capital may be conceived as a product of competing social networks. In this way, small societies considered to possess strong elements of social capital are not necessarily homogenous or stable. Rather, relatively tight social integration in any place may be an outcome of unequal power relations between social groupings, as we have demonstrated here with reference to islands.

Relative isolation and remoteness, along with intimacy and social cohesiveness are considered to stimulate democratic and consensual style politics charged with a spirit of fellowship and community, tolerance, and understanding. Yet, while intimacy can produce bonds of affection, it can also create entrenched antagonisms and hostilities. However, because people who do not like each other are compelled to interact in small-scale societies, antagonism cannot be publicly expressed or displayed (Baldacchino, 2020, p 348). Instead, inhabitants of small-scale societies are compelled to deal with each other on a regular basis while fulfilling differing societal roles. The ubiquity of such relationships may mean that private and professional interaction becomes intertwined and professional interactions may transition to personalized ones and vice versa, which may ultimately result in clientelism, patronage, or nepotism (Baldacchino, 2020, p 348). Islands foster 'in-group' and 'out-group' identities, which revolve around an often-flexible dynamic of 'belonging' (Baldacchino, 2020, p 348). In multi-island and island-mainland units across the globe, jurisdictional and administrative borders are reinforced by geographic conditions, contributing to an 'us vs them' mentality or the formulation of island ethnocentrism or nationalism that threatens state fragmentation (see Bougainville, New Caledonia, Åland, Nevis, and the Solomon Islands) (Baldacchino, 2020, p 348).

III

Much of what we have drawn on here is an extension of what has been called 'rural criminology'. However, we argue here that because of its cultural and ideological baggage, the idea of 'rural criminology' in a neo-colonial era has become anachronistic and the field has itself often played a part in reinforcing dominant cultural constructs of space and existing power-relations. To offer two examples, the strong focus on and association with agriculture has rendered places associated with natural resource extraction relatively invisible to criminological scrutiny. Nonetheless, the criminological impacts of mining are significant. Much mining occurs in regional and remote areas, but rarely have mining communities been a focus of rural criminology, being largely preoccupied as it is with agriculture. This preoccupation can also limit the scope of rural criminology to what have been constructed as 'rural crimes', such as 'farm crime' and to particular social groups who either seem to fit in a rural setting or who have the power to define what is socially problematic in a rural setting. As discussed in preceding chapters, strange and other rurals can be neglected. One such other place, of course, is the space of islands (which also regularly serve as backdrops to extractive mining endeavours, as we canvassed in Chapter 7). Islands are regularly considered remote places, but they are rarely considered 'rural'. We argue, though, that island crime merits analysis in its own right. Importantly, such analyses may help to understand and explain many aspects of crime, including rural *and* urban crime. Rather than championing 'rural criminology', it might be more useful to develop criminolog*ies*, which focus on small-scale societies and/or remote places.

Until recently, rural criminology has neglected racism and colonization. There are numerous reasons for this, including that much of the historic focus of the sub-field was homogenous, white farming communities. Nonetheless, such communities as they exist in the Global North were created at the expense of Indigenous peoples and through genocide, dispossession, and various other crimes (see Chapter 4). Islands were 'ground zero' for the imperialist colonial enterprise, and criminologies of islands cannot ignore the crimes committed to meet these ends. The very process of colonization was criminal, with dispossession/theft of property accompanied by violence, harsh (often forced) labour regimes, economic exploitation, the importation of diseases, and environmental destruction. Among such crimes, the charge of genocide has been levelled at colonizing entities (for example, West Indies and Tasmania), although the term is legally complex. With certainty, humans were trafficked into and out of islands as slaves, and later indentured labourers (Aldrich & Johnson, 2018, pp 161–3), and islanding has served as a technique of erasing Indigenous peoples and cultures the world over (see again Chapter 4).

Initial colonization of islands was motivated by the spice trade, which provided Europe with important culinary and medicinal products which had previously been inaccessible or extremely rare and expensive to import. In the 1600s sugar had become the foremost colonial crop, largely cultivated in the Atlantic. Demand for phosphates (fertilizer) and copra (soap) during the 19th century saw islands exploited in both the Indian and Pacific oceans and resulted in early environmental degradation. Islands have also been sites for mining, such as the Svalbard Islands in the Arctic (coal), Ceylon (gemstones), New Caledonia (nickel), Nauru (phosphate), and Bougainville (copper) in PNG (Aldrich & Johnson, 2018). Yet, Connell observes that qualities such as small land areas, scarce resources, distance, and other factors, limited opportunities for conventional colonial economic development in many islands, especially in the Pacific. Rather, development included penal colonies and later neo-colonial military developments, including nuclear testing sites in places such as Bikini, Marshall, Mururoa, Kwajalein, and Christmas islands, as well as military outposts (Guam, Johnston, Tinian) (Connell, 2003, p 561; Mountz, 2015).

Until recently, rural criminology also neglected green crimes. Islands can be considered at the forefront of green criminology to the extent that they are, among other things, facing an existential crisis, being sites under threat of rising sea levels due to global warming (see Chapter 7). In Pacific and Indian Ocean regions, governments are considering future relocation. Climate-induced sea level rise is the cause of a slow process of environmental migration in Pacific and other islands and, overall, it is expected that human-induced climate change will create more flooding, storm surges, ecosystem change, erosion, and water salinization, which will adversely affect nations and communities. Among the most vulnerable islands are those in Polynesia, Micronesia, and Melanesia in the Pacific Ocean (Perkiss & Moerman, 2018). The small island populations in Kiribati and Tuvalu are especially threatened. Resettlement of 'climate change refugees' has become necessary as rising sea levels claim low-lying islands such as the Marshall Islands, Kiribati, Tuvalu, Tonga, the Federated States of Micronesia and the Cook Islands (in the Pacific Ocean); Antigua and Nevis (in the Caribbean Sea); and the Maldives (in the Indian Ocean) (Royle & Brinklow, 2018). Extreme weather events and sea-level rises have also contributed to coastal erosion on islands and, with it, the destruction of property (Royle & Brinklow, 2018). Rarely, however, have small island communities themselves directly benefited from the extractive capitalism that has been a primary cause of these disastrous environmental outcomes, and which are now threatening the very existence of these same islands.

IV

If it is a discipline, criminology has not been an optimistic one and, like economics, might be regarded as being 'dismal' in character. We have tended to dwell here on the horrific aspects of islands as opposed to the idyllic, commencing with the tragic crimes associated with the Dutch East India Company ship *Batavia*, and including forays into the disastrous and enduring effects upon island peoples and communities of (settler) colonialism, extractive capitalism, and more. As suggested in the Introduction, the *Batavia* tragedy can be likened to the fictional *Lord of the Flies* (1986 [1954]), which we would like to briefly return to now.

Lord of the Flies is regarded as one of the most influential pieces of English literature of the 20th century and its title is a synonym for civil and societal breakdown. It has sold over 10 million copies, has been translated into more than 30 languages, is regularly set as a required text in schools and universities, and was adapted three times for film. Perhaps its most popular legacy has been reality television, with the creator of the original *Survivor* (2000) having paid homage to the book in interviews. The objective of this and a myriad of shows it has spawned is to survive in a remote and isolated location (often island), using only limited and natural resources. Often two teams are pitted against each other.

The inspiration for *Lord of the Flies* came to its author, schoolteacher William Golding, after reading Ballantyne's *The Coral Sea* (1857), which, as recounted earlier in this book, was a classic Victorian account of children marooned on an island. Golding's book is often regarded as having caricatured key themes and characters from Ballantyne's book. Golding, on conceiving the key idea for *Lord of the Flies*, had stated to his wife it would 'be a good idea if I wrote a book about children on an island, children who behave in the way children really would behave'. The book resolutely sides with the Hobbesian view of humanity, the island setting providing an opportunity to strip back the veneer of civilization and expose its fragility. The book might have captured something of a *zeitgeist* of its age, as nature versus nurture debates flourished, the British Empire felt the winds of change, and intellectuals such as Hannah Arendt attempted to understand the 'banality of evil' in the wake of the holocaust.

Rutger Bregman in his book *Humankind* (2019) urges us not to put our faith in Hobbes, but to follow Rousseau and his idyll, which is bound by principles of solidarity and community. Perhaps, shockingly for criminologists, humans, he argues, are at our core 'friendly, peaceful and healthy'. Bregman takes aim at Golding's depiction of schoolboys in a chapter he titles 'The real *Lord of the Flies*'. He recounts that in trying to locate a counter narrative he attempted an internet search using terms such as 'kids shipwrecked' and 'children on an island'. He eventually came across an edition of Australian newspaper, *The Age*, from 1966, with the headline 'Sunday showing for Tongan castaways', referring to a documentary that had been made the same year. The story was about six Tongan boys who had been located three weeks earlier on a rocky islet of 'Ata south of Tonga, then a British protectorate. The boys had been found by an Australian sea captain after being marooned for almost two years. He had been fishing off the island (having not been granted permission by the Tongan King to fish in Tongan waters) which had gained a reputation for having been cursed after its original inhabitants had been captured by slavers almost a hundred years prior. It had long been abandoned and forgotten. But the Australian noticed burnt areas on the islands' high cliffs and cast anchor.

To his amazement six boys aged between 15 and 17, naked and long-haired, swam to his boat. They had been students at a boarding school in the Tongan capital and had been given up for dead almost two years previously when funerals had been held for them. The boys, who had been bored with school, decided to steal a boat from a local fisherman they had disliked. They left Tonga hoping to reach Fiji or New Zealand. They took with them some bananas, coconuts, and a gas burner. None were experienced sailors and, on the first night of their journey, they made the grave error of all falling asleep, only to awaken amid a violent storm, which cast the boat adrift. On the eighth day they reached the 'Ata islet.

After some initial difficulties, they located a good place to set up camp and created a small commune with garden food, tree trunks to store water, chicken pens, and a permanent fire. They also created musical instruments and a gymnasium. The two eldest boys agreed to be leaders: one spiritual and the other practical. They agreed to work in groups of two, setting up rosters for food production and guard duty. If there was disagreement, time-out would be called and protagonists sent to separate ends of the island to cool off, after which they would mutually apologize and agree to stay friends, effectively reconciling any differences. Their days began and ended in song and prayer. The regimen proved efficient, and the boys were deemed to be in excellent physical condition when rescued. But rather than returning home as heroes, they were arrested on their return to the capital for stealing the fishing boat that they had used to reach 'Ata in the first place. However, the boys' rescuer decided to pay the boat owner for his losses and when it was discovered the boys had become international celebrities, the charges were subsequently dropped. And as for the Australian sea captain, he was invited for an audience with the Tongan King, granted permission to fish in Tongan waters, and spent his next three decades living in the islands. He and the eldest boy even went into business together and remained friends for life.

V

> Man produces evil as a bee produces honey.
>
> (William Golding)

Bregman's story seemingly counters Golding's Hobbesian narrative on humanity. But does it really speak to essential aspects of our nature as Bregman would like us to believe? Perhaps, not unlike the *Batavia* tale, which Mike Dash explained with recourse to human psychology, we cannot discount broader cultural contexts, notably here, an understanding of Māori and Pasifika ontologies and epistemologies (Vaioleti, 2006; Airini & Mila-Schaaf, 2010). Despite the diversity of Pacific Islanders, it has been argued that these cultures possess some common features. They are, for instance, typically collectivist, positing a relational self; spirituality is a central dimension of their being, inextricably linked to land, authority, and kinship; and custom consistently features as a traditional system of governance, passed on intergenerationally via oral traditions (Lilomaiava-Doktor, 2004; Suaalii-Sauni & Mavoa, 2009). We can assume that the 'Ata boys, growing up in 1960s Tonga before the challenges to traditional cultures of globalization, understood these traditions. This noted, they were also Christian, so these traditions did not exist sealed off from Western incursions, but islander agency had appropriated aspects of Western culture, such as Christianity and adapted it to local forms of islandism (such as occurred in the Torres Strait Region, discussed earlier). These traditions and ways of belonging are often at odds with Western cultures' emphasis on individualism, but Māori and Pasifika peoples believe themselves to exist only in relation to others (the relational-self) as opposed to the construct of self as existing independent of any other. The philosophy of *teu le va* means to value, nurture, and maintain social and sacred relationship spaces (Anae, 2010). It provides a framework for belonging and connectedness where people are intimately linked to others and their surrounding environment. These relationships are – in theory – meaningful, reciprocal, and respectful.

And it is here that we might wonder what we can learn from island cultures. As places, islands are situated on the periphery of peripheries. The smallest and remotest are viewed as fragile and dependent places, their value to the centre typically considered in terms of consumption. Islands, both in terms of place and space, can inform critical criminologies and form part of a criminology that challenges urban and cosmopolitan bias. On one level, island criminologies might be concerned with islands as places and analyse how crime problems are constructed and interpreted in island locales through the prism of islandness. On another level, a spatial criminology of islands might examine how the island geographies produce distinctive social networks, particular normative structures, and distinct forms of social control.

At the crux of these projects is an understanding of power structures, in terms of island societies and at a broader geo-political level. This attention to the space and place of islands in criminology is timely, given the relatively recent interest in Southern, Indigenous, and decolonizing criminologies, which similarly involve a shift away from the metropole.

What has preceded here are the first tentative steps towards finding a place for islands in a criminology informed by ecology, which we use here to refer to the relationship between people and the environment of a place. In proffering a spatial criminology of islands, we contend that the places and spaces of islands provide us with an opportunity to re-examine how fundamental concepts for understanding crime and regulation, such as social integration, community, and belonging, as well as exclusion and othering, are practised in the (seemingly) often closed and bounded networks of island ecologies. Although the cases and examples we deploy in this book go some way towards testing and stretching our understandings of crime and social regulation in relation to islands, more work is needed. Indeed, islands are not only complex and multi-layered localities, they are also dynamic, morphing both physically (for instance, with the continued ebb and flow of waters eroding the liminal space of the island beach/boundary) and conceptually (with, as Baldacchino [2016, p 97] puts it, their nature morphing 'into shady and fuzzy layers of stricture'). In these ways, islands – and indeed, island criminologies – continue to demand greater attention into the future. It is our hope that others will join with us to take up this task.

Notes

Introduction
1. See here: https://visit.museum.wa.gov.au/shipwrecks/batavia-gallery

Chapter 3
1. A Western conceptualization of sovereignty that disregards, for example, the unceded sovereignties of colonized groups the world over – a point we expand on in Chapter 5.
2. In *Discipline and Punish*, Foucault (1975) also argued that different diseases had been managed differently over time, demonstrating shifts in the way that power was mobilized and manifested. He stated, 'If it is true that the leper gave rise to rituals of exclusion, which to a certain extent provided the model for and general form of the great Confinement, then the plague gave rise to disciplinary projects. Rather than the massive, binary division between one set of people and another, it called for multiple separations, individualizing distributions, an organization in depth of surveillance and control, an intensification and a ramification of power … the great confinement on the one hand; the correct training on the other. The leper and his separation; the plague and its segmentations.' (Foucault, 1975, p 198)

Chapter 4
1. Creation in this sense cannot, however, be conceptualized as a fixed point in time like in Western ontology; it is instead, ongoing and ever-existing in a non-linear, circular sense (Yunkaporta, 2019).
2. Anderson (2018: 12) argues, though, that execution continued to be used as a frequent form of punishment *within* the New South Wales penal colony, indicating that 'transportation did not entirely replace the death sentence as a "spectacle of suffering", but incorporated it'.
3. Of course, these large stretches of desert *had* been skilfully inhabited by Indigenous peoples for millennia.
4. The definition of 'mimini' shown in square brackets here is drawn from Amery (2016, p 96).

Chapter 5
1. All interviewees referred to in this chapter participated in an Australian Institute of Criminology-funded project entitled *Crime and Justice in the Torres Strait Region*, which was undertaken by Scott, Staines, & Morton (2021) in 2018–19. The study is published in full here: https://www.aic.gov.au/crg/reports/crg-2416-17

Chapter 6

1. This is similar to the notion of *dem tull* gossip on Norfolk Island, which Latham (2006, p 81) described as an 'insidious thing that appears to undermine everything and ... [lay] a foundation of both fact and fiction on the Island'.

Chapter 7

1. The ancient Greek and Romans, for instance, assigned hard labour to slaves and 'scorned free people who did it' (Lipset, 1990: 62).
2. For example, the *UN Refugee Convention* (1951) and *UN Protocol Relating to the Status of Refugees* (1967), to which Australia became a party in 1954 and 1973, respectively. For a list of *UN Refugee Convention* (1951) participants, see: https://www.unhcr.org/en-au/5d9ed32b4; for a list of UN *Protocol Relating to the Status of Refugees* (1967) participants, see: https://www.unhcr.org/en-au/5d9ed66a4.
3. In relation to gold-mining operations in Ghana, for instance, Garvin et al (2009: 579) explained that interviews with community members and miners (n = 30) across three separate communities indicated: 'negative impacts on land tenure, security and crime, and in some cases culture. ... In terms of cultural values, members in Communities A and B believed the mining developments disrupted social norms and noted a decrease in the sense of community, family ties, strict observance of some social norms, and traditional respect for the elderly. They also identified a rise in unacceptable criminal behaviour such as prostitution and theft, and attributed these to the in-migration of a new population as well as a shift towards a monetary economy.'

    Prior to the advancement of mining in these three communities, all had small largely localized economies, consisting of agriculture and animal husbandry, small trading, small-scale mining, and gin distilling. Thus, the magnitude of social economic change that came with the transition to large-scale mining was significant (Garvin et al, 2009). Moreover, although mining promised to advance the social economic interests of the communities, and did in some ways (for example, through the partial improvement of health care and education infrastructure), most of the employment in the mines went to non-locals and the loss of arable land because of the mine meant that those who had previously used the land for subsistence and/or as an economic resource could no longer do so. This has also been found in other studies (for example, Kumah, 2006). In turn, this meant that – as was the case for Nauru and Bougainville – economic benefits flowed *away* from the communities to outsiders, including corporations, government, and outsider employees. Thus, in contrast to promises made by mining companies, the ground-level experience has often involved family disintegration, displacement from lands, environmental degradation, and *increased* economic strain.

References

Adamo, A. (2018) 'A cursed and fragmented island: history and conflict analysis in Bougainville, Papua New Guinea', *Small Wars & Insurgencies*, 29(1): 164–86.

Agamben, G. (2005) *State of Exception*, Chicago, IL: University of Chicago Press.

Agozino, B. (2003) *Counter-Colonial Criminology: A Critique of Imperialist Reason*, London: Pluto Press.

Agozino, B. (2018) 'The withering away of the law: an Indigenous perspective on the decolonisation of the criminal justice system and criminology', *Journal of Global Indigeneity*, 3(1): 1–22.

Agozino, B. (2019) 'Humanifesto of the decolonization of criminology and criminal justice', *Decolonization of Criminology and Justice*, 1(1): 5–28.

Aguirre, H. (2019) '"The girls were just so young": the horrors of Jeffrey Epstein's private island', *Vanity Fair*, 20 July.

Airini, A.M. and Mila-Schaaf, K. (2010) *Teu Le Va - Relationships across Research and Policy in Pasifika Education*, Auckland: Uniservices.

Albuquerque, K. and McElroy, J. (1999) 'Tourism and crime in the Caribbean', *Annals of Tourism Research*, 26(4): 968–84.

Aldrich, R. and Johnson, M. (2018) 'History and colonisation', in G. Baldacchino (ed) *The Routledge International Handbook of Island Studies: A World of Islands*, Abingdon, Oxon: Routledge, pp 153–72.

Altman, I. and Low, S.M. (1992) 'Place Attachment', in I. Altman and S.M. Low (eds) *Place Attachment. Human Behavior and Environment (Advances in Theory and Research)*, vol 12, Boston, MA: Springer, pp 1–12.

Altman, J. (2018) 'Raphael Lemkin in remote Australia: the logic of cultural genocide and homelands', *Oceania*, 88(3): 336–59.

Amery, R. (2016) *Warraparna Kaurna! Reclaiming an Australian Language*, Adelaide: University of Adelaide Press.

Amin, S., Girard, C., and Watson, D. (2020) 'Security, resilience and resistance in the PICs: Aligning priorities and relocating responsibility', in S. Amin, D. Watson, and Girard, C. (eds) *Mapping Security in the Pacific: A Focus on Context, Gender and Organisational Culture*, Abingdon, Oxon: Routledge, pp 231–43.

Amnesty International (2016) *Island of Despair: Australia's 'Processing' of Refugees on Nauru*, London: Amnesty International.

Amoamo, M. (2011) 'Remoteness and myth making: tourism development on Pitcairn Island', *Tourism Planning and Development*, 8(1): 1–19.

Amoamo, M. (2012) 'Fieldwork in remote communities: an ethnographic case study of Pitcairn Island. Field guide to case study research in tourism, hospitality and leisure', *Advances in Culture, Tourism and Hospitality Research*, 6: 417–38.

Amoamo, M. (2013) 'Empire and erasure: a case study of Pitcairn Island', *Island Studies Journal*, 8(2): 233–54.

Anae, M.S. (2010) *Research for Better Pacific Schooling in New Zealand: Teu le va – a Samoan Perspective. Mai Review: Special Issue. Pacific Research in Education: New Directions*, Auckland: Nga Pae o te Maramatanga, University of Auckland.

Anderson, B. (1991) *Imagined Communities: Reflections on the Origin and Spread of Nationalism*, London: Verso.

Anderson, C. (2018) *A Global History of Convicts and Penal Colonies*, Bloomsbury Academic: London.

Anderson, W. (2005) *The Cultivation of Whiteness: Science, Health and Racial Destiny in Australia*, Carlton: Melbourne University Press.

Andreas, P. and Biersteker, T. (2003) *The Rebordering of North America: Integration and Exclusion in a New Security Context*, New York: Routledge.

Anthony, T. and Baldry, E. (2017) 'Are first Australians the most imprisoned people on Earth?', *The Conversation*, 6 June.

Antonisch, L. (2010) 'Searching for belonging: an analytical framework', *Geography Compass*, 4(6): 644–59.

Archibald-Binge, E. and Wyman, R. (2020) ' "Is this Australia?": hundreds in hiding after fleeing Aurukun riots', *Brisbane Times*, 14 February.

Armstrong, S. and Jefferson, A. (2017) 'Disavowing "the" prison', in D. Moran and A. Schliehe (eds) *Carceral Spatiality: Dialogues Between Geography and Criminology,* London: Palgrave Macmillan, pp 237–62.

Australian Human Rights Commission (AHRC) (1997) *Bringing Them Home*, Canberra: AHRC.

Australian Law Reform Commission (ALRC) (2018) *Pathways to Justice*, Canberra: ALRC.

Baldacchino, G. (2004) 'Island studies comes of age', *Tijdschrift voor Economische en Sociale Geografie (Journal of Economic and Social Geography)*, 95(3): 272–83.

Baldacchino, G. (2007) 'Introduction', in G. Baldacchino (ed) *A World of Islands: An Island Studies Reader*, Charlottetown, PEI: University of Prince Edward Island, Institute of Island Studies.

Baldacchino, G. (2012) 'Islands and despots', *Commonwealth & Comparative Politics*, 50(1): 103–20, DOI: 10.1080/14662043.2012.642119

Baldacchino, G. (2016) 'Going missing: islands, incarceration and disappearance', *Political Geography*, 51: 97–9.
Baldacchino, G. (2020) 'A psychology of islanders?', in Pine, R. and Konidari, V. (eds) *Islands of the Mind: Psychology, Literature and Biodiversity*, Newcastle-upon-Tyne: Cambridge Scholars Press, pp 1–13.
Baldacchino, G. and Royle, S. (2010) 'Postcolonialism and islands: introduction', *Space & Culture*, 13(2): 140–3.
Ballantyne, R. (2013 [1858]) *The Coral Island: A Tale of the Pacific Ocean*, New York: Hesperus Press.
Ballantyne, T. (2014) 'Mobility, empire, colonisation', *History Australia*, 11(2): 7–37.
Ballard, C. and Banks, G. (2003) 'Resource wars: the anthropology of mining', *Annual Review of Anthropology*, 32: 287–313.
Bambrick, H. (2018) 'Resource extractivism, health and climate change in small islands', *International Journal of Climate Change Strategies and Management*, 10(2): 272–88.
Barrington, R. (2015) 'Unravelling the Yamajhi imaginings of Alexander Morton and Daisy Bates', *Aboriginal History*, 39: 27–61.
Bashford, A. (2003) *Imperial Hygiene*, New York: Palgrave Macmillan.
Bates, D. (1944) *The Passing of the Aborigines*, Melbourne: Oxford University Press.
Baudrillard, J. (1981) *Simulacra and Simulation*, Michigan: University of Michigan Press.
Bauman, Z. (1999) *Liquid Modernity*, London: John Wiley & Sons.
Bayley, R. (1989) 'Community policing in Australia', in D. Chappell and P. Wilson (eds) *Australian Policing*, Sydney: Butterworths, pp 63–82.
Becker, H. (1963) *Outsiders: Studies in the Sociology of Deviance*, New York: The Free Press.
Beckett, J. (1977) 'The Torres Strait Islanders and the pearling industry', *Aboriginal History*, 1(1): 77–104.
Bell, D. (1997) 'Anti-idyll: rural horror', in P. Cloke and J. Little (eds) *Contested Countryside Cultures: Otherness, Marginalisation and Rurality*, London: Routledge, pp 94–108.
Bell, D. (2006) 'Variations on the rural idyll', in P. Cloke, T. Marsden, and P. Mooney (eds) *Handbook of Rural Studies*, London: Sage, pp 149–60.
Benedict, B. (1967) 'Sociological aspects of smallness', in B. Benedict (ed) *Problems of Smaller Territories*, London: Athlone Press, pp 45–55.
Bennett, N., Whitty, T., Finkbeiner, E., Pittman, J., Bassett, H., Gelcich, S., and Allison, E. (2018) 'Environmental stewardship: a conceptual review and analytical framework', *Environmental Management*, 61: 597–614.
Birkett, D. (1997) *Serpent in Paradise*, London: Picador.
Block, A. and Klausner, P. (1987) 'Masters of Paradise Island: organized crime, neoliberalism and the Bahamas', *Dialectical Anthropology*, 24: 85–102.

Borowski, A. (2017) 'Landscapes of prison islands in the sociological perspective', *World News of Natural Sciences*, 6: 52–63.

Bourdieu, P. (1986) 'The forms of capital', in J. Richardson (ed) *Handbook of Research and Theory for Sociology of Education*, New York: Greenwood Press, pp 241–58.

Bradshaw, C., Norman, K., Ulm, S., Williams, A., Clarkson, C., et al (2021) 'Stochastic models support rapid peopling of Late Pleistocene Sahul', *Nature Communications*, 12(2440): 1–11.

Braithwaite, J. (1989) *Crime, Shame and Reintegration*, Cambridge: Cambridge University Press.

Bray, G. (1930) 'The story of leprosy at Nauru', *Proceedings of the Royal Society of Medicine*, 23(9): 1370–4.

Bregman, R. (2019) *Humankind*, London: Bloomsbury

Breidenbach, C., Frohler, T., Pensel, D., Simon, K., Telsnig, F., and Wittmann, M. (eds) (2020) *Narrating and Constructing the Beach: An Interdisciplinary Approach*, Boston: De Gruyter.

Broadfield, K., Dawes, G., and Chong, M. (2021) 'Necropolitics and the violence of Indigenous incarceration', *Decolonization of Criminology and Justice*, 3(1): 5–26.

Brown, C. (2015) 'Tourism, crime and risk perception: an examination of broadcast media's framing of negative Aruban sentiment in the Natalee Holloway case and its impact on tourism demand', *Tourism Management Perspectives*, 16: 266–77.

Bruny Island Community Association (nd) *Bruny Island Quarantine Station*. Available: https://www.bica.org.au/brunyquarantinestation

Bull, M., George, N., and Curth-Bibb, J. (2019) 'The virtues of strangers? Policing gender violence in Pacific Island countries', *Policing and Society*, 29(2): 155–70.

Bunker, S.G. (2005) 'How ecologically uneven developments put the spin on the treadmill of production', *Organization & Environment*, 18(1): 38–54.

Bursik, R.J. and Grasmick, H.G. (1993) *Neighborhoods and Crime: The Dimensions of Effective Community Control*, Lanham, MD: Lexington Books.

Cao, A.N. and Wyatt, T. (2016) 'The conceptual compatibility between green criminology and human security: a proposed interdisciplinary framework for examinations into green victimisation', *Critical Criminology*, 24: 413–30.

Carden, C. (2017) '"As parents congregated at parties": responsibility and blame in media representations of violence and school closure in an Indigenous community', *Journal of Sociology*, 53(3): 592–606.

Carrington, K. (2007) 'Crime in rural and regional areas', in E. Barclay, J. Donnermeyer, J. Scott, and R. Hogg (eds) *Crime in Rural Australia*, Sydney: The Federation Press, pp 27–43.

Carrington, K., Hogg, R., and Sozzo, M. (2016) 'Southern criminology', *The British Journal of Criminology*, 56(1) January: 1–20, https://doi.org/10.1093/bjc/azv083

Carrington, K., Hogg, R., McIntosh, A., and J. Scott (2009) *Intentional Violence – Suicide, Homicide, Assault, Sexual Assault, Family Violence, Child Abuse, Harassment and Stalking, Alcohol-related Violence, Animal Abuse, Data Report No. 2. Safeguarding Rural Australia: Addressing Masculinity and Violence in Rural Settings*, Brisbane: Queensland University of Technology,.

Castells, M. (2000) *The Rise of the Network, Volume 3 of The Information Age: Economy, Society and Culture*, Oxford: Blackwell.

Chandler, J. (2014) *Violence Against Women in PNG: How Men Are Getting Away with Murder*, Sydney: Lowy Institute for International Policy.

Cherney, A. and Chui, W. (2010) 'Police auxiliaries in Australia: police liaison officers and the dilemmas of being part of the police extended family', *Policing and Society*, 20(3): 280–97, DOI: 10.1080/10439463.2010.50528

Chesney-Lind, M. and Lind, I. (1986) 'Visitors as victims: Crimes against tourists in Hawaii', *Annals of Tourism Research*, 13(2): 167–91.

Christie, A. (1941) *Evil Under the Sun*, London: Collins Crime Club.

Chuhan-Pole, P., Dabalen, A., and Land, B. (2017) 'Mining in Africa: are local communities better off?', Washington, DC: Africa Development Forum. Available: https://openknowledge.worldbank.org/handle/10986/26110

Claudino-Sales, V. (2018) *Coastal World Heritage Sites*, Dordrecht: Springer.

Clements, N. (2014) 'Tasmania's Black War: a tragic case of lest we remember?', *The Conversation*, 24 April.

Cohen, M. and Felson, M. (1979) 'Social change and crime trends: a routine activity approach', *American Sociological Review*, 44: 588–608.

Coleman, J. (1988) 'Social capital in the creation of human capital', *American Journal of Sociology*, 94: 95–120.

Commonwealth of Australia (2010) The Senate, Foreign Affairs, Defence and Trade References Committee. *The Torres Strait: Bridge and Border.* Senate Printing Unit, Parliament House, Canberra. Downloaded 28 July 2021. Available: https://www.aph.gov.au/Parliamentary_Business/Committees/Senate/Foreign_Affairs_Defence_and_Trade/Completed_inquiries/2010-13/torresstrait/report/c08

Conkling, P. (2007) 'On islanders and islandness', *Geographical Review*, 97(2): 191–201.

Connell, J. (2003) 'Island dreaming: the contemplation of Polynesian paradise', *Journal of Historical Geography*, 29(4): 554–81.

Connell, R. (2007) *Southern Theory: The Global Dynamics of Knowledge in Social Science*, Cambridge: Polity Press.

Cook, J. (2014) [1770] *Captain Cook's Journal During his First Voyage Round the World, Made in H.M. Bark Endeavour, 1768–71*, Cambridge: Cambridge University Press.

Coorey, L. (1990) 'Domestic violence in rural areas', in M. Alston (ed) *Rural Women: Key Papers*, No. 1, Wagga Wagga: Centre for Rural and Remote Research, pp 12–42.

Crane R. and Fletcher, L. (2016) 'The genre of islands: popular fiction and performative geographies', *Island Studies Journal*, 11(2) : 637–50.

Crenshaw, K. (2011) 'Twenty years of critical race theory', *Connecticut Law Review*, 43(5): 1253–1353.

Crook, M., Short, D., and South, N. (2018) 'Ecocide, genocide, capitalism and colonialism: consequences for indigenous peoples and global ecosystems environments', *Theoretical Criminology*, 22(3): 298–317.

Cruickshank, J. and Grimshaw, P. (2015) 'I had gone to teach but stayed to learn', *Journal of Australian Studies*, 39(1): 54–65.

Cunneen, C. (1992) 'Policing and Aboriginal communities', *Aboriginal Perspectives on Criminal Justice*. Institute of Criminal Justice, Monograph Series No. 1, Canberra: 76–92.

Cunneen, C. and Tauri, J. (2016) *Indigenous Criminology*, Bristol: Policy Press.

Dash, M. (2002) *Batavia's Graveyard*, New York: Crown Publishers.

Davidson, H. (2018) 'Australia jointly responsible for Nauru's draconian media policy, documents reveal', *The Guardian*, 4 October. Available: https://www.theguardian.com/australia-news/2018/oct/04/australia-jointly-responsible-for-naurus-draconian-media-policy-documents-reveal

Defoe, W. (1719) *The Life and Strange Surprising Adventures of Robinson Crusoe*, London: William Taylor.

DeKeseredy, W. and Schwartz, M. (2009) *Dangerous Exits: Escaping Abusive Relationships in Rural America*, New Brunswick, NJ: Rutgers University Press.

Department of Aboriginal and Torres Strait Islander Partnerships (DATSIP) (2017) *Annual Bulletin for Queensland's Discrete Indigenous Communities*, Brisbane, Australia.

Department of Tourism in the West (2021) *Australia's Coral Coast*, Perth, Western Australia. Available: https://www.australiascoralcoast.com/destination/abrolhos-islands

Deveraux, C. (2014) 'Hysteria, feminism and gender revisited: the case of the second wave', *English Studies in Canada*, 40(1): 19–45.

Dinnen, S. and Braithwaite, J. (2009) 'Reinventing policing through the prism of the colonial kiap', *Policing & Society*, 19(2): 161–73, DOI: 10.1080/10439460802187571

Dinnen, S. and McLeod, A. (2009) 'Policing Melanesia – international expectations and local realities', *Policing & Society*, 19(4): 333–53, DOI: 10.1080/10439460903281539

Dinnen, S. and Walton, G. (2016) 'Politics, organised crime and corruption in the Pacific', *State, Society & Governance in Melanesia*, 24: 1–2. Available: https://openresearch-repository.anu.edu.au/bitstream/1885/142716/1/ib-2016-24-dinnenwalton.pdf

Dinnen, S., Jowitt, A., and Newton, T. (2003) 'A kind of mending restorative justice in the Pacific Islands', in S. Dinnen, A. Jowitt, and T. Newton Cain, (eds) *A Kind of Mending: Restorative Justice in the Pacific Islands*. Canberra, ACT: Pandanus Books.

Dodds, K. and Royle, S. (2003) 'The historical geography of islands: rethinking islands', *Journal of Historical Geography*, 29(4): 487–98.

Douglas, M. (1992) [1966] *Purity and Danger: An Analysis of Concepts of Pollution and Taboo*, London: Routledge.

Dudgeon, P. and Bray, A. (2019) 'Indigenous relationality: women, kinship and the law', *Genealogy*, 3(23): 1–11.

Duncan, B., Gibbs, M., and Sonnemann, T. (2013) 'Searching for the yellow fleet: an archaeological and remote sensing investigation of the prison hulk wrecks *Deborah* and *Sacramento*', *Bulletin of the Australasian Institute for Maritime Archaeology*, 37: 66–75.

Durkheim, E. (2006) [1897] *On Suicide*, London: Penguin Books.

Dvorak, G. (2020) 'Resisting the tides: responding to nuclear and environmental "insecurity" in the Marshall Islands,' in S. Amin, D. Watson, and C. Girard (eds) *Mapping Security in the Pacific: A Focus on Context, Gender, and Organisational Culture*, London: Routledge, pp 41–58.

Dwyer, A., Scott, J., and Staines, Z. (2020) 'Strangers in a strange land: police perceptions of working in discrete Indigenous communities in Queensland, Australia', *Police Practice & Research: an International Journal*, 22(1): 208–24.

Edge, A. (2000) *The Company*, Sydney: Picador.

Elias, N. and Scotson, J. (1994) *The Established and the Outsiders: A Sociological Enquiry into Community Problems*, London: Sage.

Ens, E., Scott, M., Rangers, Y.M., Moritz, C., and Pirzl, R. (2016) 'Putting Indigenous conservation policy into practice delivers biodiversity and cultural benefits', *Biodiversity Conservation*, 25: 2889–906.

Erikson, K.T. (1962) 'Notes on the sociology of deviance', *Social Problems*, 9: 307–14.

Farran, S. (2007) 'The case of Pitcairn: a small island, many questions', *Journal of South Pacific Law*, 11(2): 124–50.

Ferdon, E. (1958) 'Pitcairn Island', *Geographical Review*, 48(1): 69–85.

Feyrer, J. and Sacerdote, B. (2009) 'Colonialism and modern income: islands as natural experiments', *The Review of Economics and Statistics*, 91(2): 245–62.

Firth, S. (1978) 'German labour policy in Nauru and Angaur, 1906–1914', *Journal of Pacific History*, 13(1): 36–52.

Fletcher, L. (2008) 'Reading the news: Pitcairn at the beginning of the 21st century', *Island Studies Journal*, 3(1): 57–72.

Fletcher, L.M. (2011) '"Some distance to go...": a critical survey of island studies', *New Literatures Review*, 47–8: 17–34.
Flood, M. and Hamilton, C. (2005) *Mapping Homophobia in Australia*, Australia Institute for a Just Sustainable, Peaceful Future. Available: http://www.tai.org.au/documents/downloads/WP79.pdf
Foucault, M. (1967) *Madness and Civilization*, London: Tavistock Publications.
Foucault, M. (1977) *Language, Counter-Memory, Practice*, Cornell: Cornell University Press.
Foucault, M. (1979) *Discipline and Punish*, New York: Vintage Books.
Foucault, M. (1980) *Power/Knowledge: Selected Interviews and Other Writings*, New York: Pantheon Books.
Foucault, M. (2004) *Society Must Be Defended*, London: Penguin.
Foucault, M. (2006) [1962] *History of Madness*, Oxford: Routledge.
Frankland, K. (1994) *A Brief History of Government Administration of Aboriginal and Torres Strait Islander Peoples in Queensland*, Brisbane: Queensland Government.
Gale, S. (2016) 'The mined-out phosphate lands of Nauru, equatorial western Pacific', *Australian Journal of Earth Sciences*, 63(3): 333–47.
Gardner, L. and Shoemaker, D. (1989) 'Social bonding and delinquency: a comparative analysis', *The Sociological Quarterly*, 30(3): 481–99.
Garland, D. (1996) 'The limits of the sovereign state: strategies of crime control in contemporary society', *The British Journal of Criminology*, 36(4): 445–71, https://doi.org/10.1093/oxfordjournals.bjc.a014105
Garvin, T., McGee, T., Smoyer-Tomic, K., and Aubynn, E. (2009) 'Community-company relations in gold mining in Ghana', *Journal of Environmental Management*, 90(1): 571–86.
Gelder, K. and Jacobs, J. (1995) 'Uncanny Australia', *Ecumene*, 2(2): 171–83.
Gelderblom, O., De Jong, A., and Jonker, J. (2013) 'The formative years of the modern corporation: the Dutch East India Company VOC, 1602–1623', *The Journal of Economic History*, 73(4): 1050–76.
Goffman, E. (1961) *Asylums: Essays on the Social Situation of Mental Patients and Other Inmates*, New York: Anchor Books.
Goldie, M. (2011) 'Island theory: the Antipodes', in M. McCusker and A. Soares (eds) *Cross Cultures (Island Identities: Constructions of Postcolonial Cultural Insularities)*, 139: 1–40.
Golding, W. (1986) [1954] *Lord of the Flies*, Basingstoke, Hampshire: Macmillan Education.
Grant, K. (2007) '31 people charged in Aurukun riots', *Living Black*, 26 September.
Greenop, K. and Memmmott, P. (2013) 'Aboriginal identity and place in the intercultural settings of metropolitan Australia', in E.J. Peters and C. Andersen (eds) *Indigenous in the City: Contemporary Identities and Cultural Innovation*, Vancouver: UBC Press, pp 256–81.

Hay, P. (2006) 'A phenomenology of islands', *Island Studies Journal*, 1(1): 19–42. Available: https://gateway.library.qut.edu.au/login?url=https://www.proquest.com/scholarly-journals/phenomenology-islands/docview/1953354918/se-2?accountid=13380

Harris, C. (2004) 'How did colonialism dispossess? Comments from an edge of empire', *Annals of the Association of American Geographers*, 94(1): 165–82.

Harrison, J. (2013) '"Adopting a regular system of prison discipline": Moreton Bay and 1820s penal settlements in the "plan of punishment"', *Queensland History Journal*, 21(12): 809–18.

Harvey, C. (2004) 'Where underage sex is "like food"'. *The Australian*, 29 September, 1.

Hasan, M. (2017) *Reading Death in Paradise: Revisiting Polysemy in Televisual Pleasure*, Master's thesis, Faculty of Education, Media Education: University of Lapland.

Hayward, K. (2004) 'Space – the final frontier: criminology, the city and the spatial dynamics of exclusion', in J. Ferrell, K. Hayward, W. Morrison, and M. Presdee (eds) *Cultural Criminology Unleashed*, London: Glass House Press, pp 1–14.

Hodgkinson, T., Gately, N., McCue J., Shuhad, A., Corrado R., and Andresen, M. (2017) 'Fear of crime in an island paradise: examining the generalizability of key theoretical constructs in the Maldivian context', *International Criminal Justice Review*, 27(2): 108–25.

Hogg, R. and Carrington, K. (2006) *Policing the Rural Crisis*, Sydney: Federation Press.

Hogg, R. and Brown, D. (2018) 'Rethinking penal modernism from the Global South: the case of convict transportation to Australia', in K. Carrington, R. Hogg, J. Scott, and M. Sozzo (eds) *The Palgrave Handbook of Criminology and the Global South*, Switzerland: Springer, pp 751–74.

Hogg, R. and Scott, J. (2023) 'Masculinity, sexuality and violence in the Australian convict colonies', in R. Ricciardello and T. Bartlett (eds) *Prison Masculinities*, Abingdon, Oxon: Routledge, pp 1–19.

Holley, C., Shearing, C., Harrington, C., Kennedy, A., and Mutongwizo, T. (2018) 'Environmental security and the Anthropocene: law, criminology, and international relations', *Annual Review of Law and Social Science*, 14: 185–203.

Holt, L. (2006) 'History, honesty, whiteness and blackness', keynote paper presented at *Historicising Whiteness Conference,* University of Melbourne, November 22–26.

Howard, J. (1997) Interview with the Prime Minister, John Howard. *Face to Face* (Seven Network), 18 May.

Howard, J. and Brough, M. (2007) *Transcript of Prime Minister Hon John Howard MP joint press conference with Hon Mal Brough, Minister for Families, Community Services and Indigenous Affairs*. Canberra: Australian Government.

Hughes, R. (1987) *The Fatal Shore*, New York: Alfred A Knopf:.

Human Rights Watch (2021) 'Australia: 8 years of abusive offshore asylum processing.' Available: https://www.hrw.org/news/2021/07/15/australia-8-years-abusive-offshore-asylum-processing

Inglis, K. (2017) '*Nā hoa o ka pilikia* (friends of affliction): a sense of community in the Molokai Leprosy Settlement of 19th century Hawai'i', *The Journal of Pacific History*, 52(3): 287–301.

Jackson, R. (1988) 'Luxury in punishment: Jeremy Bentham on the cost of the convict colony in New South Wales', *Australian Historical Studies*, 23(90): 42–59.

James, E. (2013) 'The Norwegian prison where inmates are treated like people,' *The Guardian*, 25 February.

Jedrusik, M. (2011) 'Island studies, island geography. But what is an island?', *Miscellanea Geographica*, 15: 201–12.

Jenkins, R. (2014) *Social Identity*, London: Routledge.

Jewkes, R., Sikweyiya, Y., and Jama-Shai, N. (2014) 'The challenges of research on violence in post-conflict Bougainville', *The Lancet*, 383(9934): 2039–40.

Jewkes, R., Jama-Shai, N., and Sikweyiya, Y. (2017) 'Enduring impact of conflict on mental health and gender-based violence perpetration in Bougainville, Papua New Guinea: a cross-sectional study', *PLoS One*, 12(10). DOI: 10.1371/journal.pone.0186062

Jobes, P.C. (2002) 'Effective officer and good neighbour: problems and perceptions among police in rural Australia', *Policing: An International Journal of Police Strategies and Management*, 25(2): 256–73.

John, S., Papyrakis, E., and Tasciotti, L. (2020) 'Is there a resource curse in Timor-Leste? A critical review of recent evidence', *Development Studies Research*, 7(1): 141–52.

Jolly, M. (2003) 'Epilogue – some thoughts on restorative justice and gender', in S. Dinnen, A. Jowitt, and T. Newton Cain (eds) *A Kind of Mending: Restorative Justice in the Pacific Islands*, Canberra, ACT: Pandanus Books.

Karagiannis, N. and Zagros Madjd-Sadjadi, Z. (2012) 'Crime, criminal activity and tourism performance: issues from the Caribbean Worldwide Hospitality and Tourism', *Themes*, 4(1): 73–90.

Keegan, W. and Diamond, J. (1987) 'Colonization of islands by humans: a biogeographical perspective', *Advances in Archaeological Method and Theory*, 10: 49–92.

Klein, N. (2015) *This Changes Everything*, Melbourne: Penguin Press.

Kolodzjejski, A. (2014) *Connecting People and Place: Sense of Place and Local Action*, School of Environment, Education and Development: Planning and Environmental Management, Faculty of Humanities, Manchester: University of Manchester.

Kristeva, J. (1982) *Powers of Horror: An Essay on Abjection*, New York: Columbia University Press.

Kumah, A. (2006) 'Sustainability and gold mining in the developing world', *Journal of Cleaner Production*, 14: 315–23.

Lambert, D. (2018) 'Owning the science: the power of partnerships', *Griffith Review, First Things First* (60). Available: https://www.griffithreview.com/articles/owning-science-power-partnership-mungo-dna/

La Nauze, H. and Rutherford, S. (1997) 'Women's work against violence, community responses in a rural setting', *Women Against Violence*, 2: 14–21.

Latham, T. (2006) 'Norfolk Island: history and mystery', *Sydney Papers*, 18(1): 78–86.

Lauritsen, A. (ed) (2019) *Crime and Crime Control in Four Nordic Island Societies: The Faroe Islands, Greenland, Iceland and the Aland Islands*, Aarhus, Denmark: Scandinavian Research Council for Criminology.

Lea, T. (2020) *Wild Policy*, California: Stanford University Press.

Leipins, R., (2000) 'Making men: the construction and representation of agriculture-based masculinities in Australia and New Zealand', *Rural Sociology*, 65: 605–20.

Lennon, J. (2008) 'Port Arthur, Norfolk Island, New Caledonia: convict prison islands in the Antipodes,' in W. Logan and K. Reeves (eds) *Places of Pain and Shame: Dealing with 'Difficult Heritage'*, Sydney: Taylor & Francis Group, pp 165–81.

Leunig, T., van Lottum, J., and Poulsen, B. (2018) 'Surprisingly gentle confinement: British treatment of Danish and Norwegian prisoners of war during the Napoleonic wars', *Scandinavian Economic History Review*, 66(3): 282–97.

Lilomaiava-Doktor, S.I. (2004) *Fa'aSamoa and Population Movement from the Inside Out: The Case of Salelologa, Savai'i*, Doctor of Philosophy, University of Hawai'i.

Lindbergh, A. (2012) *Against Wind and Tide: Letters and Journals, 1947–1986*, New York: Pantheon.

Liu, J. (2004) 'Subcultural values, crime and negative social capital for Chinese offenders'. *International Criminal Justice Review*, 14: 49–68.

Loader, I. Girling and R. Sparks. (2000) *Crime and Social Change in Middle England*, London: Routledge.

Lockie, S. (2001) 'Rural sociological perspectives and problems: a sociological history,' in S. Lockie and L. Bourke (eds) *Rurality Bites: The Social and Environmental Transformation of Rural Australia*, Annandale, NSW: Pluto Press, pp 17–29.

Lynch, M. (1990) 'The greening of criminology: a perspective for the 1990s', *The Critical Criminologist*, 2(3): 3–4, 11–12.

Lynch, M., Stretesky, P., and Long, M. (2018) 'Green criminology and native peoples: the treadmill of production and the killing of indigenous environmental activists', *Theoretical Criminology*, 22(3): 318–41.

Macklin, R. (2013) *Dark Paradise: Norfolk Island—Isolation, Savagery, Mystery and Murder*, Sydney: Hachette Australia.

Maclellan, N. (2013) 'What has Australia done to Nauru?', *Overland Journal*, online. Available: https://overland.org.au/previous-issues/issue-212/feature-nic-maclellan/

Maglen, K. (2003) 'Politics of quarantine in the 19th century', *Journal of the American Medical Association (JAMA)*, 290(21): 2873.

Maguire, B., Faulkner, W., Mathers, R., Rowland, C., and Wozniak, J. (1991) 'Rural police job functions', *Police Studies*, 14: 180–7.

Mahabir, C. (1990) 'Book review: "Before the bulldozer – the Nambiquara Indians and the World Bank"', *Social Justice*, 17(4): 146–52.

Major, A. (2012) *Slavery, Abolitionism and Empire in India, 1772–1843*, Liverpool: Liverpool University Press.

Marks, K. (2004) 'Growing up on Pitcairn: "We all thought sex was like food on table"', *Independent*, 29 September. Available: https://www.independent.co.uk/news/world/australasia/grow - ing-up-on-pitcairn-we-all-thought-sex-was-like-food-on-table-547980.html

Marotta, V. (2017) *Theories of the Stranger: Debates on Cosmopolitanism, Identity and Cross-Cultural Encounters*, Abingdon, Oxon: Routledge.

Marston, G., Humpage, L., Peterie, M., Mendes, P., Bielefeld, S., and Staines, Z. (2022) *Compulsory Income Management in Australia and New Zealand: More Harm Than Good?*, Bristol: Bristol University Press.

Martin, D. (1993) *Autonomy and Relatedness: An Ethnography of Wik People of Aurukun, Western Cape York Peninsula*, Canberra: ANU Press.

Martin, T. (2014) '"Socialist paradise" or "inhospitable island"'? Visitor responses to Palm Island in the 1920s and 1930s', *Aboriginal History*, 38: 131–53.

McCall, G. (1994) 'Nissology: a proposal for consideration', *Journal of the Pacific Society*, 63–4(17): 99–106.

McCusker, M. and A. Soares. (2011) 'Introduction', in M. McCusker and A. Soares (eds) *Island Identities: Constructions of Postcolonial Cultural Insularity*, Amsterdam: Rodopi, pp xi–xxviii.

McCutcheon, P. (2021) 'Christmas Island future uncertain as phosphate mine starts to wind down', *ABC News*, 24 June. Available: https://www.abc.net.au/news/2021-06-24/christmas-island-future-uncertain-as-phosphate-mine-winds-down/100231824

McKay, A.L. (2021) '"Allowed to die?" Prison hulks, convict corpses and the inquiry of 1847', *Cultural and Social History*, 18(2): 163–81.

McKinley, C., Liddell, J., and Lilly, J. (2021) 'All work and no play: Indigenous women "pulling the weight" in home life (Canada)', *Social Service Review*, 95(2): 278–311.

McMahon, E. (2010) 'Australia, the island continent: how contradictory geography shapes the national imaginary', *Space and Culture*, 13(2): 178–87.

Mead, M. ([1928]2001) *Coming of Age in Samoa: A Psychological Study of Primitive Youth for Western Civilization*, New York: HarperCollins.

Mega, E. (2019) 'Prison island could be nature reserve', *Nature*, 568: 287–8.

Memmott P. Evans, N. Robins, R., and Lilley, I. (2006) 'Understanding isolation and change in island human populations through a study of indigenous cultural patterns in the Gulf of Carpentaria', *Transactions of the Royal Society of South Australia*, 130(1): 29–47.

Mennell, S. (1992) *Norbert Elias: An Introduction*, Dublin: University College Dublin Press.

Mignolo, W. (2011) 'Geopolitics of sensing and knowing: on (de)coloniality, border thinking and epistemic obedience', *Postcolonial Studies*, 14(3): 273–83.

Milgram, S. (1963) 'Behavioral study of obedience', *Journal of Abnormal and Behavioral Psychology*, 67(4): 371–8.

Moran, D. (2013) 'Carceral geography and the spatialities of prison visiting: visitation, recidivism, and hyperincarceration', *Environment and Planning D: Society and Space*, 31(1): 174–90.

Moreton-Robinson, A. (2004) 'Whiteness and knowing: whiteness, epistemology and Indigenous representation,' in A. Moreton-Robinson (ed) *Whitening Race: Essays in Social and Cultural Criticism*, Canberra: Aboriginal Studies Press, ch 6, pp 75–88.

Moreton-Robinson, A. (2015) *The White Possessive: Property, Power and Indigenous Sovereignty*, Minneapolis, MN: University of Minnesota Press.

Moreton-Robinson, A. (2021) 'The paradox of race in Australian legal thought: making the invisible visible', *Alice Tay lecture on law and human rights*, Freilich Project for the Study of Bigotry, 23 September. ANU: Canberra. Available: https://freilich.anu.edu.au/news-events/events/alice-tay-lect ure-law-human-rights-professor-aileen-moreton-robinson-paradox-race

Morris, J. (2019) 'Violence and extraction of a human commodity: from phosphate to refugees in the Republic of Nauru', *The Extractive Industries and Society*, 6(4): 1122–33.

Mountz, A. (2015) 'Political geography II: islands and archipelagos', *Progress in Human Geography*, 39(5): 636–46.

Murdoch, J. and Pratt, A. (1997) 'From the power of topography to the topography of power: a discourse on strange ruralities', in P. Cloke and J. Little (eds) *Contested Country Culture: Otherness, Marginalisation and Rurality*, London: Routledge, pp 49–66.

Murray, T. (2017) 'Islands and lighthouses: a phenomenological geography of Cape Bruny, Tasmania', in E. Stratford (ed) *Island Geographies: Essays and Conversations*, Abingdon, Oxon: Routledge, pp 32–54.

National Museum of Australia (2021) *Convict Transportation Peaks*, Canberra: National Museum of Australia.

Naviti, R. (2003) 'Restorative justice and women in Vanuatu', in S. Dinnen, A. Jowitt, and T. Newton Cain (eds) *A Kind of Mending: Restorative Justice in the Pacific Islands*, Canberra, ACT: Pandanus Books, pp 95–100.

Neame, A. and Heenan, M., (2004) *Responding to Sexual Assault in Rural Communities, Briefing No. 3*, Melbourne: Australian Institute of Family Studies.

Nelson, W. (1993) 'Criminality and sexual morality in New York, 1920–1980', *Yale Journal of Law & the Humanities*, 5: 265–341.

Nethery, A. (2012) 'Separate and invisible: a carceral history of Australian islands', *The International Journal of Research into Island Clusters*, 6(2): 85–98.

Nettelbeck, A. (2012) '"A halo of protection": colonial protectors and the principle of Aboriginal protection through punishment', *Australian Historical Studies*, 43(3): 396–411.

Nettelbeck, A. (2013) '"Equals of the white man": prosecution of settlers for violence against Aboriginal subjects of the Crown, colonial Western Australia', *Law and History Review*, 31(2): 355–90.

Neumann, C. (2012) 'Imprisoning the soul', in T. Ugelvik and J. Dullum (eds) *Penal Exceptionalism? Nordic Prison Policy and Practice*, London: Routledge, pp 139–55.

Newton. (1998) 'Policing in the South Pacific Islands', *Police Journal (Chichester)*, 71(4): 349–352. DOI: https://doi.org/10.1177/0032258 X9807100411

Newton, E. (2014) *Cherry Grove, Fire Island: Sixty Years in America's First Gay and Lesbian Town*, Durham, NC: Duke University Press.

New Zealand Herald (2004) 'Pitcairn trial a miscarriage of justice, says former islander', *New Zealand Herald*, 27 October. Available: https://www.nzherald.co.nz/pitcairn-islands-sex-abuse/news/article.cfm?c_id=700&objectid=3604142

Nguyen, B., Boruff, B., and Tonts, M. (2018) 'Indicators of mining in development: a Q-methodology investigation of two gold mines in Quang Nam province, Vietnam', *Resources Policy*, 47: 147–55.

Nielsen, M. and Robyn, L. (2003) 'Colonialism and criminal justice for Indigenous peoples in Australia, Canada, New Zealand and the United States of America', *Indigenous Nations Studies Journal*, 4(1): 29–45.

O'Connor, M. and Gray, D. (1989) *Crime in a Rural Community*, Annandale, NSW The Federation Press,.

Ogan, E. (1999) 'The Bougainville conflict: perspectives from Nasioi', *Discussion Paper – Research School of Pacific and Asian Studies*, 99(3): 1–9, Canberra: Australian National University.

Ogden, L. (2021) 'A brief biological history of quarantine', *BioScience*, 71(9): 899–906.

Park, R.E. (1928) 'Human migration and the marginal man', *The American Journal of Sociology*, 33(6): 881–93.

Parlett, J. (2020) 'The boys on the beach: Andrew Holleran's Fire Island,' in C. Breidenbach, T. Frohler, D. Pensel, K. Simon, F. Telsnig, and M. Wittmann (eds) *Narrating and Constructing the Beach: An Interdisciplinary Approach*, Boston: De Gruyter, pp 337–53.

Parthesius, R. (2010) *Dutch Ships in Tropical Waters*, Amsterdam: Amsterdam University Press.

Pascoe, B. (2013) *Dark Emu*, Broome: Magabala Books.

Passi, G. (1986) *Traditional Resource Knowledge, Western Education and Self-Management Autonomy of the Torres Strait* (Masters thesis), Brisbane: University of Queensland.

Payne, K., Berg, B., and Sun, I. (2005) 'Policing in small town America: Dogs, drunks, disorder, and dysfunction', *Journal of Criminal Justice*, 33: 31–41.

Pearce, F. (1976) *Crimes of the Powerful*, London: Pluto Press.

Pennings, J. (1999) 'Crime in rural NSW: A police perspective', Conference on 'Crime in Rural Communities: The Impacts, the Causes, the Prevention', Sydney: NSWPS.

Perkiss, S. and Moerman, L. (2018) 'A dispute in the making: a critical examination of displacement, climate change and the Pacific Islands', *Accounting, Auditing & Accountability Journal*, 31(1): 166–92. DOI: https://doi.org/10.1108/AAAJ-06-2016-2582

Pervan, J., Musulin, K., and Dorey, B. (2020) 'The path of pain: a case study in understanding trauma, acknowledging truth and enabling healing through the Bernier and Dorre Islands Lock Hospitals histories', *Historic Environment*, 32(2): 90–106.

Philo, C. (1997) 'Of other rurals?', in P. Cloke and J. Little (eds) *Contested Countryside Cultures: Otherness, Marginalisation and Rurality*, London: Routledge, pp 19–50.

Pipher, M. [1928] (2001) 'Introduction to the Perennial Classics Edition', in M. Mead (ed) *Coming of Age in Samoa: A Psychological Study of Primitive Youth for Western Civilization*, New York: HarperCollins, pp xv–xix.

Pitt, D. (1980) 'Sociology, islands and boundaries', *World Development*, 8: 1051–9.

Pochnau, W. and Parker, L. (2007) 'Trouble in paradise', *Vanity Fair*. Available: https://www.vanityfair.com/news/2008/01/pitcairn200801

Pollock, N. (2014) 'Nauru phosphate history and the resource curse narrative', *Journal de a Societie des Oceanistes*, online: 107–20.

Portes, A. (2000) 'The two meanings of social capital', *Sociological Forum*, 15: 1–12.

Povinelli E (2019) 'Driving across settler late liberalism: Indigenous ghettoes, slums and camps', *Ethnos Journal of Anthropology*, 84(1): 113–23.

Pratt, J. and Melei, T. (2018) 'One of the smallest prison populations in the world under threat: the case of Tuvalu', in K. Carrington, R. Hogg, J. Scott et al (eds) *The Palgrave Handbook of Criminology and the Global South*, London: Palgrave, pp 729–50.

Productivity Commission (2021) *Closing the Gap: Annual Data Compilation Report, July 2021*, Canberra: Productivity Commission. Available: https://www.pc.gov.au/closing-the-gap-data/annual-data-report/2021/closing-the-gap-annual-data-compilation-report-july2021.pdf

Putnam, R. (2003) *Making Democracy Work: Civic Traditions in Modern Italy*, Princeton, NJ: Princeton University Press.

Queensland Government Statistician's Office. (2016a) *Indigenous Profile: Queensland Regional Profile: Custom Region Compared with Queensland*, Brisbane: Queensland Government.

Queensland Government Statistician's. Office (2016b) *Time Series Profile— The Region over Time*, Brisbane: Queensland Government.

Quillen, J. (2015) *Inside Alcatraz: My Time on the Rock*, London: Random House.

Raineri, L. (2019) 'The Malta connection: a corrupting island in a corrupting sea', *European Review of Organised Crime*, 5(1): 10-33.

Redfield, P. (2000) *Space in the Tropics: From Convicts to Rockets in French Guiana*, California: University of California Press.

Refugee Council of Australia (2021) 'After eight years of offshore processing, where to from here?'. Available: https://www.refugeecouncil.org.au/after-eight-years-of-offshore-processing-where-to-from-here/

Reynolds, H. (2013) *Forgotten War*, Sydney: Newsouth Books.

Richards, N. and May, S. (2003) 'South Australia's "floating coffin": the diseased, the destitute, and the derelict "Fitzjames" (1852–c1900)', *The Great Circle*, 25(1): 20–39.

Rigby, N. (1997) 'Discourses of "savagery" in early pacific writing', *Wasafiri*. Available: https://www.tandfonline.com/doi/pdf/10.1080/02690059708589544

Robertson, J. (2010) 'Evolutionary identity formation in an Indigenous colonial experience: the Torres Strait experience', *Nationalism and Ethnic Politics*, 16(3–4): 465–82.

Roscoe, K. 2021) 'Islands of incarceration and empire building in colonial Australia,' in D. Hamilton, and J. McAleer (eds) *Islands and the British Empire in the Age of Sail*, Oxford: Oxford University Press, pp 172–94.

Rostila, M. (2011) 'The facets of social capital', *Journal for the Theory of Social Behaviour*, 41: 308–26.

Roukis, G. (2004) 'The British East India Company 1600–1858: a model of transition management for the modern global corporation', *The Journal of Management Development*, 23(10): 938–48.

Royle, S. and Brinklow, A. (2018) 'Definitions and typologies', in G. Baldacchino (ed) *The Routledge International Handbook of Island Studies: A World of Islands*, London: Routledge, pp 3–20.

Rumford, C. (2006) 'Theorizing borders', *European Journal of Sociological Theory*, 9(2): 155–69.

Russo, A. and Strazzari, F. (2019) 'Islands of organised crime: spatiality, mobility and confinement', *The European Review of Organised Crime*, 5(1): 1–9.

Said, E. (1978) *Orientalism*, New York: Pantheon Books.

Sampson, R., Raudenbush, S. and Earls, F. (1997) 'Neighborhoods and violent crime: a multilevel study of collective efficacy', *Science*, 277: 918–24.

Sarre, R. (2005) 'Police and the public: some observations on policing and Indigenous Australians', *Current Issues in Criminal Justice*, 17(2): 305–13.

Sartre, J.P. (2011) [1956] 'Colonialism is a system', *International Journal of Postcolonial Studies*, 3(1): 127–40.

Scannell, L. and Gifford, R. (2010) 'The relations between natural and civic place attachment and pro-environmental behavior', *Journal of Environmental Psychology*, 30(3): 289–97.

Schliehe, A. and Moran, D. (2017) 'Conclusion: reflections on capturing the carceral', in D. Moran and A. Schliehe (eds) *Carceral Spatiality: Dialogues Between Geography and Criminology*, London: Palgrave Macmillan, pp 269–83.

Schnieder, J.W. (1985) 'Social problems theory: the constructionist view', *Annual Review of Sociology*, 11: 209–29.

Scott, J. (2003) 'Prostitution and public health in New South Wales', *Culture, Health & Sexuality*, 5(3): 277–93.

Scott, J. and Jobes, P. (2007) 'Policing in rural Australia: the country cop as law enforcer and local resident', in E. Barclay, J. Donnermeyer, J. Scott, and R. Hogg (eds) *Crime in Rural Australia*, Sydney: Federation Press: pp 127–37.

Scott, J. and Hogg, R. (2015) 'Strange and stranger ruralities: social constructions of rural crime in Australia', *Journal of Rural Studies*, 39: 171–9.

Scott, J. and Staines, Z. (2021) 'Charting the place of islands in criminology: on isolation, integration and insularity', *Theoretical Criminology*, 25(4): 578–600.

Scott, J., Staines, Z., and Morton, J. (2021) *Understanding Crime and Justice in the Torres Strait Region*, Canberra: Australian Institute of Criminology.

Sehdev, P. (2002)'The origin of quarantine', *Arcanum*, 35: 1071–2.

Seuffert, N. (2011) 'Civilisation, settlers and wanderers: law, politics and mobility in nineteenth century New Zealand and Australia', *Law, Text, Culture*, 15: 10–44.

Shamir, R. (2005) 'Without borders? Notes on globalization as a mobility regime', *Sociological Theory*, 23(2): 197–217.

Shammas, V. (2014) 'The pains of freedom: assessing the ambiguity of Scandinavian penal exceptionalism on Norway's prison island', *Punishment & Society*, 16(1): 104–23.

Shapiro, H. (1928) 'Robinson Crusoe's children', *Natural History*. Available: http://www.naturalhistorymag.com/htmlsite/master.html? http://www.naturalhistorymag.com/htmlsite/editors_pick/1928_05-06_pick.html

Sharp, N. (1992) *Footprints Along the Cape York Sand Beaches*, Canberra: Australian Institute of Aboriginal and Torres Strait Islander Studies.

Shearing, C. (2015) 'Criminology and the Anthropocene', *Criminology & Criminal Justice*, 15(3): 255–69.

Shnukal, A. (2015) 'Aspects of early local administration, education, health and population on Mabuyag', *Culture*, 8(2): 55–125.

Shoemaker, N. (2015) 'A typology of colonialism', *Perspectives on History*, 53(7). Available: https://www.historians.org/publications-and-directories/perspectives-on-history/october-2015/a-typology-of-colonialism

Simmel, G. (1971) 'The stranger', in D.N. Levine (ed) *On Individuality and Social Forms*, Chicago and London: University of Chicago Press, pp 143–9.

Singe, J. (1979) *The Torres Strait: People and History*, Brisbane: University of Queensland Press.

Smith, J. (2014) 'Interrogating whiteness within criminology', *Sociology Compass*, 8(2): 107–18.

Souhami, A. (2020) 'Understanding police work in the remote northern isles of Scotland: the extraordinary ordinariness of island policing', *Edinburgh School of Law Research Paper*, No. 2020/17. Available: https://ssrn.com/abstract=3673425 or http://dx.doi.org/10.2139/ssrn.3673425

Spector, M. and Kitsuse, J. (1973) 'Social problems: a reformulation', *Social Problems*, 20: 145–59.

Spector, M. and Kitsuse, J. (1977) *Constructing Social Problems*, Menlo Park, CA: Cummings.

Staines, Z. (forthcoming) 'Social quarantining in the construction and maintenance of white Australia', *Sociology*.

Staines, Z. and Scott, J. (2020) 'Crime and colonisation in Australia's Torres Strait Islands', *Journal of Criminology*, 53(1): 25–43.

Staines, Z., Marston, G., Bielefeld, S., Humpage, L., Mendes, P., and Peterie, M. (2020) 'Governing poverty: compulsory income management and crime in Australia', *Critical Criminology*. DOI: 10.1007/s10612-020-09532-2

Stallwitz, A. (2012) *The Role of Community-Mindedness in the Self-Regulation of Drug Cultures*, London: Springer.

Strange, C. and Kempa, M. (2003) 'Shades of dark tourism: Alcatraz and Robben Island', *Annals of Tourism Research*, 30(2): 386–405.

Stratford, E. (2003) 'Flows and boundaries: small island discourses and the challenge of sustainability, community and local environments', *The International Journal of Justice and Sustainability*, 8(5): 495–9.

Sturma, M. (2002) 'Mutiny and narrative: Francisco Pelsaert's Journals and the wreck of the Batavia', *The Great Circle: Journal of the Australian Association for Maritime History*, 24(1): 14–24.

Suaalii-Sauni, T., Wheeler, A.J., Saafi, E., Robinson, G., Agnew, F., Warren, H. et al (2009) 'Exploration of Pacific perspectives of Pacific models of mental health service delivery in New Zealand', *Pacific Health Dialog*, 15(1): 18–27.

Swanson, C. R., Territo, L., and Taylor, R.W. (1988) *Police Administration*, New York: Macmillan.

Sydney Museums (nd) 'Convict hulks'. Available: https://sydneylivingmuseums.com.au/stories/convict-hulks

Tajfel, H. (1974) 'Social identity and intergroup behaviour', *Social Science Information*, 13(2): 65–93.

Tanton, R., Dare, L., Miranti, R., Vidyattama, Y., Yule, A., and McCabe, M. (2021) *Dropping off the Edge 2021: Persistent and Multilayered Disadvantage in Australia*, Melbourne: Jesuit Social Services.

Tauri, J. (2013) 'Indigenous critique of authoritarian criminology,' in K. Carrington, M. Ball, E. O'Brien, and J. Tauri (eds) *Crime, Justice and Social Democracy: International Perspectives*, London: Palgrave Macmillan, pp 217–33.

Taylor, C. (2016) *The Life of a Scilly Sergeant*, London: Random House.

Taylor, G. (2005) *Buying Whiteness: Race, Culture and Identity from Columbus to Hip Hop*, New York: Palgrave Macmillan.

Taylor, J. (2013) 'Indigenous urbanization in Australia', in C. Anderson and E. Peters (eds) *Indigenous in the City: Contemporary Identities and Cultural Innovation*, Vancouver: UBC Press, pp 237–55.

Teaiwa, K.M. (2015) *Consuming Ocean Island: Stories of People and Phosphate from Banaba*, Bloomington, IN: Indiana University Press.

Thomas, S. (2007) 'Littoral space(s): liquid edges of poetic possibility', *Journal of the Canadian Association for Curriculum Studies*, 5(1): 21–9.

Thomas, S. (2007) 'Littoral space(s): liquid edges of poetic possibility', *Journal of the Canadian Association of Curriculum Studies*, 5(1): 21–9.

Thurman, Q.C. and McGarrell, E.F. (eds) (1997) *Community Policing in a Rural Setting*, Anderson, Cincinnati, OH: Routledge.

Titlestad, M. (2013) '"Changed as to a tiger": Considering the wreck of the Batavia', *Antipodes*, 2(2): 149–56.

Tognotti, E. (2013) 'Lessons from the history of quarantine, from Plague to Influenza A', *Emerging Infectious Diseases*, 19(3): 254–9.

Tonnies, F. [1887] (1957) *Community and Society*, Michigan: Michigan State University Press.

Trigger, D. (1986) 'Blackfellas and whitefellas: the concepts of domain and social closure in the analysis of race-relations', *Mankind*, 16(2): 99–117.

Tuan, Y. (1979) 'Space and place: humanistic perspective', in S. Gale and G. Olsson (eds) *Philosophy in Geography*. Dordrecht, Netherlands: D. Reidel Publishing Company, pp 387–427. Available: https://link.springer.com/chapter/10.1007/978-94-009-9394-5_19

Tuncbilek, G. (2020) 'Quarantine(d) space: Urla-lzmir (Smyrna) Island', *Space and Culture*, 23(3): 246–52.

Turner, B. (2007) 'The enclave society: towards a sociology of immobility', *European Journal of Social Theory*, 10(2): 287–303.

Twain, M. (1879) 'The great resolution in Pitcairn', *Atlantic Monthly* 43 (March). Available: http://mysite.du.edu/~ttyler/pitcairn/1879%20-%20Twain%20-%20Great%20Revolution.htm

UNESCO (2021a) 'Sundarbans'. Available: https://whc.unesco.org/en/list/798

UNESCO (2021b) 'Rock islands'. Available: https://whc.unesco.org/en/list/1386/

United Nations (2021) 'Non-self-governing territories'. Available: https://www.un.org/dppa/decolonization/en/nsgt

UNHCR (2018) 'UNHCR urges Australia to evacuate off-shore facilities as health situation deteriorates'. Available: https://www.unhcr.org/en-au/news/briefing/2018/10/5bc059d24/unhcr-urges-australia-evacuate-off-shore-facilities-health-situation-deteriorates.html

Urry, J. (2000) 'Mobile sociology', *British Journal of Sociology*, 51(1): 185–203.

Vaioleti, T.M. (2006) 'Talanoa methodology: a developing position on Pacific research', *Waikato Journal of Education*, 12(1): 21–34.

Valentin, J. (2007) *An Independent Assessment of Police in Remote Indigenous Communities for the Government of Australia*, Government of Australia.

van den Bergh, G., Kaifu, Y., Kurniawan, I., Kono, R., Brumm, A., Setiabudi, E., Aziz, F., and Morwood, M. (2016) '*Homo floresiensis* – like fossils from the early Middle Pleistocene of Flores', *Nature*, 534: 245–8.

Vázquez, R. (2011) 'Translation as erasure: thoughts on modernity's epistemic violence', *Journal of Historical Sociology*, 24(1): 27–44.

Villalonga-Olives, E. and Kawachi, I. (2017) 'The dark side of social capital', *Social Science & Medicine*, 194: 105–27.

Vink, M. (2003) '"The world's oldest trade": Dutch slavery and slave trade in the Indian Ocean in the seventeenth century', *Journal of World History*, 14(2): 131–77.

Walters, W. (2010) 'Foucault and frontiers: notes on the birth of the humanitarian border', in U. Brockling, S. Krasmann, and T. Lemke (eds) *Governmentality: Current Issues and Future Challenges*, New York: Routledge, pp 138–64.

Walton, G. and Dinnen, S. (2020) 'Lost in space? The spatial and scalar dimensions of organised crime in the Pacific', *Asia Pacific Viewpoint*, 61(3): 521–36.

Watego, C. (2020) 'Black Lives Matter – a Brisbane Blacks Manifesto', *IndigenousX*, 15 July. Available: https://indigenousx.com.au/black-lives-matter-a-brisbane-blacks-manifesto/

Watego, C. (2021) 'Who are the real criminals? Making the case for abolishing criminology', *43rd John Barry Memorial Lecture*, University of Melbourne, 29 November.

Watson, D. and Dinnen, S. (2020) 'Contextualising policing in Melanesia: history, adaptation and adoption problematised', in S. Amin, D. Watson, and C. Girard (eds) *Mapping Security in the Pacific: A Focus on Context, Gender and Organisational Culture*, London: Routledge, pp 161–73.

Watson, I. (2008) 'De-colonising the space: dreaming back to Country', in S. Morgan, T. Mia, and B. Kwaymullina (eds) *Heartsick for Country: Stories of Love, Spirit, and Creation*, North Fremantle: Fremantle Press, pp 82–100.

Watson, J. (2010) *Palm Island: Through a Long Lens*, Canberra: Aboriginal Studies Press.

Watson, J. (2016) 'A century of activism and heartache: the troubled history of Palm Island', *Griffith Review*, (60). Available: https://www.griffithreview.com/articles/century-activism-heartache-troubled-history-palm-island/

Weaver-Hightower, R. (2007) *Empire Islands: Castaways, Cannibals and Fantasies of Conquest*, London: University of Minnesota Press.

Weber, L. (2007) 'Bridges or band aids? Another death in police custody reveals fatal flaws in the Aboriginal liaison officer concept', *Current Issues in Criminal Justice*, 19(2): 235–42. DOI: 10.1080/10345329.2007.12036430

Weber, M. (1978) [1922] *Economy and Society: An Outline of Interpretive Sociology*, Berkeley, CA: University of California Press.

Websdale, N. (1998) *Rural Woman Battering and the Justice System: An Ethnography*, Thousand Oaks, CA: Sage.

Weisburd, D., Bernasco, W., and Bruinsma, G. (2009) *Putting Crime in Its Place: Units of Analysis in Geographic Criminology*, London: Springer.

Weisburd, D., and Eck, J.E. (eds) (2017) *Unraveling the Crime–Place Connection: New Directions in Theory and Policy. Advances in Criminological Theory*, vol 22, New York: Routledge.

Weisheit, R.A. and Donnermeyer, J.F. (2000) 'Change and Continuity in Crime in Rural America', in G. LaFree, J.F. Short, R.J. Bursik, Jr, and R.B. Taylor (eds) *The Nature of Crime: Continuity and Change*, Vol 1, Washington, DC: US Department of Justice, Office of Justice Programs, pp 309–58.

Wettenhall, R. (2015) 'Victoria's yellow stain: the fleet of floating prisons', *Victorian Historical Journal*, 86(2): 250–75.

Whyte, K. (2018) 'On resilient parasitisms, or why I'm sceptical of Indigenous/settler reconciliation', *Journal of Global Ethics*, 14(2): 277–89.

Wikström, P. and Sampson, R. (2003) 'Social mechanisms of community: influences on crime and pathways in criminality', in B. Lahey, T.E. Moffitt, and A. Caspi (eds) *Causes of Conduct Disorder and Juvenile Delinquency*, New York: Guilford Press, pp 118–52.

Wild, R. (1974) *Bradstow: A Study of Status, Class and Power in a Small Australian Town*, Sydney: Angus and Robertson.

Wilkins, L. (1982) 'Crime quantification and the quality of life', in F. Elliston and N. Bowie (eds) *Ethics, Public Policy and the Criminal Justice System*, Cambridge, MA: Oelgeschlager, Gunn & Hain, pp 18–32.

Williams, B. (2005) 'The archaeological potential of colonial prison hulks: the Tasmanian case study', *Bulletin of the Australasian Institute for Maritime Archaeology*, 29: 77–86.

Willoughby, C. (2018) 'Running away from drapetomania: Samuel A. Cartwright, medicine, and race in the Antebellum South', *Journal of Southern History*, 84(3): 579–614.

Wolfe, P. (1998) *Settler Colonialism and the Transformation of Anthropology: The Politics and Poetics of an Ethnographic Event*, London: Cassell.

Wolfe, P. (2006) 'Settler colonialism and the elimination of the native', *Journal of Genocide Research*, 8(4): 387–409.

Woodhouse, A (2006) '"People are accepted as long as they don't misbehave": The relationship between social capital and crime in rural Australia', *Rural Society*, 16(1): 5–24.

World Bank (2021) 'Nauru, data dashboard'. Available: https://data.worldbank.org/country/NR

Young, M. and Woodiwiss, M. (2019) 'Organised crime and security threats in Caribbean Small Island Developing States: a critical analysis of US assumptions and policies', *European Review of Organised Crime*, 5(1): 85–117.

Young, R. (2016) *Postcolonialism: An Historical Introduction, Anniversary Edition*, West Sussex: Wiley Blackwell.

Yunkaporta, T. (2019) *Sand Talk*, Melbourne: Text Publishing.

Yuval-Davis, N. (2006) 'Belonging and the Politics of Belonging', *Patterns of Prejudice*, 40(3): 197–214.

Zimbardo, P. (1971) *The Stanford Prison Experiment: A Simulation Study of the Psychology of Imprisonment*. Stanford, CA: Stanford University Digital Repository.

Index

References to endnotes show the page and
chapter number and the note number (139ch4n2).

A
Adamo, A. 112, 120, 121, 122–3, 124, 125
The Admirable Crichton 40–1
Agamben, G. 55, 112, 118
Agozino, B. 20, 63, 64
AIDS pandemic 57
Albuquerque, K. 28, 29
Alcatraz 50–1, 53
Amnesty International 118, 119
Ancient Greece 37
And Then There Were None 34
Anderson, B. 9, 12
Anderson, C. 114, 115, 139n2
anomie 107, 122, 125
anthropology, classical 26
Armstrong, S. 19, 21, 43, 44
asylum seekers 117–20, 125
'Ata castaways 136, 137
Aurukun 70–1, 72–3, 75, 76
Australia
   asylum seeker policy 118–19
   carceral islands in desert outback 67–72
   continuing echoes 72–7
   Community Development Programme (CDP) 74
   'islanding as erasure' in settler colonial 64–77, 77–8
   penal settlements as tourist sites 58
   policing in rural spaces 93
   prison hulks 54–5
   'protection era' 67
   social disorganization and crime 23–4
   start of European settlement 65–6
   see also Indigenous groups in Australia

B
Bahamas 27
Baldacchino, G. 7, 8, 12, 14, 26, 43, 45, 61, 66, 68, 71, 77, 112, 126, 132, 138
Ballanytyne, R.M. 8, 36, 135
banking, offshore 28
Barrie, J.M. 40

Barrington, R. 48, 49
Bastøy Island 51–3
Batavia 1–4, 5–9
Baudrillard, J. 58
Bauman, Z. 44
The Beach of Falseá 40
beachscapes 14, 45
Beacon Island 1, 2, 3, 4
Bell, D. 9, 35, 37, 38
belonging 9–10, 15, 26–7, 131
   flexible dynamic 132
   place attachment informing 9, 22, 106
   politics of 10, 16, 131–2
   teu le va a framework for 137
Bentham, J. 55
Bernier and Dorre Islands 48–9
biopower 43, 47, 58
bonding ties 107, 109–10
borders
   control of Aboriginal 68, 72, 73, 74, 77
   globalization and shifting 44, 111
   the Other at 24, 43–5
Bougainville Copper Limited (BCL) 120, 121
Bougainville Island 112, 120–4
   blockade 112
   climate change 126
   comparing experiences of Nauru and 124–5
   compensation 121, 123
   copper mining 120–1
   environmental destruction 121
   policing 85
   violence and conflict 112, 121–3, 124
Bougainville Revolution Army (BRA) 121, 122, 124
boundedness, island 13–14, 42, 51, 125
Bounty mutiny 100, 103, 109
Braithwaite, J. 20, 82, 83, 84, 85, 87, 107, 109
Bregman, R. 135–6

Breidenbach, C. 14, 45
bridging ties 107
British East India Company (EIC) 114
British Isles 13, 27, 39, 80
Bruny Island 46
Bull, M. 83, 85, 86, 87, 95, 96, 97

C
Canada 48, 78
carbon capture 126, 127
carceral islands in Australian desert 67–72
   continuing echoes of 72–7
Caribbean 28–30
Carrington, K. 20, 23, 25, 26, 107
Cartwright, S. 48
castaways 7, 62, 136, 137
Cayman Islands 28
Charriére, H. 54
Chicago School 23
child sex abuse 27, 102, 103, 104
Christianity 71, 84, 87, 100, 101, 108, 137
Christie, A. 34
Christmas Island 126
classifications of islands 12–16
climate change 112, 126, 134
   resilience to 126–7
collective efficacy 22, 23, 109
colonialism
   conquering of nature 36
   crime in image of undesirable Other 23, 63–4, 66, 111
   criminal justice systems 63–4, 82–3
      transitioning from 82–5
   extractive colonialism 113–15
      on Nauru 115–20
   islands as sites for experiments in 7–8
   vs. settler colonialism 62–3
   see also settler colonialism
colonization
   Batavia mutineers mimicking brutality of crimes of 133
   of islands 7–8, 61–4, 133–4
   and spice trade 134
   Torres Strait Islands resistant to 64, 105
Coming of Age in Samoa 26, 37
Commonwealth of Australia 88, 89, 90
communitarianism 15, 23–4, 26–7, 99, 109, 131
Community Development Programme (CDP) 74
compensation for environmental damage 117, 121, 123
concept of islands 15
connectedness, isolation in tension with 15, 43, 52–3, 71
Connell, J. 12, 14, 15, 20, 32, 35, 36, 37, 40, 41, 134
Connell, R. 20–1
convict transportation 36, 39, 54, 114–15

Cook, Captain J. 39–40, 65
copper mining 120–1
The Coral Island 8, 36, 40, 135
Cornelisz, J. 2, 3, 4, 5, 6
COVID-19 pandemic 44, 46
creating islands under settler colonialism 67–72
crime
   drug trafficking 28, 29
   and extractivism through a prism of islandness 124–5
   fear of 9, 21, 22, 30
   firearm trafficking 29–30
   in Greenland 31
   hidden 17, 35, 92–3, 99
      of Pitcairn Island 102–5
   in image of undesirable Other 23, 63–4, 66, 111
   incarceration rates 75, 77
   integration, island settings and 92–6
   island insularity and 105–9, 110
   Nordic islands 30–1
   organized 27, 29, 119
   property 25, 28, 31, 89, 93, 107
   racialization of 23, 25, 76
   'rural' 23–4, 24–5, 106, 133–4
   social capital
      as crime preventative 23, 64, 109
      as crime productive 92–3, 99, 109–10
   social integration producing and preventing 98–9
   tourism and 28–9
   urban 20
   victims 25, 28, 29, 33, 38, 86, 95
   violent 6, 25, 29, 109, 121–3, 124
crime fiction 32–41
   horror 37–41, 135
   idyll 35–7
crime maps 22, 23
crime prevention 25, 29, 109
   and alternatives to extractivism 128
   place attachment and 22
   social capital and 23, 64, 109
   tight social control and 24
crime rates 28, 29, 30, 75, 80, 106
   low 30–1, 34, 64, 81
criminal body, island isolation of 50–6
criminal justice systems
   colonial transition in Pacific 82–5
   maintaining of social divisions 130
   and state sponsored violence 70
   as tools of colonialism 63–4, 82–3
criminology
   decolonization of 20
   as a 'discipline' 129
   disciplining and controlling the Other 63
   geography informing 19, 20, 129, 137–8
   neglect of islands and remote locations 20–1, 24

INDEX

Southern 20, 41
space, place and 20–4
textbooks 21
urban 19
vocational and critical approaches to 129–30
see also green criminology; rural criminology

D

'dark tourism' 4–5, 51, 58
Dash, M. 2, 3, 4, 5, 6
Death in Paradise 33, 35
decolonization of criminology 20
definitions of islands 12–16, 67
Defoe, D. 7, 35, 51
detention, administrative 49
detention camps 50, 51
detention centres, refugee 117–20, 125
Devil's Island 51, 54
Diamond, J. 61, 67
Dinnen, S. 12, 80, 82, 83, 84, 85, 86, 87, 117, 119
disease 45–50, 116, 139ch3n1
dissection of prison hulk corpses 54
domestic and family violence (DFV) 86, 87, 89–90, 92, 93, 110
Dorre island 48–9
Douglas, M. 39, 43, 45, 47, 62, 65
drug trafficking 28, 29
Dutch East India Company 6, 114
Dwyer, A. 75
dystopias, island 7, 32, 38, 40
see also horror, island

E

eco-tourism 126
economies, small island 27
Edge, A. 6
Elias, N. 10, 11, 131
empire 41, 61
see also colonialism; colonization
'enclave tourism' 28
environmental
  destruction 112, 113, 117, 121, 124, 125, 134
  compensation claims 117, 121, 123
  sociology 23
  stewardship 125, 127–8
Epstein, J. 27
Erikson, K.T. 9
escape, islands as a form of 56–7
established–outsider relations 10–11, 24, 93, 97, 131–2
exception, islands as sites of 55, 111–12, 118, 119, 125
executions 1, 3, 4, 65, 139ch4n2
exemption passes 68, 70, 73
extractive capitalism 126, 127, 134
  green criminology and 112–13

greenwashing 127
extractive colonialism 113–15
  on Nauru 115–20
extractivism 111–12
  on Bougainville Island 120–4
  and climate change 126
  understood through prism of islandness 124–5

F

Faroe Islands 30, 34
Farran, S. 100, 103, 108
fear of crime 9, 21, 22, 30
Ferdon, E. 101
fiction see crime fiction
Fiji 83, 86, 87, 116
financial centres, off-shore 27, 28
Fire Island 56–7
firearm trafficking 29–30
'First Law' 127
Firth, S. 115, 116
Flores 42
Foucault, M. 14, 43, 44, 45–6, 47, 48, 49, 56, 139ch3n1
freedom within constraints 52–3, 119

G

Galapagos 42
Garland, D. 85
Garvin, T. 123, 124, 140n3
gemeinschaft 24, 99
gendered violence 85–7, 96–7, 123
genocide 6, 35, 69, 113, 133
geographies, island 7, 8, 12, 13, 20, 45, 62, 78, 132
  and Pitcairn Island narrative 98, 99–100, 104, 105
  and Torres Strait Islands 64, 105
gesellschaft 24
Gibson, C. 56, 76
Global North 20–1, 23, 127, 133
  policing islands 80
  study of Nordic Islands 30–1
  understanding of islands as tourists sites 27–8
Goffman, E. 7, 50
Golding, W. 7, 40, 135, 137
gossip 11, 99, 104, 140ch6n1
Gray, D. 81
green criminology 111, 112–13, 125, 128, 134
Greenland 31
greenwashing 127
Guantanamo Bay 51
Gulliver's Travels 35, 36

H

habitat islands 67, 68, 72
Harris, C. 78
Hau'ofa, E. 15–16, 32
Hayes, W. 4, 5

Hobbes, T. 130, 135
Hodgkinson, T. 30
Hogg, R. 20, 21, 23, 25, 36, 38, 39
Holt, L. 70
homo floresiensis 42
homosexuality 48, 56, 57, 94–5
horror, island 32, 37–41, 135
　Batavia 1–4, 5–9
　Pitcairn Island 102–5
Houtman Abrolhos Islands 1–4, 4–5
human nature 130
hyperreal 58–9

I
identity, place and 9–10, 15, 21–2, 106
idyll, island 8, 8–9, 32, 35–7, 41, 99
　Pitcairn Island 100–1
'imagined communities' 8, 9, 12
'in' and 'out' groups 22, 43, 132
inbreeding 101
incarceration rates 75, 77
Indigenous groups in Australia
　apartheid-like policies towards 67–8
　banishment to island prisons 66–7
　colonial framing as parasites 63
　concepts of time 127
　crime rates 75
　displacement to reserves and
　　missions 68–72
　Dreaming stories 65
　in early settler criminal justice system 63–4
　exemption passes 68, 70, 73
　'First Law' 127
　impact of environmental destruction
　　on 113
　incarceration rates 75, 77
　'islanding as erasure' of 64–77, 77–8
　learning from philosophies and practices
　　of 127–8
　medicine as an instrument of
　　oppression 48–9
　as other rurals and rural Others 37, 38
　as outsiders in own lands 11
　policing of remote communities 74–5,
　　76
　in policing roles 89
　prior to settler colonization 65
　self-determination 72–3
　victims of crime 38
Industrial Revolution 36
industry 111–28
insularity 15, 32, 98–110
integration 80–97, 108
International Court of Justice 117
interpersonal violence 84, 106, 107, 110
invasion 60–79
Isla Maria Madre 126
'islanding' 59, 60, 64
　as erasure 60–1, 68
　in Canada 78
　in settler colonial Australia 64–77, 77–8
　within islands 116
islandness 9, 13–15, 53, 59, 68, 71, 105, 109
　of communities in Australian
　　outback 64, 68
　extractivism understood through prism
　　of 124–5
　as technique of invasion 60, 67, 77
　islands within islands 51, 56, 57, 116
Isles of Scilly 80
isolation 13, 42–59
　an anti-idyll 104
　enabling secrecy around harmful
　　activities 124–5
　in tension with connectedness 15, 43,
　　52–3, 71

J
Jamaica 29–30
Jedrusik, M. 12, 13, 15
Jefferson, A. 19, 22, 43, 44
Jersey 27, 28
Jewkes, R. 121, 123

K
Keegan, W. 61, 67

L
labour camps 50, 114
labour, exploiting Othered populations
　for 114–15
land, relationship with 78
landscape 36, 45
Lazzaretto Vecchio 46
legal exceptionalism 125
leprosy 45–6, 46–7, 116, 139ch3n1
LGBTQIA+ populations 94–5
Lindbergh, A.M. 80, 97
liquid modernity thesis 44
Little St James 27
lock hospitals 48–9
Lord of the Flies 7, 40, 135
　Bregman's counter narrative to 135–6

M
Mabo and Others v The State of Queensland
　(1992) 73
Maglen, K. 46
mainland/island distinction 13, 43, 106
Maldives 30, 134
Malinowski, B. 26
Malta 28
Manitoulin Island 78
Marshall Islands 126
McCusker, M. 7–8
McElroy, J. 28, 29
McKay, A.L. 54
McLeod, A. 12, 83, 84, 85, 86, 87
McMahon, E. 65, 68, 72

Mead, M. 26, 37
medicine as a site of power and oppression 48–9
Melanesia 12, 40, 80, 83, 85, 86, 87, 134
Milgram Experiment 6
mining, extractive 123, 133, 134, 140n3
  copper mining 120–1
  extreme conflict and violence as a result of 121–3
  gold-mining 140n3
  phosphate mining 115–17, 118
missions
  Aurukun 70–1, 72–3, 75, 76
  exemption passes 68, 70, 72
  and reserves as carceral spaces 68–72
Morris, J. 112, 113, 115, 116, 117–18
Mountz, A. 13, 42, 51, 53, 56, 111, 116, 126, 134

N
nature 36
  reserves 4, 126
  stewardship of 127–8
Nauru 111–12
  climate change 126
  colonization 115
  comparing experiences of Bougainville and 124–5
  compensation claim 117
  environmental destruction 117, 125
  geography 115
  phosphate mining 115–17, 118
  political corruption 124
  refugee processing 117–20, 125
neo-colonialism, extractive 112, 115–20
neo-liberalism 85
Nethery, A. 49, 56
Newton, E. 56, 57
Newton, T. 80, 81, 83
nissology 14–15, 129
'noble savages' 36, 37, 40
Nordic islands 30–1
Norfolk Island 39, 55, 66, 100, 101, 114, 140ch6n1
Northern Territory Emergency Response (NTER) 73–4
Norway, Prison Island 31, 51–3, 119
nuclear testing 126, 134

O
Ocean Island 116, 117
O'Connor, M. 81
offshore banking 28
organized crime 27, 29, 119
the Other 9
  at the border 24, 43–5
  constructions of Self and 61–2, 65, 71, 72
  crime in image of undesirable 23, 63–4, 66, 111
  criminology and controlling of 63
  disappearing of black 72
  exploiting for labour 114–15
  governing behaviour of, in remote communities 73–4, 77
  idyllization and exclusion of 41
  island spaces as a refuge for 56–7
  Pacific culture as exotic 36, 37
  racialized 61–2
  regimes of power to manage manifestation of 47–8, 57–8
  rural 25–6, 38
  as wild and savage 61
outsider–established outsider relations 10–11, 24, 93, 97, 131–2

P
Pacific Islands
  climate change 126–7, 134
  cultural and geographic groupings 80
  cultural features, common 31–2, 137
  as exotic Other 36, 37
  feminization and sexualization of 37
  gendered violence 85–7
  independence and transition of justice system 82–5
  'noble savages' of 36, 37, 40
  Pacific Ocean a uniting feature of 15–16
  Pacific Way 31–2
  population 80
  racialized geography 40
  shift away from idyllic perceptions of 39–40
  state and local notions of social order 87
  see also policing of Pacific Islands
Pacific Islands Company 115, 116
Palm Island reserve 68, 69–70, 75, 76, 78–9
Panguna copper mine 120–1
panopticon 55, 56
Papillon 54
Papua New Guinea Defence Force 121–2, 124
Papua New Guinea (PNG) 120, 123
  conflict with Bougainville 121–2, 124
  hybrid justice system 84–5
  policing 83–4, 85
  violence 83, 84, 86–7
Parker, L. 99, 100, 102, 103, 104, 105
Pelsaert, F. 2, 4
penal settlements 36–7, 39, 58, 65–6
  convicts awaiting transportation to 54, 55
  forced labour 114–15
  Norfolk Island 39, 55, 100, 114
  Port Arthur 58
  as tourist sites 58
Pervan, J. 48–9
phosphate mining 115–17, 118
Pitcairn Island 98, 99–101
  age of consent 102
  bonding capital 109–10
  child sex abuse 102, 103, 104

culture 101, 109
future 110
geography 98, 99–100, 104, 105
idyllization 100–1
legal code 102
normative structures 108–9
religion 101
sexual assault trials 102–5, 108
supportive of crime 110
place 15, 35, 137–8
  attachment 9, 22, 91, 106
  identity and 9–10, 15, 21–2, 106
  social sciences, space and 20–4
plague 46, 139ch3n1
Pochnau, W. 99, 100, 102, 103, 104, 105
policing
  of Global North islands 80
  of remote Indigenous communities 74–5, 76
policing of Pacific Islands
  community 85, 89, 90, 94, 106
  in fragmented communities 83, 93, 97
  of gendered violence 85–7
  institutionalized, external police interventions 96, 97
  integration of local police in community 92–6
  localistic versus legalistic 81–2, 89, 93–4, 97
  neo-liberal model 85
  over- 94
  Papua New Guinea 83–4, 84–5, 86–7
  Pitcairn Island 102
  police discretion 82, 94, 95
  social networks influencing styles of 97
  Torres Strait Islands case study 88–92, 93–4
  and transition to independence 82–5
Pollock, N. 115, 117
polluted bodies, island isolation of 45–50, 139ch3n1
Polynesia 26, 37, 40, 134
population, islander 12, 80
Port Arthur 58
Price, J. 55
prison hulks 54–5, 68
prisoners
  experiencing 'pains of freedom' 52–3, 119
  in Nordic islands 30–1
  political 48, 49, 50, 51
  prisoner patients 48–9
  protection through punishment for Indigenous 66–7
prisons
  borders of 44–5
  carceral islands in Australian desert 67–72
  continuing echoes of 72–7
  creating islands within islands 51
  detention centre 119

Faroe Islands 34
Greenland 31
isolated island 50–6
lock hospitals as 48–9
Norway's 'open prison islands' 31, 51–3, 119
prison hulks 54–5, 68
property crime 25, 28, 31, 89, 93, 107
prostitution 47
public health 43, 45–7, 58
Putnam, R. 99, 106, 107

Q
quarantine 46–7
Queensland Police Service (QPS) 88, 89
  Police Liaison Officer (PLO) programme 89

R
race
  classifications of self and Other 61–2
  crime, justice and 63–4
  as a defining feature of 'disease' 48
  and space 62
racialization of crime 23, 25, 76
racism 8, 40, 68–9, 133
recidivism rates 52
Redfield, P. 51
refugee detention 117–20, 125
researching islands 24–32
reserves
  in Canada 78
  exemption passes 68, 70, 72
  and missions as carceral spaces 68–72
  Palm Island 68, 69–70, 75, 76, 78–9
'resource curse' hypothesis 122, 124
restorative justice 85, 86, 87
Richard II 13
Robben Island 51
Robinson Crusoe 7, 35–6, 51
Robinsonade 35, 62
Roscoe, K. 60, 66, 67, 71, 78, 114
Rousseau, J.-J. 37, 130
'rural' crime 23–4, 24–5, 106, 133–4
rural criminology 19, 21, 23, 25, 27, 133
  invisibility of women 25
  neglect of islands and remote locations 19, 24–5
  neglected in criminology textbooks 21
  representations of place 35
rural idyll 35, 37
rural Others 25–6, 38
Russo, A. 23, 24, 27, 28, 50

S
Said, E. 61
Scotson, J. 10, 11
Scott, J. 21, 38, 39, 43, 47, 57, 64, 76, 88, 89, 93, 132
sea, islander perceptions of 15–16, 32

INDEX

sea levels, rising 61, 126, 134
secretive island spaces 55–6, 124–5
security, 'natural' 15
self-isolation, island 56–7
settler colonialism
  Australian
    creating islands 67–72
    criminal justice system 63–4
    echoes of island carcerality 72–7
    'islanding as erasure' 64–77, 77–8
  Canadian 78
  vs. colonialism 62–3
sex-trafficking 27
sexual abuse of minors 27, 102, 103, 104
sexual assault trials 102–5, 108
sexual violence 86, 102–5, 108
Shakespeare, William 13, 35
shaming 89, 109
Shammas, V. 52, 53, 119
Shapiro, H. 100, 101
Shetland Islands 27
shipwrecks 1–4, 4–5
Simmel, G. 95–6
slaves, medical conditions of 48
small-scale societies 9, 86, 130, 131–2
  social problems in 10–11
Soares, A. 7–8
social bonding 107
social capital 9, 17, 22, 64, 99
  as crime preventative 23, 64, 109
  as crime productive 92–3, 99, 109–10
  as a form of social control 106–7, 109, 132
  'negative' aspects 108, 132
  producing forms of 'closure' 95, 132
  TSIPLOs as an extension of networks of 90, 91, 93
social control
  'collective efficacy' to develop informal 23
  informal means of 90, 92, 95, 106, 132
  and social bonding 107
  social capital as a form of 106–7, 109, 132
  social fragmentation and weakening of theory 107
  tight networks of 24, 89, 106, 109
social disorganization 23–4, 25, 106
  extractive mining, violence and 120–4, 125
social experimentation 6, 40–1
social integration 23, 24, 109, 130, 131–2
  crime and 98–9, 106
social justice 112, 119
  move towards stewardship and 125–8
social order 9, 24, 32, 35, 131
  Batavia mutineers subversion of 5–6, 7
  state and local notions of 87
Solomon Islands 80, 83, 86, 122
Solovetsky Islands 50
space 15, 137–8
  extractive mining and strains on 112, 125
  hidden 55–6, 68, 71, 118
  island idyll as an exclusive and exclusionary 35, 36, 41
  island space on *terra firma* 60, 67–72
  islands as uncanny 39
  as an object of dread 38
  race and 62
  social sciences, place and 20–4
spice trade 134
Staines, Z. 64, 74, 75, 76, 77
Stallwitz, A. 27
Stanford Prison Experiment 6
Stevenson, R.L. 40
stranger, concept of 95–6
Strazzari, F. 23, 24, 27, 28, 50

T

The Tempest 35
terra nullius 65, 73
teu le va 137
textbooks, criminology 21
Thomas, S. 13, 42, 50, 129
time, concepts of 127
Timor-Leste 123
Titlestad, M. 2, 3, 6
Tonga 86, 136, 137
Torres Strait Islands 64, 105–6
  culture 91–2, 105–6
  geography 64, 88, 105
  local authority structures 106
  policing 88–92, 93–4
  schooling 91
Torres Strait Islands Police Liaison Officers (TSIPLOs) 89, 90, 95
'total institutions' 7, 50
tourism 27, 28, 126
  crime and 28–9
  'dark' 4–5, 51, 58
transportation, penal 36, 39, 54, 114–15
Twain, M. 98

U

UNESCO World Heritage Sites 42
United Nations High Commissioner for Refugees (UNHCR) 118
US Virgin Islands 27, 29
utopias, island 7, 8–9, 35
  see also idyll, island

V

victims of crime 25, 28, 29, 33, 38, 86, 95
violence
  domestic and family 86, 87, 89–90, 92, 93, 110
  extractive mining resulting in extreme conflict and 112, 121–4
  gendered 85–7, 96–7, 123
  interpersonal 84, 106, 107, 110
  outbreaks in Aurukun 76

in Papua New Guinea 83, 84, 86–7
sexual 86, 102–5, 108
weak social capital and high rates of 106–7
youth gangs 83

W
Walton, G. 117, 118, 119
Watson, D. 80, 84, 85, 86, 87
Watson, I. 78
Watson, J. 68, 69, 70, 76, 79
The White Lotus 33, 35
Whyte, K. 11, 62–3
The Wicker Man 39
Wik Peoples v Queensland (1996) 73
wilderness 36, 51, 62

'Winston Parva' 10
women 25, 48, 94, 97
violence against 85–7, 96–7, 123
Woodiwiss, M. 29

Y
'Yellow Fleet' 55
Young, M. 29
youth unemployment and violence 30, 83
Yunkaporta, T. 78, 127, 128

Z
Zeewijk 5
zona franca 27

www.ingramcontent.com/pod-product-compliance
Lightning Source LLC
Chambersburg PA
CBHW071707020426
42333CB00017B/2182